Latinx Studies Curriculum in K-12 Schools

Other books by the authors:

David Colón:

Between Day and Night: New and Selected Poems 1946-2010 by Miguel González-Gerth (edited)

The Lost Men

Max Krochmal:

Civil Rights in Black and Brown: Histories of Liberation and Struggle in Texas (edited, with Todd Moye)

Blue Texas: The Making of a Multiracial Democratic Coalition in the Civil Rights Era

Latinx Studies Curriculum in K-12 Schools

David Colón, Max Krochmal, and Contributors

Foreword by Jacinto Ramos, Jr.

Department of Comparative Race & Ethnic Studies
Texas Christian University (TCU)

In partnership with the Social Studies Department
Fort Worth Independent School District (FWISD)

TCU
Press

Fort Worth, Texas

Copyright © 2022 by David A. Colón and Maximilian Krochmal

Library of Congress Cataloging-in-Publication Data

Names: Colón, David A., author. | Krochmal, Max, author.
Title: Latinx studies curriculum in K-12 schools : a practical guide /
  David Colón, Max Krochmal, and contributors ; foreword by Jacinto
  Ramos, Jr.
Description: Fort Worth, Texas : TCU Press, [2022] | Includes
  bibliographical references. | Summary: "Created by an interdisciplinary
  team of researchers in partnership with a large urban school district,
  this guidebook helps teachers and school district leaders in Texas and
  beyond learn how to overlay Latina/o/x Studies content on top of
  existing state standards, providing a practical roadmap toward
  historically accurate, culturally relevant curricula and instruction
  that can be injected into all K-12 social studies classes. Following a
  detailed introductory essay synthesizing the field for new
  practitioners, it provides detailed explanations of seven major themes
  that define Latinx Studies across time and space, each accompanied by
  embedded "enduring understandings" and "essential questions" to
  jumpstart the process of backward design. For Texas teachers and school
  districts, the guidebook also includes content maps that provide
  guidance on sample lessons for specific units in each course and grade
  level. Finally, educators can draw upon detailed annotated
  bibliographies to identify supplemental resources, guidance for learning
  activities outside the classroom, and a scope and sequence for a
  high-school Latino/a Studies elective. This is essential reading for
  teachers and district leaders who seek to provide culturally relevant
  instruction to improve student outcomes among the nation's largest and
  fastest-growing ethnic group"-- Provided by publisher.
Identifiers: LCCN 2022028813 | ISBN 9780875658193 (paperback)
Subjects: LCSH: Hispanic American children--Education--United States. |
  Curriculum planning--United States. | Latin America--Study and
  teaching--United States. | BISAC: EDUCATION / Curricula | SOCIAL SCIENCE
  / Ethnic Studies / American / Hispanic American Studies | LCGFT:
  Instructional and educational works.
Classification: LCC LC2670.3 .C65 2022 | DDC
  371.829/680764--dc23/eng/20220707
LC record available at https://lccn.loc.gov/2022028813

TCU
Press

Fort Worth, Texas

TCU Box 298300
Fort Worth, Texas 76129
To order books: 1.800.826.8911

Design by Bill Brammer

Front cover artwork, *The Builders*, courtesy of Babatola Oguntoyinbo

Vision

The goal of the Fort Worth Independent School District is to prepare students for college, career, and community leadership through learning about the individual histories and cultures of people represented in the FWISD community. Going into the future, this curriculum supports:

- Leading innovative experiences that develop students' understanding of history, ethnicity, culture, and identity;

- Empowering stakeholders to forge bridges between district and community about history, ethnicity, culture, and identity;

- Encouraging students to value unity in the midst of their diverse cultures and histories;

- Sparking lifelong learners of Latino/a history and culture;

- Empowering students to be centered in their own culture and authors of their personal narrative;

- And creating conditions that afford students the opportunity to explore their own story with a freedom to be their authentic selves.

Mission

This document lives to create equity within the curriculum by providing multiple historical and cultural narratives that enhance students' understanding of themselves and foster authentic relationships grounded in mutual understanding.

Contents

Foreword

Growing up in the North Side and Diamond Hill community in Fort Worth, Texas, I was surrounded by my "gente." I never had to question who I was or where I came from. My parents immigrated from Mexico; Spanish was my first language; and we visited Coahuila and Michoacan each and every year. Still, I don't recall any conversations or lessons about the history of my people. My father has an eighth-grade education, and my mother completed high school. My grandparents, aunts, and uncles shared stories of our struggles in Mexico as well as their dreams for all the children in the family. It always started and ended with getting a great education.

When I entered the school system I began to wonder where my people were in the context of history. Aside from learning that my people were conquered, I began to receive messaging I was not welcome in the country. I was called a beaner, wetback, and illegal from time to time. I read school books with the "N" word, and my teachers tried to teach me to turn the other cheek. They justified it by stating it was language condoned in those times. I read and memorized material explicitly dehumanizing my community, such as the depictions of lazy, criminal Mexican "bandits" in Texas. On top of that, I was quizzed and tested to prove I had learned the material. There was a lot of internalizing as well as growing self-doubt.

When I got to the university, I began to learn that what I had been taught was not by accident. One of my professors was Dr. José Angel Gutiérrez, a co-founder of La Raza Unida political party. He sparked a fire in me by sending me down a journey where I was asked to look for the counternarrative to what mainstream America was teaching in PreK-12 school systems. The spark turned into a full-blown passion by the time I got my undergraduate degree. I felt as if I could crack the codes used regularly in my everyday interactions. Daily microaggressions began to trouble me more than ever. Knowing the history of how things came to be became infuriating. There were times I wished I had not become so conscious. Resistance and immersion were stages in which I struggled, and eventually felt I had to pick a side. My options were to either sit on the sidelines and perpetuate the cycles or lean in and find a way to take a stand.

The journey allowed me to learn about my own indigenous lineage, the Purepecha People. It gave me a deep sense of empowerment. I began to carry myself very differently. I found my true and authentic self. I studied my American, Mexican, and indigenous history to make sense of the social construct of race. I understood what my mentors were trying to teach me: "You can't love the fruit, if you don't love the root."

My mentor, Rickie Clark, once asked me, "Name me a time when people of color were free and in power. More specifically, name me a time when Black people were free and in power." That question stumped me. I had not been alone. I have watched him ask professors with PhDs in history, school board members, and school superintendents only to see them remain quiet. Most people struggle with that question. As one trustee on an urban school board, I do not want that cycle to continue. Frankly, I refuse to continue it.

I have asked young people all over the country to name five White, five Black, five Brown, and five Asian American leaders having impacted the course of US history. They are quick to name five White men (usually presidents). They are a bit slower to name five Black people. They usually name Dr. Martin Luther King, Jr., Malcolm X, Harriett Tubman, Rosa Parks, and President Barack Obama. Now, when we get to five Brown people . . . they really begin to struggle. Most young people name Cesar Chavez. A distant second person will be Dolores Huerta. After that, they struggle and begin to reach for actors and musicians. Selena is often thrown in the mix. The activity is further exacerbated when I proceed to ask them to name five Asian Americans and five native Indigenous leaders. The room usually goes silent, and in that moment, I ask them to get in touch with their feelings. Young people often tell me they feel sad for not being able to name five influential Brown, Asian American, and native Indigenous people. They feel sick to their stomachs for never really thinking about the subject. They feel angry for not being able to clearly articulate why it is important that they see themselves in the history of our country. When young people process their feelings, they begin to ask great questions. The main one tends to be, "Who decides what goes in our school curriculum and why have we been omitted?"

Our work in Fort Worth Independent School District (FWISD) began in 2013. When I was first elected as a trustee, my perception was that the school board was divided by race and would soon be divided by generations. The board was composed of four people of color and five white people, and further divided between three people under the age of forty and six over sixty, but we would be called to work together as a team. Previously, the board had not been focused on student outcomes, and the trustees did not have the tools to talk about race. Our new board came together by participating in racial and ethnic equity training through Glenn Singleton's Courageous Conversations About Race. We established a common language about the social construction of race and explored our own racial identities. It was powerful. Our board then began to take a deep dive into our district's data. It was apparent that we didn't differ from other urban districts. Our children of color have and continue to be at the bottom of the data charts. We agreed it was unacceptable. We found ourselves being able to talk about race without triggering one another.

I am appreciative of the Texas Christian University team as well as the Comparative Race and Ethnic Studies department. They wrote this guidebook that is allowing FWISD to revise its entire social studies curriculum. But before they wrote it, they engaged the FWISD community with forums and teacher trainings. Listening to the students, parents, and community stakeholders was imperative. The feedback from the FWISD community is engrained in the material. They showed the upmost respect to the people whom they intend to include in academia.

I encourage other school districts to consider Latinx studies. Brown children are the majority in Texas public schools. A mentor taught me, "Education is more than reading, writing and arithmetic. It must teach you who you are and whose you are." If you and/or the students in your schools cannot name five Brown people that helped make this country what it is, then I think you have enough evidence that this work is needed in your school system.

As I reflect on the journey, I am in awe of what it has taken to get to this point. The year is 2022, and the resistance to creating academic space for Brown children to learn about themselves and how their people have contributed to our society is now in full effect. The push against Critical Race Theory (CRT) has brought people into school board rooms who could potentially sideline the anti-racist work needed in our PreK-12 public school systems. I call it as I see it. We have more people of color and more racially conscious people serving as school board trustees. But our educational system was designed to serve White, male, heterosexual, and wealthy people. Our educational curriculum materials have been written and controlled by people pertaining to those identities and committed to keeping the hierarchies of race, class, gender, and sexuality in place. It is big business. This material in your hands is the counter to more than a century's worth of brainwashing.

We must acknowledge that people of color are now a majority and not a minority. Continuing to design curriculum without purposely including them is an injustice. Luckily, district leaders across Texas and the US are now having the right conversations. As a school board trustee, I do not have the luxury of time to address the inequities in our system. With a worldwide pandemic further widening the learning gaps, the topic of ethnic studies cannot take a back seat. I pray it will go hand-in-hand with the future of education. Research shows that when students see themselves reflected in the curriculum, they are more likely to be engaged. It just makes sense. Why would I want to learn about everyone else and not about myself?

Dr. Jacinto A. Ramos, Jr.
#AsiDerechito

Acknowledgments

With any undertaking of this scope and magnitude, there is an indebtedness owed to those sincere and dedicated individuals whose support made it possible. Indeed, many people assisted in preparing this curriculum guidebook. Their commitment, expertise, and passion in developing this curriculum is greatly appreciated.

....

Latinx Studies Curriculum Writing Team

Academic Consultants

David Colón, PhD, *Primary Author*
Professor of English, TCU
Director, Latinx Studies (2014–2018)
College Diversity Advocate, School of
    Interdisciplinary Studies (2018–2019)

Max Krochmal, PhD, *Principal Investigator*
Associate Professor of History, TCU (2017–
    2022)
Founding Chair, Comparative Race & Ethnic
    Studies (2015–2020)

Santiago Piñón, PhD
Associate Professor of Religion, TCU
Director, Latinx Studies Program (2017–2021)

Emily Farris, PhD
Associate Professor of Political Science, TCU
Comparative Race & Ethnic Studies Interim
    Chair (Fall 2018)

Melita Garza, PhD
Associate Professor of Journalism, TCU (2022)

Gabriel Huddleston, PhD
Associate Professor of Curriculum Studies, TCU

Michelle Bauml, PhD
Winter Professor in Early Childhood Education,
    TCU

Sylvia Mendoza, PhD
Lecturer in Comparative Race & Ethnic Studies,
    TCU (2018–2019)

Orlando Lara, MFA
Associate Director of Comparative Race &
    Ethnic Studies, TCU (2018–2019)

Cecilia Sánchez Hill, MA
PhD Candidate, History; Graduate Assistant,
    Comparative Race & Ethnic Studies, TCU
    (2018–2021)
Finalist, FWISD Teacher of the Year (2017)

Social Studies Department Staff

Joseph Niedziela
Executive Director of K-12 Social
    Studies and Curriculum Support

John Fernández
Core Coordinator

Xavier Pantoja
Core Coordinator

Mishelle Hall
Core Coordinator

Kathleen Hall
Administrative Associate

Ongoing leadership & support from:

FWISD C&I, Academics
FWISD Equity and Excellence
FWISD Equity Committee
FWISD School Leadership
FWISD Communications
FWISD Historic Stop Six Initiative
FWISD Teachers

Community Members

1. Overview

FWISD's mission is to "Prepare ALL students for success in college, career, and community leadership." Being prepared for success means a FWISD graduate should independently be able to articulate ideas and exhibit behaviors that cultivate teamwork, critical thought, and communication skills needed to function in a culturally diverse workforce and global community. The overlay curriculum sets the narrative, understandings, and questions to guide the infusion of Latinx history and culture into the core curricula across grade levels and courses beyond what is defined in the Texas Essential Knowledge and Skills (TEKS). A living document, this curriculum remains a work in progress. It will evolve in response to future TEKS iterations and, until then, be improved upon to best serve the FWISD learning community.

What is an "Overlay" curriculum?

An overlay curriculum serves as a support and guidance document for curriculum writers, teachers, administrators, and anyone else who is interested in knowing what FWISD students are learning about Latinx history and culture. It does not take the place of the core district curriculum, nor is it a separate unit of instruction. Rather, the overlay curriculum informs what's written into the core curriculum just as grade/level course TEKS are used.

How is the curriculum organized?

The content narrative of Latinx Studies is organized according to seven themes. The themes were developed by Dr. Max Krochmal (Principal Investigator) and Dr. David Colón (Primary Author) and refined as part of a joint collaboration between members of the Curriculum Writing Team, the district's Social Studies Curriculum Team, and members of the FWISD community. The themes are intended to systemically infuse the experience of Latinxs throughout the district's Social Studies curricula.

The themes are:
1. Pre-Colonial Indigenous American Civilizations and Iberian History

2. Spanish America and the Colonial Era

3. US Imperialism and Latin American Nationalisms

4. Migration and the Making of Latinx Communities

5. The Long and Wide Civil Rights Movement

6. Radical Movements, Critiques, and Legacies

7. Emergent Shifts and Contemporary Issues

Living up to the mission and vision of this document means that students learn to understand—at progressively deeper levels—that they are able to transfer their understanding of Latinx Studies to novel contexts while they are in school or upon high school graduation. In support of this aim, the curriculum's structure is primarily influenced by Grant Wiggins and Jay McTighe's *Understanding by Design* (UbD) framework. Understandings and questions are mapped at two levels:

- Overarching Understandings and Overarching Essential Questions
- Theme Level Enduring Understandings and Essential Questions

What are "Enduring Understandings" and "Essential Questions"?

An *enduring understanding* is a "big idea" that gets to the core of content. It is what we want students to remember after they have forgotten many of the details. An enduring understanding provides the larger purpose for the learned content, having enduring value beyond the classroom. It answers the question, "Why is this topic worth studying?" It goes beyond discrete facts and is transferable to situations beyond the content.

An *essential question* is a "big idea" question that shapes the materials and activities that will guide student thinking and inquiry into theme-related content. Essential questions probe the deepest issues confronting us; complex and baffling matters that elude simple answers; and issues such as courage, leadership, identity, relationships, justice, conflict, or prejudice. They are open-ended and are framed to provoke and sustain student interest.

How should teachers and administrators use this curriculum guide?
Similar to learning standards, the overlay curriculum informs the "what" behind the district's written core curriculum. Therefore, if teachers are planning their daily instruction using the core curriculum, then they are by consequence also teaching the "overlay/infusion curriculum." Where applicable, the core curriculum will include annotations that refer back to this guidebook.

In lieu of day-to-day planning, this guidebook is envisioned to better serve teachers and administrators as a reference and learning tool throughout the year. It provides a comprehensive account of the content, how it plays out, and curates a list of aligned resources. Administrators and teachers can also use this guidebook to inform professional learning priorities and plan campus-based special events.

2. Introductory Essay
Latinx Studies: Origins, Histories, Presents, Futures

I. Origins and History of Latinx Studies

Preface: Revolutionary Americans

In April of 1777, Colonel George Morgan, the Continental Army's commander of Fort Pitt, sent a flotilla of empty ships down the Ohio and Mississippi Rivers to New Orleans, where his crew would appeal to Spanish Louisiana for aid in the war against Britain. Four months later, the ships returned to Pennsylvania stocked, thanks to Louisiana's governor, Bernardo de Gálvez (1746–1786). After some admonishment and disregarding the advice of Spanish authorities, Gálvez would continue to aid the American Revolution. In 1778, the Second Continental Congress signed a treaty with France to join forces against the British and as a result, England concentrated its war efforts to the South, encroaching on Spanish-controlled territory. So Gálvez financed George Rogers Clark's Siege of Fort Sackville, Illinois (1779), a key victory for the Americans that turned the tide in the Midwest.

Soon after, Spain declared war against England. Gálvez subsequently amassed a fighting force of 667 men—a group that combined free Native Americans, African Americans, Creoles, and Spaniards[1]—to combat British forces along the Gulf of Mexico, aiding the revolutionaries further by making the British fight on two fronts. Between 1779 and 1781, Gálvez's mixed battalion defeated the British at Fort Bute, Baton Rouge, Natchez, Mobile, and finally Pensacola, thereby ending British occupation of Florida. Meanwhile, in the Northeast, George Washington allied with Jean-Baptiste-Donatien de Vimeur, comte de Rochambeau, to prepare a new campaign fraught with challenges. Diseases like smallpox and yellow fever killed as many soldiers as did combat; the Royal Navy dominated the Atlantic; and the recently adopted Articles of Confederation (1777) prevented Congress from taxing states to generate revenue, relying on voluntary contributions from states to fund the war. As a result, Washington desperately needed supplies and money to pay exhausted soldiers' salaries long overdue.

One of Gálvez's officers, Don Francisco Saavedra de Sangronis, who had been stationed in the Caribbean after the Siege of Pensacola, was dispatched for the task. Saavedra quickly secured one hundred thousand silver pesos from Santo Domingo and another five hundred thousand from private donors in Havana (in today's value, into the tens of millions). Saavedra then committed Spain's navy to protect French interests in the Caribbean so that the French West Indies full battle fleet of thirty warships could be deployed to deliver the money to Washington. When the French ships arrived, they blockaded the Chesapeake Bay, where British General Charles Cornwallis had camped his nine thousand battle-weary soldiers. Washington at the time was in White Plains preparing to attack New York City when he heard the news of the French fleet's arrival. He hastily set out on the famous "celebrated march" to Virginia with Rochambeau, three thousand Continental troops, and four thousand French soldiers. When they crossed Philadelphia, the Americans were fed up with Washington's promises and demanded their wages in coin, not the inflated paper currency they deemed worthless. Washington borrowed what gold he could from Rochambeau to pay his soldiers enough to end their halt and continue on to Virginia.

When Washington's army arrived at Williamsburg, the French naval bombardment of the British at Chesapeake Bay had been underway for weeks. Thousands more fatigued soldiers rendezvoused with the troops under Washington's command, and Saavedra's silver provided the means necessary for Washington to recoup his infantry and engage the British at the Siege of Yorktown (1781). This hidden influx of cash from the Spanish Caribbean reinforced the Continental Army and took Cornwallis by surprise. The British were defeated at Yorktown; the escape route out of the Bay was closed; and Lord Cornwallis, along with seven thousand of his soldiers, surrendered. Washington's success at Yorktown was the pivotal victory that led to negotiating the Treaty of Paris (1783), which ended the American Revolution and officially recognized the United States of America as free, sovereign, and autonomous.

Latinx Influence

The question *What major contributions have Latinxs made to the United States of America?* should not be hard for anyone to answer. Latinxs throughout history have made some of the most important and celebrated contributions to our country—and the world. As the prior section attests, it could be said that between Spanish Louisiana financing the efforts in Pennsylvania and Illinois, Gálvez's Latino battalion earning victories in Louisiana, Alabama, and Florida, and Saavedra's massive fundraising in Cuba and the Dominican Republic to pay for Yorktown, Latinxs had an indispensable role in the very founding of our nation—and a lasting one. Nearly a century later, they were also officers on both sides during the American Civil War. Colonel Ambrosio José Gonzales, a native Cuban, served as the Confederate artillery commander for South Carolina, Georgia, and Florida. For the Union, Diego Archuleta, a native New Mexican, became the first Latino to reach the rank of brigadier general in the US military.

But fighting in critical US conflicts is just one of the numerous areas in which Latinxs have made important contributions to society. For example, from 1942 to 1964, a US congressional initiative called the Bracero Program issued 4.6 million contracts to hire temporary farm workers from Mexico to remedy the US labor shortage crisis and ensure domestic crop harvests during World War II and the Cold War. Today, of the five most widely consumed crops in the world, three (corn, potatoes, and cassava) are indigenous to Latin America, thanks to ten thousand years of horticulture there. The majority of roofers, painters, flooring installers, and agricultural workers in the US labor force are Latinx. In contemporary politics and government, Rep. Alexandria Ocasio-Cortez is the youngest woman ever elected to Congress, and Justice Sonia Sotomayor is a leading voice on the Supreme Court. In entertainment, performers ranging from Anthony Quinn to Benicio del Toro, Celia Cruz to Rita Moreno, Nancy López to Oscar de la Hoya, Carlos Santana to Cardi B have kept Latinxs at the forefront of the American cultural imagination for decades. The Broadway musical *Hamilton*, nominated for a record sixteen Tony Awards, was written and headlined by Lin-Manuel Miranda. Any shortlist of the Texas Rangers' all-time great players would include Latinos so widely known among baseball fans that they simply go by nicknames: Pudge, Igor, El Indio, Big Sexy. As of 2019, there are over fifty-eight million Latinxs living in the US, our country's largest non-Anglo ethnic group and larger than the entire population of England. Latinxs produce a share of the US gross domestic product (GDP) that stands at $2.13 trillion per year, a sum surpassed by the GDPs of only six countries worldwide.[2] Here in Texas, State Demographer Dr. Lloyd Potter wrote in 2014: "Our population projections suggest the Hispanic population will likely surpass the Anglo population in Texas by 2020" and will "make up a majority of the Texas population [by] 2042."[3] The city of Galveston is named after none other than Governor Bernardo de Gálvez, who in 2014 was only the eighth person ever awarded honorary citizenship by the US Congress. If the question *What major contributions have Latinxs made to the United States of America?* is at all challenging to suitably answer, it is not because Latinxs haven't made major contributions: it is because our educational system, by longstanding design, has avoided formally educating us on the subject of Latinx Studies.

History of Latinx Studies

The field of Latinx Studies encompasses all areas directly related to the histories, cultures, politics, economies, and civic engagement of people in the US who are of Latin American descent. Thus Latinx Studies is by nature interdisciplinary. And like other fields of Ethnic Studies, Latinx Studies began as a curricular corrective: it emerged to amend mainstream educational systems by reacting critically to the historical exclusion of Latinx subject matter in education. The longstanding absence of Latinx subject matter left many students, teachers, and scholars with a false impression that Latinxs were a people without a history, without achievements, without a worthy place in US culture and society. It took painstaking efforts to correct this widespread omission in schools, colleges, and libraries: efforts by key people who resisted the institutionalization of Anglo/European exceptionalism in education, recovered primary texts and media long forgotten or ignored, and organized material into archives, histories, and courses at times when political resistance to such progressive change was far more powerful and unabashed than it even is today. In short, the history of Latinx Studies as an academic field is a history of activism.

Although establishing the field of US Latinx Studies was catalyzed by events and protests during the late

1960s, there were several important innovators before the height of the civil rights era who produced bodies of research that set precedents for the viability of this area of scholarship and study. The art historian and critic Arturo (Arthur) Alfonso Schomburg (1874–1938)—who was of African and German descent—was born and raised in Santurce, Puerto Rico, and self-identified in his own terms as an "Afro-Borinqueño," or "Afro-Puerto Rican"[4]—had amassed such a large collection of rare books, manuscripts, photographs, and art of the African diaspora that in 1926 he sold it for $10,000 to the 135th Street Branch of the New York Public Library (NYPL). This archive still exists today as The Schomburg Center for Research in Black Culture and is noteworthy not only for being one of the finest archives of African diasporic culture in the world, but also for its scope, which was inclusive of the extensive African diaspora present throughout Latin America and the Spanish Caribbean. Schomburg's work was an early precursor of Afro-Latinx studies and comparative studies in race and ethnicity. Another preeminent Puerto Rican, the lauded poet William Carlos Williams (1883–1963), spent a yearlong sabbatical at the NYPL to research and write *In the American Grain* (1925). This pioneering book treats American history as not national but rather *transnational* ("America" as in the Americas, not simply the US), including chapters on Cotton Mather, Daniel Boone, Aaron Burr, and Abraham Lincoln alongside ones on Hernán Cortés, Montezuma, Jacataqua, and Juan Ponce de León. On his motive to recast American history as inclusive of both Anglo-America and Spanish America, Williams grounded his stance on the importance of the Native American legacy that unites us as a people: "History! History! We fools, what do we know or care? History begins for us with murder and enslavement, not with discovery. No, we are not Indians but we are men of their world. The blood means nothing; the spirit, the ghost of the land moves in the blood, moves the blood."[5] And Julia de Burgos (1914–1953), a venerated Puerto Rican Nationalist, poet, and journalist for the newspaper *Pueblos Hispanos* in New York City, reported on extensive ethnographic research she conducted while covering the burgeoning Puerto Rican populations of New York's Lower East Side and other working-class neighborhoods.

At the same time, innovative scholars in the Southwest were working to provide the groundwork for establishing Mexican American Studies. George I. Sánchez (1906–1972) was one such immediate forebear. Born and raised in Albuquerque, New Mexico, Sánchez received his EdD in 1934 from the University of California at Berkeley, became the first professor of Latin American Studies at the University of Texas at Austin (UT), and "was an effective, relentless, and cantankerous Hispanic leader in the fights against the rank racism leveled at Mexican-Americans in New Mexico and Texas from the 1930s through the 1960s."[6] Carlos E. Castañeda (1896–1958) became the first curator of UT's Latin American collection in 1927. For his seven-volume masterwork, *Our Catholic Heritage in Texas* (1936–1958), Castañeda was dubbed a Knight of the Holy Sepulchre by the Pope, and a Knight Commander in the Order of Isabella the Catholic, in Spain. Julian Samora (1920–1996), the first Mexican American to ever receive a PhD in Sociology, pioneered the field of medical anthropology with his work on Mexican American communities in the Southwest and the Midwest. Born and raised in Brownsville, Texas, Américo Paredes (1915–1999) wrote *With His Pistol in His Hand: A Border Ballad and Its Hero* (1958), a groundbreaking ethnography of Gregorio Cortez Lira, who shot and killed a Texas Ranger in self-defense. Paredes would go on to publish many books on Mexican American folklore and music and would found the Center for Mexican American Studies at UT Austin. Ernesto Galarza (1905–1984) was a model scholar-activist whose book, *Merchants of Labor: The Mexican Bracero Story* (1964), documented the negligence and abuses of administrators of the Bracero Program, in part leading to the program's demise. Schomburg, Williams, Paredes, Burgos, Sánchez, Castañeda, Samora, Paredes, and many others (e.g. Juan Gómez-Quiñones, Manuel Gamio, Paul Taylor, and Herbert Eugene Bolton) provided crucial precedents for US Latinx Studies, leading up to its establishment as a recognized field of research and scholarly inquiry.

In the wake of the Civil Rights Act (1964), numerous multiethnic/multiracial coalitions and activist groups pressured school and college administrators to diversify curricula and reflect more accurately the histories and achievements of people of color. In the spring of 1968, some fifteen thousand Mexican American students in East Los Angeles walked out of public schools to protest the practice of corporal punishment for speaking Spanish in school and to demand more Latinx teachers, administrators, and curricula that included bilingual education.[7] Later that year, college students involved in these "blowouts" also organized their efforts to make similar demands on various university campuses in California, including California State University-Los Angeles, where the first Mexican American Studies program was founded in the US.[8] At San Francisco State University, a multicampus group called the Third World Liberation Front coordinated the largest student strike in US history, from November 1968 to April 1969, and issued a statement of demands to administration to create a College of Ethnic Studies that housed the Latina/Latino Studies Department. At the University of California at Berkeley, parallel efforts came from the Mexican American Student Confederation, the African American Student Union, and the Asian American Political Alliance: a multiethnic consortium working together for lasting improvements to curriculum and staffing.[9] The composition and dissemination of *El Plan de Santa Bárbara: A Chicano Plan for Higher Education* (1969) brought these efforts to a head in April of 1969, when the newly formed Chicano Coordinating Council on Higher Education drafted this 155-page plan to address social justice and curriculum. *El Plan* resulted from a conference at the University of California at Santa Barbara, at which students representing a dozen Californian universities organized a new coalition, MEChA (*Movimiento Estudiantil Chicanx de Aztlán*), which nationally has some four hundred affiliated chapters on college campuses today. In 1970, the creation of Latinx Studies programs and departments proliferated throughout the country, ranging from the Puerto Rican Studies Department at Brooklyn College-CUNY to the Chicano/a Studies Department at the University of Texas-El Paso, the first such program in Texas.

Since then, the field of Latinx Studies has grown in profound ways. Decades of advancement in Latinx Studies research and teaching have produced a long and wide body of scholarship on Latinxs in the US. From the start, a major motivation for this movement in education was to reverse the prevalent negative, biased portrayals of Latinxs in culture and media, from literature to journalism to film to television to politics. While this focus has shifted somewhat over the years as Latinx scholars have made strides in recovering the accuracy of our own portrayals, this impetus is still present in contemporary educators' efforts. And history has taught us that schools with large (if not majority) populations of Latinx students inherently have the collective self-esteem to advocate for proper change and assert their influence as a constituency to improve administration and curricula. For these reasons, our cohort of faculty and staff affiliated with TCU's Comparative Race & Ethnic Studies Department (CRES) have developed and designed this curriculum overlay in collaboration with the Fort Worth Independent School District (FWISD). It is intended to infuse the existing Texas Essential Knowledge and Skills (TEKS) curriculum with material that helps FWISD teachers and administrators be more accurate, efficient, and confident in teaching Social Studies that stay true to, for lack of a better word, reality. Effectively incorporating Latinx Studies content into Social Studies curricula avoids cultural exclusion, ethnic marginalization, and distorted perceptions that undermine the success of all students from all backgrounds. By empowering teachers and curriculum specialists with information and resources, we intend to help prepare FWISD students of all ages and levels to understand more thoroughly the social complexities of the US and Texas at a historical moment when the term "racial or ethnic minority" refers to every demographic in Texas that we know—"non-Hispanic whites" included.

II. Origins and History of US Latinxs

Contents:

1. Pre-Colonial Indigenous American Civilizations and Iberian History
2. Spanish America and the Colonial Era
3. US Imperialism and Latin American Nationalisms
4. Migration and Communities in Early Twentieth Century
5. Depression, WWII, and Cold War Civil Rights
6. Radical Movements, Critiques, and Legacies
7. Emergent Shifts, Contemporary Issues, and Local History

1. Pre-Colonial Indigenous American Civilizations and Iberian History

Considering the long history of the American hemisphere, the ancestry of US Latinxs is extraordinarily diverse. The modern term *Latinx* refers to all people with heritage from Latin America, including greater Mexico, Central America, South America, and the Spanish Caribbean. The wide range of descendants of indigenous American peoples and a variety of colonists, immigrants, and peoples brought in bondage (combined or separated to varying degrees, depending on the region and time period) results in a history that involves cultures from all over the world. Understanding them and their long history is a challenge for students, teachers, and scholars alike because the history spans many thousands of years and covers many millions of square miles. New artifacts, archaeological sites, testing methods, and findings are being revealed by the day, constantly rewriting the history of Latin America's first peoples.

Even with the best of intentions, Social Studies curricula can tend to pay an undue amount of attention to Anglo/European societies and their relationships with indigenous peoples whenever American indigenous peoples are meant to be the focus of study. Such a distraction trades adequate attention to the full range of indigenous cultures and experiences in exchange for a narrow focus on reductive generalizations conceived by Westerners. This has developed a misleading binary in the ways we think about events in world history. We know that in the Americas, indigenous civilizations have risen and fallen. They were often in competition with neighboring Native American civilizations that existed at the same time. Other times civilizations effectively evolved into new species of social order, impacted by numerous environmental and cultural factors. Therefore, it is key to remember that before Iberian colonizers arrived at the American hemisphere in the 1490s, many languages, political systems, religions, ethnicities, and wars arose between indigenous peoples without any interference from Anglos or Europeans whatsoever. (Just as many key events in modern Texan and US history that shaped our present condition involved factors and participants who did not self-identify as being of Anglo/European ancestry or heritage.) This awareness can help you *decolonize* your curriculum: to distinguish between facts and reason on the one hand, and ideology and propaganda on the other. As the saying goes, "History is written by the victors," and what we inherit from our forebears as the official account of the past is invariably a narrative intended to proclaim and preserve the virtues of authority. Oftentimes this inheritance is patently unfair, even inaccurate, as the drive to preserve authority can come with the price of disempowering groups of people who do not deserve it. To *decolonize* your curriculum is to actively audit your teaching materials and practices to purge them of contents and scopes that unduly or inaccurately privilege the values and perspectives of Anglo/European colonizer culture over those of non-Western, indigenous, or—as has recently entered scholarly parlance—*Global South* cultures. This way, you can avoid the default reflex (especially when the material is unfamiliar or obscure) to center Anglo/European importance even in topics that clearly do not include Western civilization. The importance of non-Anglo/European civilizations does not begin with colonization. It begins with indigenous sovereignty.

Indigenous American Civilizations

The earliest people known to have lived in what is now Latin America did so at least 12,000 years ago, confirmed in part by the discovery in 1975 of an 11,500-year-old fossilized human skeleton (the Luzia Skeleton) in Lapa Vermelha, Brazil. Recent studies in carbon dating and genetic analysis support claims that well after the original dispersal of humans from Africa, people migrated from Siberia to North America across the Bering Strait about twenty-three thousand years ago. They then continued on a gradual southern descent over the following ten thousand years to thoroughly populate both American continents. DNA analysis results published in 2015 reveal slight traces of Australo-Melanesian genes in indigenous American ancestry, meaning that at some point in time a different, smaller wave of prehistoric migrants arrived in the Americas from Australia, New Guinea, and/or the Andaman Islands.[10] Precisely how these human migrations happened is still an unanswered question that archaeologists, linguists, and geneticists continue to try to solve.

Pre-civilized people in what is now Latin America lived for millennia as hunter-gatherers in small nomadic communities of probably less than one hundred members. Low population density afforded adequate natural resources that were easily renewed. Efficient weapons for hunting, such as a spear-thrower called the *atlatl*, were developed. Around 8,000 BC, systems of agriculture began to appear in Mexico, yielding crops such as beans, corn, peppers, and squash—foods that are still Latin American staples today. While communities remained small in size, farming required settlements to replace nomadic culture, and thus villages were established that have left behind fossil remains of pottery, milling stones, looms, huts, and an assortment of woven products like mats and baskets.[11] This rise in material culture, as a result of agricultural societies, is likely the foundation of the more complex social structures that appeared after 3,000 BC.

At the moment, the earliest known civilization to have existed anywhere in present-day Latin America is the Norte Chico civilization (3,100–1,800 BC) of Peru.[12] The Norte Chico civilization—which created Huaricanga, the first city in the Americas—is considered one of the world's six *pristine civilizations,* meaning original civilizations that were unique and developed independently without outside influence. These six are the ancient cultures of the Andes, Mesopotamia, Egypt, India, China, and Mesoamerica.[13] Norte Chico produced terraced pyramids, sunken plazas, and irrigation techniques that might have led to their eventual migration out of the region[14]—innovations that could have influenced the later Chavín civilization (900–200 BC), also of Peru. The Chavín had long been considered the true *pristine civilization* of the Andes until carbon dating of Norte Chico remains in 2001 revealed that they were thousands of years older than the Chavín (as old, in fact, as the ancient Egyptians). Such remains include a fragment of a Norte Chico gourd bowl depicting the "Staff God," previously known to be the chief deity of the Chavín.[15]

To the north, the approximately four hundred remaining texts written in ancient iconic script[16] along with varied archaeological evidence tell us that the Olmec civilization (2,000–400 BC) was the first in Mesoamerica, an area spanning what today is all or parts of Mexico, Guatemala, Belize, Honduras, and El Salvador. The Olmec civilization established the first urban center in Mesoamerica, at San Lorenzo, Mexico.[17] It is currently regarded as one of the world's six pristine civilizations, but some writers, notably Ivan Van Sertima in his book *They Came Before Columbus* (1976), have challenged this version of history by speculating that the Olmecs descended from pre-Columbian African migrations across the Atlantic Ocean. This view has been uniformly discredited by scholars,[18] however, for its reliance on premises based on narrow impressions and hearsay taken out of context. The most comprehensive and current evidence we have empirically supports the claim that the Olmec civilization emerged from native peoples *sui generis*, or on its own. While the Olmec civilization is most widely known for its cultural production of giant stone heads some three thousand years ago, it is just as important to note that the Olmec was one of the world's three ancient civilizations, along with the Sumerians of Mesopotamia and the Shang Dynasty of China, where writing first emerged and developed independently.[19] In 1999, road workers in Veracruz discovered the Cascajal Block, a stone measuring 14.2 x 8.2 x 5.1 in. with sixty-two glyphs written on it in measured rows. Prof. Caterina Magni, a member of the team of researchers who published the first findings, has said that the Cascajal Block dates from at least 900 BC and contains writing that most likely has religious significance.[2]

The first Andean and Mesoamerican civilizations probably began as "cultural archipelagos," meaning that several small, organized communities interacted over commerce, religion, and art without a single center of political authority.[21] This credible perspective on the likely decentered nature of the original American civilizations contrasts later social formations in the Americas that were clearly hierarchical and often resulted from conquest. After the emergence of the Norte Chico and Olmec civilizations, many others evolved over time throughout present-day Latin America. *Maya civilization* is an encompassing term often used to refer to all indigenous Mesoamerican cultures and societies from 8,000 BC until the fall of the last Mayan city, Nojpetén of northern Guatemala, in 1697 AD. It should be noted that the modern *Maya peoples* (or simply *Maya*) have continuously lived in Mesoamerica into the twenty-first century. Apart from vast populations of Spanish-speaking or otherwise integrated Mayan descendants, the modern Maya population spans several countries and is estimated at nearly six million people speaking at least twenty-five Mayan languages.[22] But historically speaking, the Classic Maya civilization (250–900 AD) produced cities with tens of thousands of inhabitants, including Chichén Itzá and, earlier, Teotihuacán (City of the Gods), which was given this name by the Aztecs (1325–1521 AD) after they discovered its ruins and revived it many centuries later. The sites of Teotihuacán and the Aztec capital of Tenochtitlán are both contained within present-day greater Mexico City, and fifty miles further out lies the site of Tula, the capital of the Toltec civilization (900–1175 AD). The Mexican state of Oaxaca originated from the Zapotec civilization (700 BC–1563 AD) with the ancient cities of Monte Albán and Mitla.

The Inca (1438–1533 AD) of Peru, as well as the Taíno, Arahuaco, and Lokono of the Caribbean basin, were just some of the indigenous cultures thriving in the Americas when Spanish colonists first arrived. The pre-Columbian achievements of indigenous Latin American civilizations are extensive, as their urban centers exhibited well-engineered pyramids, temples, apartment complexes, irrigated farmlands, astronomical calendars, ball courts, and plazas. But beyond the remains of technology and commerce, indigenous Latin American culture yields insight into studies of values and ideals. For example, Mayan gods are closer to embodiments of personality types than they are perfect role models, thereby challenging our contemporary understandings of the very idea of worship. In Mayan languages, virtues such as correctness, truth, and honor are generally conveyed through words that simultaneously denote actual behaviors or physical things, not just abstract concepts as in English. Understanding this unity of the material and the metaphysical (encoded into the fundamental level of how the language operates) gives insight into an entirely different paradigm of thinking about body and spirit, or temporary and eternal. It is a way of thinking about existence that does not make those sorts of divisions, or at least not in the same ways that we do: holism instead of dualism. In a bygone culture like the Aztec or Classic Maya, who performed ritual human sacrifice and raised children with harsh physical discipline,[23] the flesh and the soul inhabited a singular condition—not *together*, but *the same*. A comparable example of pre-Columbian *epistemology* (i.e., basis of knowledge) misaligning with European tradition comes from the Amazon, and pertains to gender. The very name *Amazon* derives from Francisco de Orellana's experience fighting a battle in 1542 against the Tapuyas, who deployed both men and women equally in combat, shocking European invaders and reminding them of the mythical Amazons immortalized by Herodotus.[24] Numerous indigenous societies, from the Aztecs to the Taínos, kept kinship and inheritance systems that were matrilineal, not patrilineal as traditionally in the West. The careful study of pre-Columbian civilizations has numerous educational benefits, not least among them a greater insight into the sustainability of cultures different from our own here and now.

Iberian History

Spain before 1492 is itself a history of colonization. Even Spain's prehistory suggests that the Iberian Peninsula was a longstanding site of cycles of conquest. Hominins have inhabited what is now Spain for over a million years, with Neanderthals living there from about 200,000 BC until at least 40,000 BC. This period overlapped with the presence in Spain of *anatomically modern humans* (AMH) for at least several thousand (and perhaps tens of thousands of) years.[25] The last pocket of Neanderthal remains found in the Iberian Peninsula was cornered in Gibraltar, the tiny peninsula on Spain's southernmost coast, suggesting to archaeologists that pure Neanderthals might have gone extinct by losing out natural resources to expanding AMH communities descended from more recent arrivals.

The town of Valencia de la Concepción in Seville has yielded ancient artifacts revealing that it was an important copper smelting town (~2,700 BC) in the transition from the Iron Age to the Bronze Age.[26] The ancient civilization of Tartessos (900–500 BC) appeared later in that same region and for centuries existed concurrently with the colonial presence of the Carthaginian Empire (814–146 BC) from present-day Tunisia. After the three Punic Wars, the Roman Republic conquered Carthaginian Spain in 205 BC and, after declaring its Empire in 27 AD, Rome ruled Spain until about 439 AD. At this time, Germanic tribes such as the Visigoths and the Vandals had been migrating into Spain because of pressure from the east by the Huns, an era known as the Gothic Migration Period. For several centuries, Spain was controlled mostly by the German Visigoths and intermittently by the Byzantines. But in the Arabian Peninsula far to the East, Islam spread rapidly after Muhammad's death in 632 AD. The Umayyad Caliphate (660–750 AD) of Mecca—which at its height controlled a territory from Portugal to India, spanning all of northern Africa and

Asia Minor—invaded Spain in 711 AD, and once this Moorish Empire took power in 718 AD, Spain was continuously subjected to Muslim rule until 1492.

The cultural, linguistic, and religious changes that Spain underwent for centuries were dramatic. In Spain, the Romans established the authority of the Catholic Church after the Edict of Thessalonica (380 AD) made Christianity the official religion of the Roman Empire. In the seventh century, Spain's Germanic rulers established the Visigothic Code of law that equally protected all ethnic groups under a single protected category of people, which historians often refer to as the "ethnogenesis" of medieval Spain.[27] Then, the Moors brought Islam; by the tenth century, most inhabitants of Spain were native Spaniards who had converted to the Mohammedan religion. The Moorish influence in Spain extended through all reaches of culture, as seen in the nonrepresentational art and architecture of the city of Granada, home to the famous Alhambra citadel. In language, a large contingent of Spanish vocabulary, such as the words for cotton (*algodón*), sugar (*azúcar*), pillow (*almohada*), orange (*naranja*), neighborhood (*barrio*), hopefully (*ojalá*), algebra (*álgebra*), and guitar (*guitarra*) derive from loaned cognates of Arabic and Berber. Muslim leaders took an approach to Jewish communities in Iberia different from that of prior Gothic kings, who systemically persecuted Jews. At a time when many other European nations were expelling Jews from within their borders, in Spain the Jewish population steadily rose to 200,000 by 1450, or about 5 percent of the total population— one of the largest Jewish communities in the world.[28] Traditional *flamenco* music and dance, as well as the Roma people and *gitano* (Gypsy) culture, arose from interactions and migrations that combined northern African, near Asian, and native Andalusian peoples, languages, and styles. The very language "Spanish" is really Castilian (*Castellano*): Basque, Catalán, Aragonese, Asturian, and several other variants are spoken and officially recognized as distinct languages in modern Spain[29]—a testament to the cultural diversity and complex history of this unique country.

The history of Spain is one of many cycles of conquest and colonization within the Iberian Peninsula. It should be understood that Spain as we know it in the modern era differed greatly from ancient and medieval Spain. The Carthaginians, the Romans, the Goths and Vandals, and the Berbers and Moors all appropriated Spain and imposed new governments and economic systems in turn. Even the ancient Greeks established colonies in Spain, founding the city of Ampurias in the sixth century BC.[30] These civilizations, whose founding or capital cities existed outside of the Iberian Peninsula, controlled Spain for the better part of two thousand years. The last vestige of the Moorish Caliphate ceased control in Spain mere months before Christopher Columbus embarked on his first Transatlantic voyage. Therefore, we should understand that the Spain we know of today, with a formidable, autonomous, centralized government, is vastly different than the condition Spain was in at the end of the fifteenth century, when it began to colonize the American hemisphere.

2. Spanish America and the Colonial Era

It is for good reason that well-informed teachers remove the word "discovery" from their vocabulary in discussing European contact and American colonization. When Columbus arrived at the Americas, there were at least forty-five million indigenous inhabitants already here,[31] with William Denevan's famous estimate suggesting a population of fifty-four million.[32] Using the terminology "discovered" or "discovery" implies that there is a cultural perspective to favor on the subject of colonization, and that this privileged perspective is Anglo/European. Using the term "discovery" reaffirms, if not sanitizes, an outsize importance given to the Anglo/European point of view. It delegitimizes the experience and history of indigenous Americans for whom first contact could not reasonably be referred to as their own "discovery." It might have seemed like "discovery" within the narrow awareness of European colonists, but that is simply a byproduct of Europeans' ignorance of the existence and sovereignty of indigenous peoples in the Americas at the time. Moreover, the motivating intention of Anglo/European aristocrats, i.e., the patrons of the first colonizers, was to extract as much profit out of the Americas as possible, with no regard to the civil rights, human rights, or inherent property claims of the Native Americans and African people subjected to enslavement. The First Charter of the Virginia Company of London (1606), which founded Jamestown, granted its colonists the

> license to make habitation, plantation and to deduce a colony of sundry of our people into that part of America commonly called Virginia, and other parts and territories in America either appertaining unto us or which are not now actually possessed by any Christian prince or people [... and to] bring the infidels and savages living in those parts to human civility. [...Colonists should] have all the lands, woods, soil, grounds, havens, ports, rivers, mines, minerals, marshes, waters, fishing, commodities and hereditaments whatsoever [in America].

A century earlier, King Charles I of Spain (King Charles V) issued a decree on August 18, 1518, allowing his councilor Lorenzo de Gorrevod to transport four thousand enslaved Africans to Spanish colonies in the Caribbean directly from African soil (Guinea). It was the moment that initiated what we now know as the Transatlantic Slave Trade.[33] From the very beginning of Anglo/European arrival at the American hemisphere, the intention of investors was clear. It was to exploit the territories and peoples of the Americas as thoroughly as possible for their own enrichment. Therefore, it is not accurate to characterize this endeavor as one with the neutral connotation of "discovery." The primary sources of historical record reveal the certainty of Anglo/European colonists' initial intentions: to mine all of America's natural wealth, including its people, that there was to be had.

Columbus's first voyages to the American hemisphere are well-documented and popularized, perhaps to the diminishment of other insightful historical narratives. Textbooks, stories, and histories of Spanish America popular in K-12 education always emphasize Columbus's first expeditions; the subsequent arrivals of conquistadors like Vasco Núñez de Balboa (1475–1519) and Hernán Cortés (1485–1547); the concomitant arrival of European diseases that decimated massive numbers of Native Americans; and other such keynotes of official colonial history. While certainly important, these histories should be supplemented with marginalized histories that can reconfigure our present-day impressions of Spanish America to be more accurate and inclusive. This can help to decolonize our ways of understanding, shifting attention to events that complicate grand narratives originally intended to cement the virtues of Western colonizers.

For example, Spanish exploitation of the Americas was resisted in various ways by a diverse range of actors. In 1510, Fray Antonio de Montesinos (1475–1545) arrived to the island of Hispaniola (Dominican Republic/Haiti) with the first group of Dominican missionaries. The Dominican Order's express purpose was to protect and advocate for indigenous Americans. On December 21, 1511, soon after the *cacique* (chief) Agüeybaná II (1470–1511) was killed at the outset of the Taíno-Spanish War (1511–1518) in present-day Puerto Rico, Montesinos gave a sermon that harshly denounced the Spanish treatment of native Taíno people, calling the abuses "mortal sin," "cruelty," and "tyrannical." Montesinos targeted the Spanish *encomienda* system, a mechanism of "plunder economy."[34] In it, entire Native American communities were subjected to forced collective labor and taxes ("tributes") demanded by Spanish entitlements that were owned and passed through family inheritance. Bartolomé de las Casas (1484–1566), a slaveholder and the first priest ordained in the Americas, heard the sermon and was affected. While he did not rescind his titles to slaves right away, in a few years he was committed to ending Spanish abuses of Native Americans. Montesinos and de las Casas both held audience with King Charles V to lobby for reform, and over the span of several decades, the Laws of the Indies—including the Laws of Burgos (1512) and the New Laws (1542)—restricted or ended many Spanish practices exploitative of indigenous peoples: regulations widely considered by historians as the first humanitarian laws created by Europeans in the Americas. De las Casas was assigned to the administrative office of *Protectoría de indios* (Protector of the Indians) and authored the highly influential letter to King Charles V, *A Short Account of the Destruction of the Indies* (1542, published 1552). But while de las Casas advocated for the emancipation and fair treatment of Native Americans, he suggested a more expansive system of African slavery to replace the lost labor force of Indians. De las Casas, like so many figures in history, is a surprising, conflicted figure by the measure of our contemporary values.

Native Americans, Spaniards, and *criollos* (creoles, i.e. Spaniards born in America) were not the only people to resist the Spanish Empire. Africans and their descendants throughout the Americas, when in bondage, often fought for freedom, too, and often were successful. One of the earliest African slave rebellions in the Americas was the San Miguel de Guadalupe Rebellion (1526) in Winyah Bay, South Carolina.[35] After funding several scouting trips, Lucas Vázquez de Ayllón (1475–1526) set sail from Puerto Plata, Hispaniola, with some five hundred Spaniards and one hundred Africans, intending to establish the first European settlement on present-day US soil. He meant to land in Florida but instead wound up at the mouth of the Jordan River, well to the north. Upon arrival, the expedition's flagship ran aground and sank with all of its cargo.[36] Ayllón's party spent several difficult months on land exploring the region for an ideal site to found San Miguel de Guadalupe, and during this time cold weather and a lack of supplies took a hard toll. Ayllón fell ill and died in October 1526, and when Spanish infighting resulted among the colonists, the slaves seized their chance for freedom, setting fire to the houses they were forced to build and fleeing inland to establish one of the first "maroon societies." *Maroon societies* were colonies of black people emancipated as a result of revolt, shipwreck, escape, the demise of captors, or purchasing freedom through the longstanding Spanish system of manumission called *coartación*.

The prevalence of maroon societies in colonial Spanish America challenges narrow views on both the nature of Latinx ethnicity and the history of slavery. In practice, Spanish American slavery was neither universal nor absolute. It did not reign everywhere and was not always permanent, although not for lack of effort by the Spaniards. Through ingenuity, cooperation, and perseverance, Africans in the Americas often achieved freedom and sovereignty even when grossly outmatched by population, resources, and threat. Despite the pervasiveness of slavery in the Spanish Empire, the creation of maroon societies as well as the practice of *coartación* liberated more people than the abolition of slavery did. In 1800, the ratio of freedmen to slaves in Venezuela was 2.5 to 1; in Puerto Rico, it was 5 to 1; in Colombia and Ecuador, 5.25 to 1; in Mexico, it was 30 to 1.[37] As early as the 1560s, Africans who had escaped slavery were allying with Indians to raid Spanish settlements, establishing strategic base camps known in Spanish as *palenques*.[38] Maroon societies existed in vast numbers in Spanish America, and many were so large, self-sufficient, and strong that Spanish colonies had to establish treaties with them to ensure their own stability. Such legally documented maroon societies existed in what is now Brazil, Colombia, Cuba, Ecuador, Surinam, Jamaica, Mexico, Haiti, and the Dominican Republic.[39] In 1570, in Veracruz, Mexico, Gaspar Yanga led a successful slave rebellion that ultimately resulted in a well-sustained maroon society. For over thirty years, Yanga—a man of noble descent from Gabon—was the leader of this eponymously named community, thriving with over one hundred adults. Beginning in 1609, Yanga withstood years' worth of attacks by a force of 450 Spanish troops, in the end negotiating a peace treaty that established their sovereignty with Spanish officials, who renamed it San Lorenzo de los Negros. In time San Lorenzo ceased to be an exclusively Afro-Mexican community, not through conflict but rather peacefully, after several generations of family mixing with new non-African arrivals.[40] San Lorenzo de los Negros eventually restored its original name, and today the municipality of Yanga in Veracruz has a population of over fifteen thousand people.

The intermixing of Iberian, Native American, and African peoples into new ethnicities was one of the most profound and lasting legacies of colonization. In the sixteenth and seventeenth centuries, Spanish and creole society grew increasingly concerned with racial identity and lineage, even if reference to a "white race" did not appear in any known Spanish writings until the eighteenth century.[41] With the culmination of the *Reconquista* and the Alhambra Decree (1492), both Moors and observant Jews were systematically expelled from the Iberian Peninsula; and during the Iberian Union (1580–1640), Portugal was officially considered part of Spain. Subsequently, Spanish culture became more preoccupied with race, ethnicity, and nationality as a means to stratify society. The Spanish developed their *casta* (caste) system, which designated ethnic categories representing the range of races and racialized admixtures developing in the colonial Americas, e.g. *español* (Spanish), *indio* (Indian), *mestizo* (Spanish-Indian), *mulatto* (Spanish-African), *pardo* (Spanish-Indian-African), *zambo* (African-Indian), and *negro* (African). Many new cultures emerged that are distinctive for their *syncretism*, in other words their aspects of combination or blending. The Caribbean religion of *santería* combines Yoruba polytheism with the Catholic practice of ceremonial devotion to the saints. The *Garífuna* people (sometimes referred to as "Black Caribs"), who originated on the island of St. Vincent and have grown to a population of about six hundred thousand across present-day Central America, share an African heritage, yet speak a unique language derived mostly from indigenous Caribbean Arawak. Key figures in Latin American history themselves reflect the largely syncretic nature of Latinx culture. "El Inca" Garcilaso de la Vega (1539–1616), who wrote *La Florida* (1605), the definitive account of Hernando de Soto's expedition, was a native speaker of Quechua, born to the Incan princess Palla Chimpu Ocllo and a Spanish *encomendero*. La Virgen de Guadalupe, the patron saint of the Americas, is believed by Catholic faithful to have presented herself in a series of apparitions to St. Juan Diego Cuauhtlatoatzin (1474–1548) in 1531. The definitive account of this Marianist event contained in the pages of the *Huei Tlamahuiçoltica* (The Great Event, 1649) states that the Virgin Mary took the form of an indigenous woman and spoke Nahuatl. Vicente Guerrero (1782–1831), Mexico's second president, who in 1829 issued the law that abolished slavery, was of mixed Afro-Mexican ancestry and more fluent in Zapotec dialect than Spanish in his youth.

These are just some of the remarkable outcomes of Spanish American colonization that, when infused into a Social Studies curriculum, can inform students and teachers alike of the astonishing diversity of Latinx history and culture. For example, it might be surprising to learn that in 1541, a woman, Beatriz de la Cueva (1498–1541), was appointed by Spain to be governor of Guatemala. It might also be surprising to learn that the New Laws of 1542 that made Indian slavery illegal and officially put an end to the *encomienda* system led to a new yet similar system of forced Indian labor called *repartimiento*, which lasted another century, evolving thereafter into myriad systems of enslavement as Spanish control of America expanded into Texas, New Mexico, and California. The enslavement and forced labor of Native Americans by the Spanish, while unrecognized by the Crown, was central to Spanish American economies and lasted well into the nineteenth century. In what is now the Southwestern US, the system even relied on Comanche and Ute warriors to kidnap adults and children from Apache, Jumano, Kiowa, Pawnee, and other tribal settlements in order to meet the Spanish demand for slave labor.[42] The Pueblo Revolt (1680) in New Mexico saw the Pueblo Indians kill hundreds of Spanish colonizers and drive out thousands more, liberating the province for a dozen years. After owning slaves was outlawed in the US in 1863 and the Civil War ended in 1865, the US Congress passed the Peonage Act (1867), which explicitly banned the continued, unlawful practice of Indian slavery, particularly in New Mexico.

With the turn of the nineteenth century, Spanish America experienced a change in the scale of resistance movements against the Empire. Napoleon Bonaparte (1769–1821) led French forces to invade Iberia in 1808, installing Napoleon's brother Joseph as king of Spain, and the Peninsular War (1807–1814) that ensued weakened Spain's control over its colonies throughout the world. In the Americas, revolts and rebellions were replaced with larger-scale revolutions. In a small town in the state of Guanajuato, Mexico, on the morning of September 16, 1810, Father Miguel Hidalgo called his congregation together to hear his call-to-arms against Spanish rule. This event is known as the *Grito de Dolores* (Cry of Dolores) and instigated the Mexican War of Independence (1810–1821) that resulted in the demise of New Spain and the establishment of Mexico as a sovereign country. In the Caribbean, the *Grito de Yara* (1868) in Cuba was launched with a call to insurrection by the sugar farmer Carlos Manuel de Céspedes (1819–1874), and this rebellion initiated the Ten Years' War (1868–1878), a bloody campaign that caused over two hundred thousand casualties. Céspedes's initiative was inspired in part by the Puerto Rican Nationalist Ramón Emeterio Betances (1827–1898) and his orchestration of the *Grito de Lares* (1868) in Lares, Puerto Rico, which happened just weeks before the *Grito de Yara* but was suppressed quickly by the Spanish military. The nineteenth century was the final phase of Spanish rule throughout the Americas, capped by the Spanish-American War (1898) and the US annexation of the territories of Puerto Rico, Guam, and the Philippines, which also had been under Iberian control for centuries. The exploitation that Latin America and its peoples had endured from four centuries of Iberian colonization is a legacy that can never be purged from our history. But perhaps the key lesson is that across a dozen generations, and in the making of some thirty countries, the will to freedom and self-determination persisted throughout the evolution of the Latinx people.

3. US Imperialism and Latin American Nationalisms

US Imperialism

In the wake of the American and French Revolutions, the circulation of politically subversive Latin American literature began to influence the public. This transnational dialogue in letters increasingly involved intellectuals and activists within the US, particularly in Philadelphia, and added a little-known rhetorical, community-building dimension that was key to the large-scale revolutionary efforts to overthrow Spain's colonial control.[43] Soon after the Treaty of Córdoba (1821) was signed, thus ratifying the Plan of Iguala that established Mexico's independence, El Salvador, Nicaragua, Costa Rica, Venezuela, Colombia, Panama, Ecuador, Guatemala, and the Dominican Republic joined Peru as the newest Latin American territories to gain sovereignty from Spain. These victories were largely due to the success of the extraordinary leader Simón Bolívar (1783–1830), the Venezuelan military commander who served as president of three Latin American countries, including the one named for him, Bolivia.

It would not be long before the US was deeply involved in these new nations' domestic affairs. The Louisiana Purchase (1803), which nearly doubled the land mass of the US by adding six states, portions of nine more, and lands in two Canadian provinces, changed our country's ambitions by changing what was possible. James Monroe's presidency (1817–1825) gave rise to the Monroe Doctrine, an ideology of foreign policy asserting that European nations must never seek to recolonize any part of the Americas and must permanently remain out of the Pan-American sphere of government. While Bolívar and other Latin American leaders ostensibly supported the *continentalist* positions of the Monroe Doctrine (as it was principally articulated by Monroe's Secretary of State, John Quincy Adams), others were dubious—and with reason. In subsequent years, liberated Latin America endured waves of immigration by modern-day colonists known as *filibusters*. These were US citizens seeking to illegally establish English-speaking plantation colonies in neighboring American countries. A noteworthy case was the Tennessean William Walker (1824–1860), who in 1853 led a band of mercenaries to take over Baja California and Sonora, Mexico. He eventually pushed on to sack León, Nicaragua, in 1856 and install himself as the nation's president until his capture and execution by the Honduran military in 1860.

Such efforts to undermine the sovereignty of Latin Americans in order to conquer lands for Anglo American profit were publicly defended in the US by the rhetoric of *manifest destiny*, a term coined in 1845 by the journalist John L. O'Sullivan: "the fulfillment of our manifest destiny to overspread the continent allotted by Providence for the free development of our yearly multiplying millions."[44] While counter to the continentalist spirit of universal autonomy in the Monroe Doctrine, manifest destiny, while contested by many, became the driving force of the US in hemispheric foreign affairs. Coordinated efforts set precedents for positioning manifest destiny as our nation's chief political philosophy, a dynamic that entwined US domestic policies with those of our neighbors, particularly Mexico. After achieving independence, the Mexican government wanted to spur economic growth in its recovery from war, but while the government "no longer supported the [Catholic] missions as colonizing institutions," it also "did not have the population to settle the north."[45] Thus it revitalized the old Spanish land grant program that recruited foreign *empresarios* to arrange for hundreds of families at a time to relocate into Mexico, especially the territory of *Tejas* (Texas), in order to settle lands fit for large-scale agricultural production. In 1821, Stephen F. Austin (1793–1836) inherited the empresarial contract that his recently deceased father Moses had been awarded by Spain prior to Mexican independence. The government newly formed by the Mexican Constitution of 1824 continued to honor empresarial contracts, whose terms varied depending on context and interest. As an *empresario*, Austin negotiated a grant for 297 families, each family receiving, free of cost, 320 acres for farming, 640 acres for ranching, 200 acres for the head-of-household's wife, 100 acres per child, and 50 acres per slave[46]—a total ranging from about 1,000 to 2,000 acres per family, or a grand total of several hundred square miles of real estate. Austin became the first *empresario* to settle the state of Coahuila y Tejas, maintaining an entrepreneurial spirit in the process (although the land came free, Austin schemed to charge families 12.5 cents/acre).[47]

The fact that the land came for free did demand of *empresarios* certain contractual stipulations. In exchange for the space to establish farms, ranches, and homes, the Mexican federal government required Anglo-American settler families to submit to Mexican law: to speak Spanish, practice Catholicism, pledge allegiance to Mexico, not bring guns, and (after 1829) neither hold nor traffic slaves. Besides the fact that President Vincente Guerrero was himself of mixed African and indigenous American descent, a major motivation of the Mexican abolition of chattel slavery was a well-grown moral opposition to the scope and scale of human rights violations endemic to imported Anglo-American plantation systems. (Remember that at this moment, there were about thirty times as many free African Mexicans as there were enslaved African Mexicans.) Anglo-American empresarial settlers primarily intended to establish cotton plantations worked by slaves, however. To protect and defend this purpose, these settler-colonists often brought guns; to efficiently conduct their commerce, they often spoke English; to morally justify the system in a country that denounced its evil, they consistently upheld manifest destiny and their heritage way of life with the ethno-nationalist rhetoric of "God and Country." (It was "Providence" that granted the right for Anglo-Americans "to overspread the continent" in "the fulfilment of our manifest destiny.") The open defiance of the nearly twenty thousand Anglo settlers occupying the state of Coahuila y Tejas instigated tensions with the Mexican government, which passed the Bustamante Act in 1830, altogether outlawing US immigration to Mexico.

Nevertheless, from 1830 to 1836, the Anglo population in Tejas practically doubled. Unauthorized immigration was so rampant that by 1836, Anglos outnumbered native Tejanos ten to one. Even enslaved African Americans exceeded Mexicans in the territory.[48] Moreover, in 1832, after being convicted of assaulting a congressman who accused him of fraud in relation to providing goods to Native Americans displaced by the Indian Removal Act (1830), Sam Houston fled to Mexico. A former senator, former governor, and veteran of the War of 1812, Houston (1793–1863) immediately became a leader of the Anglo-American secession cause in Coahuila y Tejas. Houston represented Nacogdoches at the controversial Convention of 1833 that advocated for Tejas to secede as its own nation-state, a pivotal event in the lead-up to the Texas Revolution (1835–1836).

The next two decades were years of endemic violence in northern Mexico. After a six-month war, Houston became the first president of the Republic of Texas (1836–1846). Although his vice president was Lorenzo de Zavala (1788–1836), fifty-three of the fifty-six men who signed the Texas Declaration of Independence (1836) were Anglos. The "ten men" that Stephen F. Austin hired in 1823 to guard his Mexican settlements were organized in 1835 as the Texas Rangers, a unit soon expanded to roughly three hundred armed officers. The Rangers proved a staunch paramilitary asset for the Texas Republic in numerous skirmishes against Tejanos, Mexicans, and Cherokees, which included the Córdova Rebellion (1838) and the Battle of Salado Creek (1842). In the 1840s, Texas's troubles began to weaken its economy, and President John Tyler, a Virginian and zealous supporter of both slavery and manifest destiny, led the initiative to annex Texas. Tyler signed the annexation bill into law on March 1, 1845, but Mexico's challenge of Texas's southern border began an ongoing dispute that culminated in the Mexican-American War (1846–1848).

This period of Texas history is familiar territory for FWISD Social Studies teachers. The Mexican-American War concluded with the Treaty of Guadalupe Hidalgo (1848), which not only defined Texas's southern border, but also permitted the US to annex a continuous territory that included Arizona, California, Nevada, New Mexico, Utah, and portions of Colorado and Wyoming—over half of Mexico's land mass—as essentially spoils of war. The $15 million that the US paid Mexico through the deal was compensation to ensure in writing that the territory's existing infrastructure (e.g. roads, buildings) would remain intact for the US upon receipt of the land. The Gadsden Purchase (1854) completed modern Arizona, a soft option compared to the All Mexico Movement that was vocally supported by many members of US government, including Senators Edward Hannegan, Stephen A. Douglas, and Lewis Cass. After the Louisiana Purchase and the Treaty of Guadalupe Hidalgo tripled the territorial size of the US in little more than a generation, the All Mexico Movement voiced an extreme side of the expansionist debate: a position that argued for further under-threat-of-invasion diplomacy to annex the entirety of Mexico as a US territory. The initiative was fraught with opposition (including abolitionists, Monroe Doctrine ideologues, pacifists, and anti-Catholic segments of the population), and thus the ultimate goal of the All Mexico Movement was never realized.

The practical lesson here is that the well-trod area of Texas history is one with many points of view. The perspective most familiar to us via formal education is that figures like Stephen F. Austin and Sam Houston were among "the great men of Texas": indomitable visionaries who willed into being a stronger, fuller, and more modern version of Texas and our country as a whole. Nevertheless, a vital and competing point of view on this history comes directly out of Latinx Studies. By conservative estimate and not including Texas, there were far more than 100,000 people living in the territories of the Mexican Cession, and over 90 percent of these people took the legal option to stay and become US citizens after the Treaty of Guadalupe Hidalgo. Between the Treaty of Guadalupe Hidalgo and the Gadsden Purchase, Mexico lost over 55 percent of its territorial mass. In our present moment, the US-Mexico border itself, considered as an actual thing, is widely seen as static: a fixed site that is defended, in places even militarized, and while it is surely dynamic for being crossed by many people, the coordinates of its location are not open for debate or negotiation. But the facts of the nineteenth-century history of Texas and the US-Mexico border are quite clear in demonstrating how this was not always the case: how the border massively moved across the Mexican people, not the other way around.

There is much to consider when regarding this period of US history, because one's cultural point of view can deeply affect the character of the historical narrative. For one, while Austin and Houston did have virtues and enjoyed tremendous successes by the measures of capital and power, they also had moral flaws and endured extraordinary failures. While Houston as a teenager had lived for years with the Cherokee—even becoming a Cherokee citizen, marrying a Cherokee woman, and gaining fluency in the language—the efficacy and sincerity of his "advocacy" of Cherokee rights wavered dramatically throughout his lifetime. As a first lieutenant in the US Army, he oversaw the forced removal of Cherokees from Tennessee. As president of Texas, his treaty to apportion over a million acres of land to establish a Cherokee reservation was overturned by the Texas congress in a matter of months. While he resisted Texas joining the Southern Confederacy and publicly advocated against the slave trade, he held office in Texas (president, then senator) when its constitution not only upheld slavery, but also made it illegal for free African Americans to live anywhere in the state. Houston even ignored the $500 civil judgment he was ordered to pay to the congressman he assaulted, instead exiling himself to Coahuila y Tejas two years after Mexico revoked his legal right to immigrate. Houston's collaborator Austin did succeed in legally securing at least five empresarial contracts to settle Texas, but he also spent the entire year of 1834 in jail during the administration of President Antonio López de Santa Anna (1794–1876) for charges of inciting insurrection, charges that were certainly true. Austin's persona as a high-profile leader—the man who brought "The Old 300" to Texas—was tainted by childhood experiences. The business setbacks of his affluent father Moses during Stephen's childhood struck so frequently that it bred a "persecution complex"[49] among the Austin family: "Moses's wife and children, even more than Moses himself, developed something of a siege mentality—Austins alone against the world. [...] The Austin children imbibed this conspiratorial view of the family's enemies and carried it with them into adulthood."[50] This is a toxic mentality we can observe surviving in numerous Texas communities today, an attitude programmed by an aggrieved self-interest that is hostile to the validity of any values not their own. And it would seem that at least one strain of this culture, this cognitive distortion of privilege as an inalienable right that is being assailed by "outside" forces, may be traced across generations and back to the personal motivations of Texas's founding fathers.

Alongside Anglo-American icons such as Austin and Houston, there are further influences to be considered in understanding the impact of this time period. Jesús F. de la Teja's anthology, *Tejano Leadership in Mexican and Revolutionary Texas* (2010) contains eleven biographies of early Tejano leaders such as José Antonio Saucedo (first official administrator of Coahuila y Tejas) and Ramón Múzquiz ("the ultimate insider"), in a recent attempt to recover the marginalized histories of Mexican influence in Tejas/Texas. But apart from modern politics, the longstanding origin story of the *Mexica* people, corroborated by the textual remains of pre-Columbian Nahuatl codices, suggests that a massive southern migration of people happened beginning in the eleventh century from a region somewhere in the present-day Southwestern US, a site known as *Aztlán*. The legend of Aztlán as a Mexican homeland would become a rhetorical cornerstone in the 1960s during the Chicano/a Movement: a uniquely combined spiritual, historical, and ecocritical justification of the inherence of Chicano/a civil rights. Although Anglo-American settler-colonists may have seen the Southwest as a "frontier" primed for "discovery," indigenous Americans and the Mexican people had longstanding, even ancient connections to the lands usurped by Anglo colonists, expansionists, and later *squatters*.

Latin American Nationalisms

Moving the border halfway into Mexico was but one means for the US to co-opt Latin America into Anglo America. The Santa Fe Trail (1821–1880), established by William Becknell in conjunction with Mexican independence, intended to provide direct passage and commerce from interior US territory to free settlement opportunities in Mexico. "America's first great international commercial highway,"[51] the Santa Fe Trail connected the capital of Nuevo México with Franklin, Missouri. In its entirety and including its numerous variations—it had been blazed by French-Canadian traders and travelled by Pedro Vial in planning a route to San Antonio[52]—the Santa Fe Trail was large enough to disrupt bison migrations, and it transported US troops during the Mexican-American War. The advent of the Santa Fe Railroad put an end to the need for the trail, as the continual emergence of new industrial technologies issued layer upon layer of settler-colonist infrastructure.

Because of the powerful network to usurp Latin American sovereignty coordinated by the federal government, state governments, military, and private citizenry of the US, nineteenth-century Latin American politics, identity, and culture coalesced to become a foundation for resistance to the US as a *neo-imperialist* power. We can trace this consistent theme of resistance through a broad range of cultural works, including law and history but also literature and the arts. María Amparo Ruiz de Burton (1832–1895), a California woman and the first known Mexican American novelist, wrote two novels that explore ideological resistance to US imperialism: *Who Would Have Thought It?* (1872) and *The Squatter and the Don* (1885).[53] The Gold Rush outlaw Joaquín Murrieta (1829–1853) and his vigilantism against the malice he suffered at the hands of corrupt Anglo/European prospectors served as the basis for John Rollin Ridge's dime novel *The Life and Adventures of Joaquín Murrieta* (1854), widely recognized as the inspiration for Johnston McCulley's famous fictional adventurer Zorro. Américo Paredes, in his essay "The United States, Mexico, and *Machismo*" (1971), examines folklore (including fiction and the lyrics of *corridos*, or "border ballads") to argue that the hyperbolic masculinity commonly known as *machismo* was not purely a product of Latinx society but rather a more culturally "universal" trait with curious historical roots in post-Revolutionary Anglo America, when the national ethos was shifting centers from New England to the Western Frontier:

> The man of the forest—the frontiersman dressed in animal skins—becomes a political force, and the aristocrats of the coast look with horror at the vulgarity of the new leaders. [...] In the United States the sense of manliness is exaggerated during the 1820s and 1830s, because of a growing sense of nationalism, resulting in greater participation by the common man in the democratic process of the country, as well as in a marked feeling of hostility and inferiority toward Europe, especially toward England.[54]

Honoring at once manifest destiny and the Monroe Doctrine, the unrooted, dangerous, prospecting, lone frontiersman with a horse and a gun who drinks whisky in a brothel replaces the upstanding, family-oriented, established pillar of the community as the ideal of American manliness. But this emergence caused trouble for the rhetoric of Anglo-American exceptionalism; if the tough, insatiable frontiersman symbolized Anglo-American determination and individualism, then the patriarchal, law-abiding citizen of the Southwest would conversely imply Mexican social order. If Anglo-American superiority was to be asserted in this binary propaganda, the Mexican would need to be recharacterized as having questionable morals. To gain the upper hand in this contest of character, Anglo-American propaganda stereotyped Mexicans as neither courageous like the rough Anglo frontiersman, nor as pillars of society. Instead, two well-known tropes emerged: the drunkard and the layabout (the docile savage), or the horse thief and the bandit (the criminal). And in the early nineteenth-century contact zones, where grossly outnumbered Anglo men precariously encroached upon Latin America, the embodiment of Anglo Puritanical, masculine self-centeredness transforms into the *macho*, not because Mexicans were the machos but because they were the ones who gave it a name: hence *machismo*. The skepticism that Paredes shows in reexamining the white supremacist conviction that Latinx culture is more sexist than Anglo culture follows a well-established Latinx intellectual tradition. The overt antagonism the US exhibited toward Latin America was an attitude that, over time, many Latinxs, domestic and foreign, began to reciprocate in the form of resentment toward the US. While at times both attitudes grew into species of prejudice, a key difference was that the former antagonistic impulse was colonial; the latter, *decolonial*.

Between 1859 and 1861, in the Rio Grande Valley, the cattle rancher Juan Nepomuceno Cortina (1824–1894) led several deadly attacks on units of the US Army, Confederate States Army, Texas Rangers, and Brownsville Tigers militia. His mother was a major landowner of Matamoros and Brownsville. Cortina complained that Anglo-American authorities in Texas were brutal and exploitative, lamenting when these "flocks of vampires, in the guise of men, came and scattered themselves in the settlements, without any capital except the corrupt heart and the most perverse intentions." He described them in his Proclamation to Texans (1859) as "a perfidious inquisitorial lodge to persecute and rob us, without any cause, and for no other crime on our part than that of being of Mexican origin, considering us, doubtless, destitute of those gifts which they themselves do not possess."[55] According to Arnoldo de León, in his book *They Called Them Greasers: Anglo Attitudes Toward Mexicans in Texas, 1821–1900*, "Cortina's movement escalated into a 'war' because of the setting and the emotional circumstances surrounding the threat that he posed to white supremacy. For one thing, whites were very much alert to their minority status on the frontier, where Mexicans outnumbered them ten to one; in certain communities along the border the proportion was twenty-five to one."[56] The Cortina Wars overlapped with the US Civil War Era (1861–1865), and while most Civil War history has fixated on the battles of the Deep South and the Eastern seaboard, recent scholarship has begun focusing more on events at the fringes of US geography and demographics. The rationale in doing so is that such events on the margins, by testing the outermost limits of centralized authority, made the issue of national sovereignty and sustainability the dominant legacy of the Civil War and Reconstruction.[57]

Latinxs participated extensively in the Civil War. The Thirty-Ninth New York Volunteer Infantry Regiment, D Company, known as the "Spanish Company," was composed of Latin Americans, mostly Cuban and Puerto Rican, who fought at Gettysburg. The New Mexico Volunteer Infantry of the Union Army had the most Latino officers of any outfit in the Civil War. Certain units on both sides of the war were so fully manned by Latinos that their names reflected their membership: the Benavides Regiment (Texas), the Spanish Guards (Alabama), and the Cazadores Espanoles Regiment (Louisiana) among them. Some Latinas had important roles in the Civil War, too. Lola Sánchez (1844–1895) was a Confederate spy whose intelligence provided the advantage to win the Battle at Horse Landing (1864). The Cuban American Loreta Janeta Velázquez (1842–1897) disguised herself as a man and used the alias Lieutenant Harry T. Buford in order to fight for the Confederate Army at the Battles of Bull Run, Ball's Bluff, Fort Donelson, and Shiloh.

The Civil War and its aftermath had profound effects on Latinx communities both here and abroad. Benito Juárez (1806–1872) served as president of Mexico (1858–1872) in a time of extraordinary tumult. Born in Oaxaca to poor Zapotec *campesinos* and orphaned at the age of three, Juárez studied to become an attorney before beginning a successful career as a statesman, successful primarily for his advocacy of Mexican sovereignty, indigenous peoples' rights, and resisting attempts at all forms of political, economic, or cultural recolonization by European powers. In 1859, he enacted the Law of Nationalization of the Ecclesiastical Wealth, which outlawed the Catholic Church from owning property in Mexico. In 1861, Juárez issued a moratorium on repaying French, English, and Spanish debts. A domestic policy tug-of-war between Juárez's progressive liberals and the European-supported conservatives grew increasingly volatile, and while the US was mired in its Civil War, France, seeking repayment of Mexico's outstanding debts, took the opportunity to challenge the Monroe Doctrine and invaded Mexico, initiating the Second French Intervention (1861–1867). The defeat of the French at the Battle of Puebla on May 5, 1862, is to this day celebrated as Cinco de Mayo, a microcosm of Mexico's commitment to resist European exploitation and a symbol on which still rests Juárez's heroic reputation.

Latin American and US Latinx resistance to neo-imperialism in the late nineteenth century manifested in a number of forms and places. Much as Juan Cortina did in the Rio Grande Valley, brothers Juan, José, Pablo, and Nicanor Herrera founded *Las Gorras Blancas* (The White Caps) in 1889 in the New Mexican Territory to actively resist Anglo-American squatters and the fraud they were committing in their business of selling stolen lands to wealthy Anglo speculators. Las Gorras Blancas' platform stated that their "purpose is to protect the rights and interests of the people in general; especially those of the helpless classes."[58] Their tactics included vandalism, arson, and raids in response to the deeply corrupt dealings of a local Anglo establishment of lawyers and investors known as the Santa Fe Ring. In 1890, Las Gorras Blancas formed *El Partido del Pueblo Unido* (United People's Party), getting three members elected to the New Mexico Legislature. Meanwhile, on the Texas-Coahuila border, the journalist Catarino Garza (1859–1895) organized a fighting force of over a thousand men in Texas and invaded Mexico in defiance of President Porfirio Díaz (1830–1915), whose neoliberal approaches to foreign investment, *laissez-faire* economics, and wealth concentration had made him unpopular with the agrarian and working classes in Mexico.

As mentioned earlier, the final phase of the demise of the global Spanish Empire extended through the 1890s and was centered in the Caribbean. It should be noted that the insurrections of 1868, known as *El Grito de Lares* (Puerto Rico) and *El Grito de Yara* (Cuba), occurred before slavery was outlawed on either island; abolition laws weren't passed for Puerto Rico until 1873, for Cuba until 1886, and de facto slavery continued to exist in remote regions for years more. The Cuban War of Independence (1895–1898) was publicly declared when revolutionaries José Martí (1853–1895) and Máximo Gómez (1836–1905) published their "Montecristi Manifesto." Issued from exile in the Dominican Republic, their words present an inspiring vision of a Latinx *postcolonial* society free from Spain, a Cuban nationalism predicated on racial equity, mutual reliance, and inclusivity:

> The Cuban black has no schools of wrath there, and in the war not a single black was punished for arrogance or insubordination. Upon the shoulders of the black man, the republic, which he has never attacked, moved in safety. Only those who hate the black see hatred in the black, and those who traffic in such unjust fears do so in order to subjugate the hands that could be raised to expel the corrupting occupier from Cuban soil.[59]

In these final lines, Martí and Gómez critique the strategic practice of Spanish authorities to incite racial divisions among Cubans in order to suppress decolonization. Martí's close friend and fellow revolutionary, Juan Gualberto Gómez (1854–1933), was a grassroots activist and publisher of the newspaper *La Fraternidad* (The Brotherhood), whose work in advocating for Afro-Cubans' and veterans' rights was instrumental in the racial coalition-building necessary for the success of the Revolution. Nevertheless, what really quickened the liberation of Cuba was the mysterious ruin of the USS *Maine*, a naval battleship that was in Cuba protecting US interests from the island's ongoing violence when a massive explosion onboard tore open its hull and sank it in Havana Harbor. This immediately spawned the Spanish-American War (1898), which lasted barely longer than the summer but resulted in the fateful Treaty of Paris (1898). This agreement not only granted Cuba independence, but also assigned Puerto Rico, Guam, and the Philippines as territorial possessions under US control. Thus, the year 1898 marks a political sea change for greater Latin America and the entire Global South. The transfer of colonial ownership of Puerto Rico, Guam, and the Philippines from Spain to the US introduced a new era. With abolition and democracy universally recognized as the natural order, a new species of postcolonial state, the modern *unincorporated territory*, entered the sphere of Latin American political reality. To this day, Puerto Rico has remained an "unincorporated territory" of the US, allowing a perpetual precedent for the viability of foreign (especially US) interference in Latin American sovereignty. After the turn of the twentieth century, a nationalist identity could be relabeled as a *commonwealth status*. The concept of citizenship would evolve to the point where it would require modifiers and variants for precision: *transnational* citizenship, *cultural* citizenship, the *non-citizen national*. The complexities of sociopolitical derivatives that resulted from the 1898 Treaty of Paris were so profound that the potential for Latinx nationality to emerge in the Pacific Rim of Asia was no longer a logical incongruity beyond the realm of possibility.

4. Migration and the Making of Latinx Communities

Before continuing on to examine Latinx communities in the twentieth century, it is worthwhile for our purposes to take a moment and consider the Philippines. About two hundred miles south of Taiwan's coast, this Western Pacific country provides an interesting set of cultural circumstances that allow us to raise thought-provoking questions with students about the fundamental (*epistemological*) nature of what it means to be Latinx. With a present-day population (one hundred million) over six hundred times greater than that of Guam, the Philippines has a colonial past remarkably similar to the nations of Latin America. Seeking out the Spice (Maluku) Islands off the coast of Indonesia, Ferdinand Magellan (1480–1521) arrived at the Philippines in March of 1521—the same year Cortés conquered Tenochtitlán. In only a month's time, Magellan and his men converted some two thousand natives to Christianity. In 1542, Ruy López de Villalobos (1500–1544) set sail from Jalisco, Mexico, with six galleons and four hundred men to cross the Pacific Ocean and establish permanent Spanish colonies in the East Indies. While he, like Magellan, did not live long enough to complete his mission, it was he who named the archipelago after King Philip II. In 1565, Miguel López de Legazpi (1502–1572) succeeded in finishing what López de Villalobos started, and from 1565 to 1821, the Philippines was ruled by the Viceroyalty of New Spain until that authority transferred to Madrid after Mexican Independence. The Philippines was ruled by Spain for a total of 333 years, then controlled by the US for decades until World War II. Filipino nationalists resisted US neo-imperialism during the Philippine-American War (1899–1902), but to no avail. Today, over 90 percent of Filipinos self-identify as Christians (80 percent Roman Catholic). Linguists estimate that between 20 percent and 33 percent of the vocabulary of the Filipino language (standardized Tagalog) derives from Spanish,[60] and there are hundreds of words with Nahuatl etymology. Filipino cuisine, while heavily influenced by Chinese cooking, offers many popular dishes familiar to Latin Americans in both flavor and name: *lechón* (roast pork), *pata* (pig's feet), *longganisa* (sausage), *torta* (omelet), *empanada* (fritter), and *champorado* (pudding), among many others. Traditional Filipino folk music employs a *rondalla*, or guitar/string ensemble (originated in Catalonia, Spain) and sounds very much like traditional *décimas* and acoustic *bachata* music from the Dominican Republic. Considering the Philippines may help students contemplate the extent to which being *of the Americas* is crucial to the fundamental question *What is Latinx?* How did the Spanish Empire impact Filipino culture and economy in comparison to the Americas? How did Mexico, during the centuries when it was a Spanish territory, play a role in the trans-Pacific colonization of the Philippines? Is the Philippines a *Latin Asian* country in a way comparable to a *Latin American* country? What makes it different? Is it merely geography, or do the particular cultural, linguistic, ethnic, and historical factors of the indigenous peoples present upon colonization make distinct and meaningful differences between Latin America and Latin Asia? Are there elements of present-day Latinx culture that were originally imported from the Philippines during the Spanish Empire? Does studying the Spanish colonial history of the Philippines, as a record of Latin American influence and exchange in Asia, make Latinx culture seem more *integral* to the Global South? These questions and more can come out of class discussions, especially when students volunteer personal knowledge of Latinx culture and immigrant-diaspora communities here in Fort Worth.

That said, a major impact on Latin America of the 1898 Treaty of Paris—much as in the case with the Treaty of Guadalupe Hidalgo—was absorbing a significant number of Latin Americans into the US population. According to the 1899 US census of Puerto Rico, there were over 953,000 inhabitants of the island, a population many times higher than that of the Mexican Cession of 1848 and, at that time, higher than any US city besides New York, Chicago, and Philadelphia. And once annexed, Puerto Rico's fortunes fluctuated greatly. The Foraker Act (1900) established a provisional government for the island with very limited elected representation, giving the president of the US sole authority to appoint Puerto Rico's Governor as well as all members of its eleven-seat Executive Council (including the Attorney General and Chief of Police). The Foraker Act also created a US District Court to claim federal jurisdiction over the island. Puerto Rican representation in the US Congress was limited to a non-voting Resident Commissioner. And although the US owned and controlled the island, inhabitants were not initially considered US citizens but rather "Puerto Rican citizens"—a condition soon tested. In 1902, Isabel Gonzales (1882–1971) sailed on the SS *Philadelphia* from San Juan to New York City and upon arrival, US officials detained all passengers on board who were either pregnant or travelling with less than ten dollars, labelling them as "alien immigrants" likely to become burdens as "public charges"—i.e. people with the potential to require welfare for basic needs. Gonzales legally challenged her detention, and the landmark US Supreme Court case *Gonzales v. Williams* (1904) ruled in her favor: that while not technically full-fledged US citizens, Puerto Ricans were neither "aliens" nor subject to immigration laws that would bar them from entry to the mainland US.

In a two-year span during World War I, three US legislative acts worked together to effectively repurpose Puerto Rican men for military service. The National Defense Act (1916) reordered and expanded the US military, preparing the transformation of the Puerto Rico Regiment of Infantry into the Sixty-Fifth Infantry Regiment of the US Army, renamed after returning from deployment (1917–1919) to protect the newly built Panama Canal. The Jones-Shafroth Act (1917) voided "Puerto Rican citizenship" and instead declared all Puerto Ricans US citizens. The Selective Service Act (1917) imposed *conscription* (i.e. a draft) as a solution to the insufficient numbers of US male citizens volunteering for service during World War I. These three acts quickly enabled the US to get many thousands of Puerto Rican men on the front lines[61] of the war, but the Jones-Shafroth Act in particular had further implications. Once assured passage to and from the mainland US without legal restrictions, Puerto Ricans began engaging in *revolving-door migration*, in which Puerto Ricans freely travelled back and forth to the US for extended periods of time, either to attend to family matters, pursue seasonal work, manage property, or sundry other reasons.

The Merchant Marine Act (1920) established *cabotage laws* that, to this day, require all seafaring vessels transporting cargo between US ports to be owned and staffed entirely by US citizens. With Puerto Rico a US territory but geographically situated closer to Venezuela, Colombia, the Dominican Republic, Haiti, Jamaica, Cuba, and every nation of the Antilles than it is to the US, the imposition of US cabotage laws has inflated costs for all goods on the island, contributing to a perpetual poverty and pursuit of employment that feeds revolving-door migration. Coupled with failed early twentieth-century US policies meant to industrialize Puerto Rico's agrarian economy in hopes of reducing unemployment, this quickly led to the Puerto Rican migration boom that spiked later in the 1950s and cemented New York City as the hub of the Puerto Rican *diaspora*.

In the landlocked Southwest, US Latinxs had more routes for migration. As most Anglo-American settlers in the nineteenth century came to either farm cotton (Texas) or prospect for gold (California), the long-standing Spanish tradition of ranching was largely left to Mexican Americans. After both Texas and California were granted statehood (1845, 1850), Anglo-Americans invested more in the ranching industry, but the skilled trades of raising cattle and horse breeding continued to be primarily the work of *vaqueros*. The methods, techniques, equipment, dress, and overall lifestyle of the *vaquero* is recognized as the basis of the cowboy: a *buckaroo* in *chaps* who can *corral* a *remuda*, lasso a *bronco*, fit it with a *hackamore*, and *vamoose* to the *rodeo* (all italics are modern Spanish-origin words). More importantly, the *vaquero* lifestyle was inherently migratory, which shaped Latinx communities throughout the *borderlands*. In the nineteenth century, *vaqueros* ranged over large open territories with grazing herds and traded hides, handicrafts, and provisions at an array of border zones and ports, from San Francisco to the Santa Fe Trail to Corpus Christi. Furthermore, the nineteenth-century population boom of the Southwest gave rise to commercial agriculture. California's population increased from about thirteen thousand to nearly one hundred thousand in the year 1850 alone.[62] Between 1836 and 1900, Texas's total population rose from less than fifty thousand to just shy of four million.[63] From 1820 to 1930, approximately 1.3 million Latin Americans immigrated to the US: nearly 750,000 from Mexico and about 425,000 from the Caribbean.[64] The Civil War disrupted and displaced innumerable communities, and the era of Porfirio Díaz's presidency of Mexico (known as the *Porfiriato*, 1876–1911) produced dramatic inequality and poverty among the Mexican working classes. Furthermore, in the Rio Grande Valley, the percentage of low-wage "unspecialized laborers" in the Mexican American work force increased from 0.3 percent in 1850 to 54.5 percent by 1900; and from 1866 to 1899, "the wages of day laborers on Texas farms declined by about 30 percent."[65] This combination of factors led to increased immigration along the border. Díaz's daylong coup, the Battle of Tecoac (1876), was one of many armed insurrections in Mexico in the 1870s—including by Yaqui and Apache communities—that drove Mexican immigrants to the US at a time when their labor was needed here. The global economic depression that resulted from the Panic of 1873 hit Fort Worth in particular at a vulnerable time, as the Civil War and Reconstruction had just wiped out the slavery-based economy, dropping Fort Worth's population to about 175 and threatening its very sustainability. But the Texas and Pacific Railway opened in Fort Worth in 1876, enabling efficient, large-scale transportation of commercial merchandise as well as of borderland refugees escaping violence to seek safety and work. With cattle selling in the Northeast for ten times their value in Texas, access to a national railroad system, vast market opportunity, and a diverse labor force reinvigorated Fort Worth, soon establishing it as the center of the cattle industry and earning it the moniker "Cowtown." Mexican American communities grew in Fort Worth as workers in the more industrialized sectors of meatpacking, manufacturing, construction, and railroading settled the city's early *barrios* (Latinx neighborhoods), such as *La Diecisiete* and *La Corte* downtown in the early 1890s, and Northside right after the turn of the century.[66] From 1880 to 1900, the city's population quadrupled. In subsequent decades and before World War II, a small entrepreneurial class of Latinx grocers, barbers, and restaurant owners soon developed in Fort Worth.

The Mexican Revolution (1910–1920) plunged the transnational Mexican community into deeper turmoil, with the war's violence inflicting an estimated 2 million Mexican casualties. During the conflict, Mexican immigration to the US increased sharply, but reception was mixed at best. The Anglo population was soaring in southern Texas, too, as the new petroleum industry, agriculture, and railroad travel grew in the region. A struggle for hegemony continued, for while Mexicans in the early twentieth century made up only about 5 percent of the Texas population, they were largely concentrated in border communities where they voted, held office, owned businesses, and served on juries. Anti-Mexican prejudice only grew in Texas, which saw the spread of "Juan Crow" laws and practices akin to Jim Crow systems of discrimination and disempowerment that African Americans were subjected to throughout the South. Contemporaneous with the Mexican Revolutionary War and World War I, many smaller-scale, reactionary insurrections broke out along the borderlands. This includes what was known as the Plan of San Diego (1915), in which a group of Mexican men issued a manifesto to incite violent rebellion against Anglo-Americans and thereby overthrow US authority in the Southwest. They called on Mexican, African, and Japanese Americans to organize a "Liberating Army of Races and Peoples" that would free Texas, New Mexico, Arizona, California, and Colorado from the US and form an independent republic with the potential to return to Mexican statehood.[67] These actors committed raids in Texas during a period of time (1915–1919) that has become known in textbooks as the Bandit Wars but is increasingly referred to by contemporary historians as *La Matanza* (The Massacre). The Plan of San Diego was not at all successful in its aims and caused relatively little damage, but the backlash at the hands of the Texas Rangers and local Anglo-American militias was severe. *La Matanza* was the killing of hundreds if not thousands of Mexican Americans[68] as a response to the Plan of San Diego, and the subsequent 1919 Texas Legislative Investigation of the Rangers' actions toward Mexican Americans during this period determined that they were guilty of crimes: "the first time that the Texas Rangers had ever been called to be held accountable for atrocities against the Texas-Mexican community by the legislature."[69]

Events like this became the impetus for US Latinx community-building and political action in the early twentieth century. Thanks to the railroad, automobiles, and Texas reserves, the nature of Latinx labor was spreading from agriculture into petroleum, and World War I added extra demand on the emerging oil industry. With labor a central concern of the Mexican Revolution and unions like the American Federation of Labor (AFL) and the Industrial Workers of the World (IWW) gaining vast membership, Mexican labor on both sides of the border began to grow and radicalize. The Oil Field Strikes (1917) were transnational; in

May 1917, the *International Herald Tribune* reported that "numerous strikes are paralyzing all commercial and industrial activity in Mexico," especially because of the strike at the Eagle Oil Company in Tampico, Tamaulipas, the source from which labor union organization and strikes began "spreading southward like wildfire" in Mexico.[70] In the US, oilfield strikes followed shortly thereafter, as "a union strike vote resulted in the walkout of approximately ten thousand workers in seventeen Texas and Louisiana oilfields on November 1, 1917."[71] Motivated by the demands of the vast working classes, the Mexican Constitution of 1917 (in place to this day) added several articles that empowered laborers, including the government's right to expropriate property owned by foreign entities exploiting Mexican workers; explicit protections of labor unions to organize and collectively bargain; the establishment of fair workloads; and the setting of a minimum wage.

Public discourse on Latinx affairs in the early twentieth century developed through the growth of Latinx media. Ignacio E. Lozano Sr. (1886–1953) founded the influential Spanish-language daily newspapers *La Prensa* (1913; ceased publication in 1963) in San Antonio and *La Opinión* (1926) in Los Angeles. Both papers circulated widely, helping to define a Mexican American consciousness at local, national, and international levels. Lozano's newspapers supported initiatives and funding drives for civil rights causes, including legal cases argued by the League of United Latin American Citizens, or LULAC (1929). They also covered vital news from Mexico during the Revolution and later the bloody Cristero War (1926–1929), when the *Federales* fought the Catholic clergy over the anticlerical measures of the 1917 Constitution that set out to eliminate Church authority and suppress public displays of religious celebration. As their population dramatically grew, Latinxs had keen interest in news from back home as well in US domestic matters that impacted Latinxs—such as the immigration reforms of the Johnson-Reed Act (1924), which issued a $10 tax on Mexican immigrants and created the US Border Patrol. The growth of Latinx media within the US fostered the sorts of publics and *counterpublics* necessary to maintain large populations of Latinxs that were increasingly experiencing the integration, assimilation, bias, and hybrid nationalism inherent to an ethnic group subjected to the pressures of *Americanization*. The early twentieth century was a period in which the social foundations of many US Latinx communities settled into a semblance of permanence, and grew increasingly urban.

5. The Long and Wide Civil Rights Movement

The migrations that planted the roots of Latinx communities across the US resulted in regional enclaves distinctive for their national origins. From 1900 to 1930, geography, well-orchestrated migratory routes, and family/neighbor connections settled different Latinx groups in different places. Mexican immigrants and migrants predominantly settled into communities throughout the Southwest and in pockets of the Midwest, especially in Chicago in the 1910s, when factory jobs attracted Mexican male workers (most with ties to the central states of Guanajuato, Jalisco, and Michoacán) to the Pilsen and Little Village neighborhoods. By the time Rafael Trujillo (1891–1961) launched his *coup d'état* and assumed the presidency of the Dominican Republic in 1930, Ellis Island in New York City was the preferred gateway of Dominican immigrants. Cuban immigrants had longstanding connections to Texas, Louisiana, New York, and Florida, with New Orleans, New York City, and Key West as chief destinations. Puerto Ricans travelled primarily to New York City on commercial ocean liners, initially settling in East Harlem and then in the South Bronx before the Great Migration boom that began in the 1940s brought Puerto Ricans to various parts of Manhattan and Brooklyn. Therefore, in the early decades of the twentieth century, Latinx communities were strongly aligned by umbilical ties to specific national origins. Mexican, Puerto Rican, Cuban, and Dominican neighborhoods arose before more integrated and diverse "Latinx" ones developed, and the legacies of these *barrios* most often have retained distinctive identities based on national origin that are palpable to this day.

This happened, yet again, in the face of powerful opposition. For example, between 1890 and 1930, millions of Anglo/European Midwesterners migrated to California, and they "brought with them a familiar Protestant worldview" as well as a "distinctly anti-urban ethos [...] hoping to perpetuate the communal familiarity which characterized their former rural and small town lives."[72] To that end, Hiram Johnson, the governor of California (1911–1917) and a member of the Progressive Party (1912–1918), created the Commission of Immigration and Housing (1913–1923). Its purpose was to enact the "Social Gospel" tradition of the Progressive *social reformers* and pursue initiatives to thoroughly integrate all immigrants by means of "distributing" them from congested cities; teaching them English and holding them to strict English-only standards; having them abandon their own cultural and religious practices distinct from mainstream Anglo American society; and generally assimilating them into "the American way of life" under the banner of "Americanization."[73] Many of these efforts worked, and over time countless Latinxs and their descendants changed, adopting Anglo-American social norms, ways of speaking, cultural tastes, religious denominations, personal ambitions, spouses, and even disdain for their heritage. Nevertheless, the making of sizable Latinx communities in the US was the groundwork for organizing and political action in the name of civil rights. From the 1930s to the 1960s, there was tension between US Latinxs working toward equity and US policies prioritizing the extraction of profit from Latinx communities. The Great Depression (1929–1939) saw Latinx immigration fluctuate—nearly half a million Mexican persons living in the US, including US-born children, repatriated to Mexico over this decade[74]—but the areas already established as Latinx communities in the mainland US survived. And this survival was the fundamental experience that bred the Latinx social justice cause in what is increasingly being referred to as the *long and wide Civil Rights Movement*:[75] the sum of efforts to increase equal opportunity and protections that networked radical social protest with mainstream legislation, built coalitions across distinct ethnic/demographic groups, and occupied a historical moment far longer than a single decade.

For Latinxs of Caribbean descent, the long and wide Civil Rights Movement began offshore. Opposing the Jones-Shafroth Act that declared Puerto Ricans US citizens, local leaders organized the *Asociación Nacionalista de Ponce* (Ponce Nationalist Association) in 1917. In 1922, this group united with the *Juventud Nacionalista* (Nationalist Youth) and the *Asociación Independentista* (Independence Association of Puerto Rico) to establish the *Partido Nacionalista de Puerto Rico* (Puerto Rico Nationalist Party, or PRN). Pedro Albizu Campos (1891–1965) was elected president of the PRN in 1930, and he called for drastic change. His leadership attracted both working and intellectual classes, and the PRN organized marches and protests throughout the island. Inspired by Ireland's *Sinn Féin* nationalist liberation movement, he created the *Cadetes de la República* (Cadets of the Republic), a paramilitary organization that adhered to strict, disciplined training and a loyal commitment to revolution, wearing uniforms as they marched in files at rallies.[76] Responding to the Rio Piedras Massacre (1935) in which police killed four nationalists at a student protest, two *cadetes*, Hiram Rosado and Elías Beauchamp, assassinated Puerto Rico's chief of police, former US Army Colonel Elisha Francis Riggs, leading to Albizu Campos's eventual arrest and imprisonment. Albizu Campos ordered a series of deadly uprisings, known by historians as the Puerto Rican Nationalist Party Revolts of the 1950s, and PRN action extended to the US mainland. A failed assassination attempt on President Harry Truman in 1950 cost the life of a White House police officer. And in 1954, Lolita Lebrón (1919–2010), who joined the PRN in New York City in 1946, led a group of men in an attack inside the chambers of the US House of Representatives, shooting pistols from a vantage in the visitors' gallery and wounding five congressmen. Along with Lebrón, scores of Puerto Rican women were deeply involved in the PRN, forming *Las Hijas de la Libertad* (Daughters of Liberty), the feminist branch of the movement.

The feminist cause in Puerto Rico was shaped under unique circumstances. The passage of Law 116 (1937) regulated contraception and introduced a state-sponsored *eugenics* program on the island with the intention to socially engineer a more sustainable labor pool: "demographic formulations which were developed by American scientific organizations and foundations in response to the need of American corporations to protect capital earnings and holdings in the island colony beginning with the depression of the thirties."[77] Law 116 introduced the practice of *forced or coerced sterilization* among Puerto Rican women, and the fifty-three sterilization clinics that opened on the island in the 1930s made the forced or coerced sterilization of women so common that the procedure was simply known colloquially as *"la operación."* A 1949 survey showed that 18 percent of women who gave birth in Puerto Rican hospitals were medically sterilized as a routine postpartum procedure, regardless of consent. "By 1965, approximately 34 percent of women of child-bearing age had been sterilized, two thirds of whom were still in their early twenties." By 1970, statistics showed that Puerto Rico had "the highest proportion of its reproductive population sterilized of any country in the world—male or female."[78]

The US government's interest in reproductive control was rooted in its investment in the Puerto Rican economy. The large-scale push to completely transform the island from an agrarian economy to an industrialized one led to a 46 percent decrease in agricultural employment between 1940 and 1960. Soaring overall unemployment on the island was answered by the Industrial Incentives Act (1947), which afforded major tax rebates to US corporations that set up operations on the island, but the measures only added to growing unemployment. What resulted from this project, known since 1949 as "Operation Bootstrap," was a massive influx of Puerto Ricans into the US mainland. A net total of 470,000 Puerto Ricans (out of a total population at the time of 2.2 million) migrated to the mainland US during the 1950s.[79] With the primary destination being New York City, the Puerto Rican New Yorker, better known as the *Nuyorican*, emerged as a salient identity. Subsequent waves of *secondary migration* took thousands of Nuyoricans to other destinations, including Chicago's Lincoln Park and Humboldt Park neighborhoods. It was in Chicago where José "Cha-Cha" Jiménez (b.1948), inspired in part by the Black Panthers, reinvented a neighborhood street gang into the civil and human rights organization the Young Lords in 1968, on the hundred-year anniversary of the *Grito de Lares*. The Young Lords advocated for local/neighborhood empowerment, improved education and public services, and Latinx self-determinism. Within a year, the Young Lords opened chapters in many cities across the country and became increasingly inclusive in membership: an activist model for community-building across different nationalities of Latinxs that reflected the growing diversification that many *barrios* were experiencing at the time.

In the early period of the long and wide Civil Rights Movement, an array of Latinx social justice initiatives emerged throughout the country as the result of ranging factors. A prominent Latinx organization in contrast to the Young Lords is the aforementioned League of United Latin American Citizens (LULAC, f.1929). Established in Corpus Christi by a small, influential group of Mexican American business leaders,[80] LULAC was supported by corporate and government funds and had a *reformist* platform that encouraged Americanization. LULAC's approach to social issues "incorporated a number of seemingly contradictory goals," because by staunchly supporting the virtues of US institutions and free enterprise, "their prescriptions for social change sprang from a world view in which individual initiative and achievement were central, and where economic processes and class power were minimized or ignored." While "LULAC was proposing to dismantle a harsh system of racism, its values were such that racism was virtually the only problem it identified as oppressing Mexican American people."[81] Because numerous LULAC members left to serve in World War II, many activities ceased for years, but the return of LULAC veterans facilitated collaboration with the congressional-chartered Latinx veterans' group, the American GI Forum (f.1948). LULAC and the GI Forum together had leading roles in myriad social causes for Latinxs, such as school desegregation, fair political representation, and legal residence for immigrants. LULAC and the GI Forum provided the *pro bono* attorneys who successfully argued the landmark US Supreme Court case *Hernández v. Texas* (1954), which ruled that excluding Mexican Americans from jury selection violated the equal protection clause of the Fourteenth Amendment.

Other Latinx organizations promoting social justice took on a variety of issues, including housing, labor conditions, wages, women's rights, community policing, veterans' affairs, healthcare, and the law. Luisa Moreno (1907–1992), a Guatemalan American labor organizer who worked for both the AFL and the Congress of Industrial Organizations (CIO, f.1936) decades before the AFL-CIO merger in 1955, organized *El Congreso de Pueblos de Habla Española* (Spanish-Speaking People's Congress, 1939) in Los Angeles. An effort "of a Communist 'Popular Front' strategy to encourage ethnic minorities in the United States to join them in a fight against racial and class oppression,"[82] *El Congreso* was modeled after the National Negro Congress (1935)—one of many instances of inter-ethnic influence in the struggle for civil rights—and co-organized with fellow activist Josefina Fierro de Bright (1914–1998), the daughter of refugees of the Mexican Revolution. Fierro de Bright would later arrange for the defense committee in the Sleepy Lagoon

Murder Trial (1942), a case in which some six hundred Latinos were detained and nine were convicted of second-degree murder in the death of José Gallardo Díaz. Lacking witnesses, evidence, and a cause of death consistent with murder, the case was overturned on appeal in 1944. But in the California social atmosphere of Japanese internment camps, and with the failure of Progressivist Americanization to dilute immigrant concentrations in LA neighborhoods, ethnic tensions were extremely high. The Sleepy Lagoon case would become a bellwether of challenging the overt racism practiced widely by courts and police forces throughout the country. Because the prosecution, trying to tap jurors' fears and prejudice to assure convictions, put so much emphasis on how the young defendants were dressed—in the urban *pachuco* style of oversize *zoot suits* and long hair popular amongst Latinx, Filipino, and African American youths—Sleepy Lagoon was an immediate forebear of the Zoot Suit Riots (1943). In the Zoot Suit Riots, thousands of on-leave Navy servicemen, off-duty police, and local civilians went on a week-long rampage in East LA in order to, according to prominent journalist Carey McWilliams's firsthand account, "beat up every zoot suiter they could find."

Early Latinx civil rights efforts were equally dedicated to both urban and rural communities, and a strong tie that bound both demographics was labor. African American civil rights pioneer and labor leader A. Philip Randolph (1889–1979) leveraged threats of large-scale peaceful protests to pressure President Franklin D. Roosevelt into implementing Executive Order 8802 (1941), which prohibited racial discrimination in the defense industry. It also established the Fair Employment Practices Committee that spurred labor organizing throughout the Latinx US. According to House Concurrent Resolution 253 (2007), between four hundred thousand and five hundred thousand Latinxs served in the US military during World War II, but since the total number of US soldiers exceeded sixteen million, the country suffered a massive labor shortage in essential industries. To remedy the agricultural labor shortage, Congress enacted the aforementioned Bracero Program (1942–1964). Over the span of two decades, 4.6 million contracts were issued to Mexican workers brought to the US to work in the fields. These contracts were intended to be short-term, but many laborers signed multiple contracts to extend their work periods, and some wound up staying stateside after their contracts expired (either by applying for citizenship or visas or else remaining as undocumented residents). Apart from maintaining necessary levels of agricultural production, the Bracero Program saw two significant results. First, from the 1940s to the mid-1950s, farm wages plummeted relative to all manufacturing wages since *braceros* and other non-citizen laborers were denied full rights and protections from workplace mistreatment and discrimination, including being denied legal means to negotiate pay or collectively bargain with employers. Second, subsequent postwar legislation between 1947 and 1951 transferred the program's oversight and expenses from the federal government to the private sector.[83] Renewed ethnic resentment, coupled with disagreements with the Mexican government over *braceros'* compensation, caused a sociopolitical backlash that resulted in a campaign to deport Mexican residents of the US, an initiative known as Operation Wetback (1954). As declared in the 1954 Annual Report of the Immigration and Naturalization Service (INS), and unflinchingly using the offensive slur for a Mexican person: "In order to gain control over a situation which had assumed such alarming proportions, the Attorney General announced on June 9, 1954, that the Border Patrol would begin an operation on June 17 to rid Southern California and Western Arizona of 'wetbacks.'" That year, the INS deported a record 1,104,541 Mexicans, many of whom were neither *braceros* nor undocumented immigrants but actually lawfully residing Mexican nationals, or even US citizens.

Agricultural working conditions deteriorated through the 1950s and into the 1960s, and as a result, labor strikes proliferated throughout California, such as those in El Centro (1959), Fresno County (1962), and Linell (1965). Local unions continued to partner and consolidate into larger organizations, and one of the most historic of such mergers was the formation of the United Farm Workers (UFW) in 1965. A field worker born in Yuma, Arizona, who became a civil rights advocate for the Community Service Organization (CSO) in 1952, César Chavez (1927–1993) organized farm laborers in the San Joaquín Valley. In 1962, he partnered with fellow activist Dolores Huerta (b.1930) to create the National Farm Workers Association (NFWA). The NFWA merged with the Agricultural Workers Organizing Committee (AWOC), led by Filipino American Larry Itliong, to form the UFW. Their fight to raise workers' subminimum-wage pay led to the Delano Grape Strike (1965–1970), a major collaboration between Latinx and Filipino communities and a watershed moment in the history of labor activism. The social politics of the UFW and the cultures it spawned in the 1960s as the multiracial Civil Rights Movement drew closer to fruition set precedent for the rhetoric of the *Chicano Movement* of the late 1960s and 1970s. The UFW's fight in the struggle for self-determination and economic stability became one of the pillars of Latinx social conscience entering the second half of the twentieth century.

6. Radical Movements, Critiques, and Legacies

The sum of efforts in the long and wide Latinx Civil Rights Movement established historic precedents at the heart of its legacy. For one, several legal cases regarding schools resulted in landmark decisions that transformed our educational system on a national level. The Supreme Court case *Méndez v. Westminster* (1947) ruled that separating Mexicans and Anglos into different primary schools in Orange County was unconstitutional, setting precedent for the paradigmatic case *Brown v. Board of Education of Topeka, Kansas* (1954). In *Minerva Delgado v. Bastrop ISD* (1948), LULAC attorneys earned a permanent restriction against segregated classes within white schools.[84] *Hernández v. Driscoll CISD* (1957), the fruit of a ten-year effort by LULAC and the GI Forum and one of the first school segregation cases litigated after *Brown v. Board of Education*, ended the common practice in the Southwest of requiring Mexican American children to complete the first grade three times—in "low," "beginner," and "high" classes—a practice ostensibly for the sake of not slowing down the progress of Anglo schoolmates. Beyond the scope of education reform, the aforementioned case *Hernández v. Texas* (1954) established that while the US Census regarded Latinxs as "white," they were clearly treated as "a class apart"—an argument made so eloquently by LULAC's lawyer Gustavo García (1915–1964) that he was permitted to speak an extra sixteen minutes over the time he was customarily afforded: the only time the Supreme Court has made such an allowance in its history.

Other historic precedents emerged outside of the courts. In 1955, Raúl Cortez (1905–1971) founded KCOR-TV in San Antonio, the first exclusively Spanish-language television station in the US. It was eventually sold, merged, and transformed into the Spanish International Network (SIN) in 1962. The opening of more Spanish-only stations in cities such as Chicago, Fresno, Houston, Paterson, Phoenix, and San Francisco eventually formed the media conglomerate Univision in the 1980s. In the fields, the 1965 merger of the NFWA and the AWOC (as an "association" and a "committee," respectively) into the UFW labor union granted new leverage in negotiations and campaigns like the strikes in 1966–67 in the Rio Grande Valley, their five hundred-mile march to Austin, and grassroots boycott campaigns in cities across Texas in the late 1960s and into the 1970s. This movement to empower farm workers was paralleled by efforts to recover Latinx entitlement to the very land itself. Reies Lopez Tijerina (1926–2015), the son of Texan migrant farm-workers, founded a utopian colony in Arizona in 1956 with seventeen families—an ethnic reversal of the filibustering and settler-colonization the region experienced up through the nineteenth century. He moved to New Mexico in 1960 and, having spent time researching primary documents elucidating the terms and agreements of *land grants* and entitlements in New Mexico (such as the aforementioned Laws of the Indies and the Treaty of Guadalupe Hidalgo), he soon began his own movement to reclaim lands stolen over the centuries from Mexican and Native American families. In 1963, he and a group of fellow activists formed the *Alianza Federal de Mercedes* (Federal Alliance of Land Grants) to make their case, and the *Alianza* secured a weekly radio show on Spanish-language station KABQ in Albuquerque in order to inform the public of their cause. Seeking legal means to reclaim property never officially rescinded, the *Alianza* failed to convince US politicians of their position, and so they became increasingly radical in their tactics. Protests, rallies, raids, and standoffs with law enforcement ensued throughout the 1960s, and Tijerina's reputation as a radical activist grew as he networked with other like-minded Latinx leaders such as José Ángel Gutiérrez (b.1944) and Rodolfo "Corky" Gonzales (1928–2005) in the burgeoning *Chicano Movement*.

But not all legacies of the Latinx Civil Rights Movement were above reproach. As grassroots action spread across the country in the name of Latinx social justice, cultures arose around their organizations: cultures that—for better and for worse—reflected wider social attitudes and trends that pervaded the greater American social fabric. By a certain measure, the Chicano Movement was no different from the African American movement in that it, too, was plagued by sexism in its ranks across numerous organizations, from Huey Newton's Black Panther Party to Martin Luther King, Jr.'s Southern Christian Leadership Conference. In the words of veteran *New York Times* reporter Paul Delaney, "to top leaders of the [black] civil rights movement—all men—women were a nuisance and a pain, best kept at a distance so as not to challenge their hegemony. The proof was not so secret in those days of sexism and chauvinism. Their credo could have been the James Brown hit, 'It's a Man's World.' The civil rights movement was run as a male preserve."[85] As Delaney notes, sexism and misogyny were prevalent throughout America in the politics and leadership of the vast majority of demographics. In the Ninety-First US Congress (1969–1971), out of one hundred Senators, only one was a woman, and just ten of the 435 members of the House of Representatives were women—a total congressional representation of 2 percent. Likewise, and in spite of a rich history of female participation in the cause for social justice, from Lolita Lebrón and Luisa Moreno to Dolores Huerta and the garment workers of El Paso's Farah Strike (1972–1974), the leadership of Chicano activist organizations was disproportionately male and patriarchal in attitude. Nevertheless, many Chicanas did play vital roles in organizing the movement, both at its core as well as in autonomous spaces specifically for women. For example, Rosie Castro (b.1947) of San Antonio (and the mother of prominent present-day politicians Julián and Joaquín) ran for city council on the Committee for Barrio Betterment ticket, making her one of the first cohort of Chicanas to ever seek elected office in Texas and the Southwest.

The *Conferencia de Mujeres por la Raza* (National Chicana Conference) was the first national assembly of Mexican American feminists in the US, where more than six hundred Chicanas from twenty-three states convened at the Magnolia Park YWCA in Houston on May 28-30, 1971. A crucial aspect to understand about this conference is that while it sought empowerment for women within the Chicano Movement and thereby was a reaction to the movement's male-centrism, it was equally (if not more so) a response to mainstream Anglo-American feminism, which elided Latinas' issues and concerns from public consideration. The National Chicana Conference was organized around four main workshops on the topics of marriage and childcare, sex and birth control, education and employment, and religion. This discourse was at once a critique of the larger Chicano Movement's sexist tendencies to ignore concerns specific to women as well as a critique of Anglo *second-wave feminism*, which was primarily motivated to pursue career opportunities, financial independence, property rights, equitable political representation, and protection from domestic violence for middle-class white women who refused to live as subordinates of white men. Chicanas at the conference emphasized a different set of goals because of the intersections of economic class, ethnicity and race, and neo-imperialism: they wanted welfare reform and expansion, fuller access to birth control, free childcare for working women (since Chicanas were employed in the labor force at a significantly higher rate than their white counterparts), and greater tolerance for secular lifestyles within more religious, traditionalist working-class communities. Given all these aims, the conference was contentious since its participants represented a wide range of opinion on the role of feminism in the Chicano cause, and the final day of the assembly ended with a walkout due to ideological conflicts, as nearly half of the participants thought that racism was a more pressing concern than sexism and feminist goals.[86] Soon after, the *Comisión Femenil Mexicana Nacional* (National Mexican Women's Commission) was founded in 1973 to continue working for feminist concerns particular to Chicanas.[87] In time, Chicana feminism and activism would expand into the mainstream debate that cultural historians regard as the *feminist sex wars*, in which lesbians countered the *heteronormative* status quo of broad second-wave feminism. The 1980s saw a substantial growth in critical and creative literature produced by queer Chicanas, such as Gloria Anzaldúa (1942–2004), Cherríe Moraga (b.1952), and Ana Castillo (b.1953). Anzaldúa and Moraga coedited and published *This Bridge Called My Back: Writings by Radical Women of Color* (1981), a multiracial anthology of feminist thought that announced the intervention of *third-wave feminism*, i.e. feminism focused on how race, ethnicity, class, religion, and sexual orientation complicate gender discourse—a dynamic that the African American scholar Kimberlé Crenshaw would dub, in 1989, as "intersectionality."

The emergence of new terminology—like *intersectionality*, or the replacement of "Chicano" with the more saliently gender-inclusive "Chicano/a"—was instrumental in the proliferation of *identity politics*. The very term "Chicano," to refer to a Mexican American person, is a modern manifestation with disputed origins. The four prevailing conjectures of the etymology of the word *Chicano* are 1) a corruption of the word *Mexicano* that happened in US *barrios*, 2) a shortening of the word *Mexicano* that happened in Mexico, where indigenous peoples would use the term to distinguish Spanish-based Mexican culture from Nahuatl-based indigenous culture, 3) an altered form of *chilango*, the slang term for a Mexico City native, and 4) a variation of *Chichimeca*, the indigenous people of Guanajuato. The word may be a product of *caló*, the colloquial dialect originating from pre-World War II *pachuco* urban culture that poetically blends Spanish, English, and certain Spanish archaisms especially common to New Mexican regional Spanish (and from which we get familiar expressions such as *vato* "dude," *carnal* "bro," and órale "come on," "right on"). Regardless of its etymology, *Chicano* is universally considered a term that at one point was a slur but evolved to be reclaimed as a distinction of ethnic pride. Activists and sympathizers adopted the term Chicano to signal the politically conscious Mexican American subject in the unique time and place of the US in the mid-twentieth century. In the Puerto Rican community, the term *boricua* became popular, derived from the Taíno word for a native of *Borinquen*, "Island of the Brave Lord," the indigenous name of Puerto Rico before Spanish colonization. Likewise, *Quisqueya* was the original Taíno name for Hispanola, meaning "Great Land," and people of the Dominican Republic commonly refer to each other as *quisqueyanos*. Such new self-identifiers recognized Latinx indigeneity and emphasized independence from the constrictive power of Anglo/European labels. Rather than view themselves as immigrant ethnics, many took pride in having survived colonization and celebrated our indigenous roots—declaring that they were "Brown," calling for "Brown Power," rejecting their prior status as hyphenated Americans, and embracing cultural nationalism instead. The Chicano Movement also helped US-citizen Chicanos/as see themselves as one community (*pueblo*) along with more recent Mexican immigrants ("*un pueblo sin fronteras*," "a people without borders"), leading US Latinxs to become increasingly and overwhelmingly pro-immigrant. The radical cultural politics of the post-Civil Rights Act era were also impacted by the success of the Cuban Revolution (1953–1958) and the Marxist vocabulary of proletarian oppression and capitalist exploitation espoused by its leaders Fidel Castro (1926–2016) and Ernesto "Che" Guevara (1928–1967). Guevara in particular became a heroic icon of Latinx self-determinism and ideological revolution immortalized, along with other radical predecessors like Emiliano Zapata and Pedro Albizu Campos, in the public murals, paintings, poetry, magazines, and music of the Chicano Arts Movement that paralleled civil rights activism.

When discussing the social atmosphere of protest politics in the Vietnam Era, historical literature often uses the term *radical* to describe the moment. And for some, implicit in the frequency of using the term *radical* for this period compared to prior epochs of Latinx history is that the 1960s were inherently a more radical period than any that came before. However, it would better serve our understanding to say that it was not the extreme rhetoric and drastic measures of late-1960s social protest that were uniquely radical and different from anything ever attempted before, but quite the opposite: that to "fight the power" ultimately became widespread, socially acceptable, and even, one could say, mainstream. The counterculture became the culture; the revolution was indeed televised, every day. The struggle for civil rights entered public domains with intensity, commitment, and a vast number of participants. The "revolution" was aided by population density and new media that made unprecedented efforts in networking and grassroots organizing efficient and successful. The movement had permanent effects on US society and institutions in ways that the Pueblo Revolt of the 1680s or *Las Gorras Blancas* of the 1890s or Puerto Rican Nationalist militancy in the 1930s did not. The protest movement took hold in public schools, colleges, and universities; branches of the Armed Forces; professional and amateur sports; Hollywood; news broadcasts; the recording industry; churches, and nearly every area of American public life. It spread to uncharted areas of US culture and enjoyed its victories.

In 1966, high school students in LA created the group Young Citizens for Community Action (YCCA) to organize efforts against police brutality, racial inequity in public schools, high unemployment, and several other challenges in the community. A year later, Sal Castro (1933–2013), a teacher at Lincoln High School, met with the group and became an influential mentor. The YCCA took to wearing their signature hats, soon adopting the name the Brown Berets, and quickly inspiring local branches to open in over half a dozen states, especially in metropolitan centers with sizable Latinx populations experiencing similar challenges, such as a dearth of bilingual education and inadequate preparation for students aspiring to attend college. Beginning at five high schools in East LA in the spring of 1968, Latinx students across the nation walked out to protest inferior resources and poor treatment in public schools, including the practice of corporal punishment for speaking Spanish on school grounds. Latinx student activists who did manage to enroll in college—typically the first generation to do so—likewise demanded that universities serve their specific needs and give back to their larger communities. They called for equity and demanded curricula in Chicano/a Studies, Mexican American Studies, Puerto Rican Studies, and related fields. They rapidly built large membership organizations such as the *Movimiento Estudiantil Chicanx de Aztlán* (MEChA), which opened hundreds of chapters across the nation.

Texas was a pivotal site of the Chicano Movement, in labor, education, and politics. Inspired by the UFW's strikes in southern Texas, youth activists in Crystal City and San Antonio created many of the key organizations of the movement and, by extension, much of its cultural identity. The Mexican American Youth Organization (MAYO), founded in 1967 by five students (including José Ángel Gutiérrez), gained popularity across the state and also grew nationally, its ethos following the *migrant trail* to the North and West. MAYO coordinated school walkouts, protest marches, community education institutes, and poverty programs, among other initiatives. In 1970, it transformed into La Raza Unida Party, a political party that challenged Democrats and Republicans alike and raised the consciousness of hundreds of thousands of Chicanos/as. Such efforts attempting to establish new political competition at the fundamental level of elected representation often required far-reaching collaboration across racial and ethnic lines. "Brown" Chicano/a and Puerto Rican activists formed strong ties with African American "Black Power" activists across the country. In California, the aforementioned Third World Liberation Front at San Francisco State University included Chicanos/as, African Americans, Asian Americans, and Native Americans in their successful efforts to establish permanent ethnic studies programs. In Texas, Black Power activists worked with La Raza Unida Party; and in New York State, the Young Lords helped lead the 1971 uprising at Attica State Penitentiary, a watershed in the movement for prisoners' rights and a precursor to the action taken in *Ruiz v. Estelle* (1980), which reformed prison conditions through class action. Meanwhile, homegrown Latinx student movements also emerged south of the border. Student demonstrations and public protests impacted Mexico City, much of Latin America, and the Caribbean. In 1968, Mexican armed forces opened fire on students protesting the upcoming Olympics in the Tlatelolco Massacre in Mexico City, killing forty-four people and possibly as many as three or four hundred. There, and across the region, activists continued to protest US interventions in their domestic politics and economy, largely for the repressive regimes they had to endure under governments that were propped up by the US. From 1930 to 1961, Rafael Trujillo imposed his notoriously brutal dictatorship over the Dominican Republic, but his assassination provided the Dominican people an opportunity to exert their will in a free election. They elected their beloved statesman Juan Bosch (1909–2001) after his return from a long exile in Puerto Rico during the *Trujillato*. But the US government did not approve of Bosch's sympathies for the Cuban Revolution and, after only seven months in office, Bosch was deposed by a CIA-sponsored coup d'état. In 1965, US Marines invaded the Dominican Republic to support the junta that opposed Bosch, and the US was successful in installing Joaquín Belaguer (1906–2002), another military dictator styled after Trujillo. Overall, Latinx activists joined in protesting US neo-imperialism in the hemisphere, and they frequently visited their allied counterparts across the Americas, visits that included liaisons with Castro's government in Cuba. Puerto Rican activists on the US mainland regularly traveled to and from the island, where some joined the pro-independence and student movements. Many US Latinxs, of a group that had long sought citizenship through military service, now questioned American patriotism and militarism, and many protested the Vietnam War.

Latinx youth movements spawned a host of "second-generation" organizations, including softer versions with diluted political agendas. Cultures of social resistance became increasingly in vogue, and many second-generation movements capitalized on the opportunity to create new groups pursuing social justice that were clearly more palatable to moderates. Often calling themselves "Hispanic" or "Mexican American" as opposed to "Chicano/a" and its more radical connotations, such groups continued the legacy of the legal campaigns endemic to the early phases of the long and wide Civil Rights Movement. The Mexican American Legal Defense and Education Fund (MALDEF, f.1968) specialized in pursuing reform through legal channels rather than the often extralegal resistance efforts of its radical counterparts. MALDEF was supported by liberal institutions like LULAC, the NAACP Legal Defense Fund, and the Ford Foundation, and the latter "awarded MALDEF 2.2 million dollars over five years to be spent on civil rights legal work, 250,000 of which to be channeled for scholarships to Chicano law students."[88] Along with the Southwest Council of La Raza (f.1968), this pair of organizations eventually became the most influential Latinx civil rights advocates in the country. When the Voting Rights Act (1965), which prohibited discrimination against non-white voters, was amended in 1975 to include *language minorities* under its protections, MALDEF and the Southwest Council of La Raza gained a new legal instrument with which to sue states and localities for racist gerrymandering: a means to literally redraw the nation's political maps. As a result, voting in Texas became subject to preemptive judicial review for forty years, and the number of Latinx elected officials dramatically increased (in 1981, San Antonio elected the first Latinx mayor of a major US city in more than a century). MALDEF lawyers successfully argued *Cisneros v. Corpus Christi ISD* (1970), the first case that applied the *Brown v. Board of Education* decision to the context of Mexican American school segregation. In the process, it revoked the premise of *Hernández v. Texas*, which, although asserting that Mexican Americans were "a class apart," did not challenge the notion that they were officially "white." The new paradigm that issued from *Cisneros v. Corpus Christi ISD* became that Latinxs were an "identifiable racial minority." MALDEF won other important legal challenges in the sphere of public education, such as *Edgewood ISD v. Kirby* (1989), which reversed *San Antonio ISD v. Rodríguez* (1973) and established the "Robin Hood Plan" (1993): affluent neighborhoods' property tax revenues earmarked to finance public education were to be redistributed more equitably among all Texas school districts. Such judicial successes for Latinx communities were a far cry from earlier attempts at modest gains that were easily quashed by the establishment. By the 1980s, the turbulent social climate of the Civil Rights Movement during the Vietnam Era had waned, with Latinxs comprising a nationwide community that was culturally, politically, ideologically, linguistically, geographically, and economically diverse.

7. Emergent Shifts and Contemporary Issues

In the US, the waning of the turbulent social climate of 1960–1980 was really more a product of cultural impressions and changing attitudes than it was of political fact. The 1980s were a context different from the very public upheaval in the years between the Civil Rights Act (1964) and the end of the Vietnam War (1975). Nevertheless, global politics continued to grow increasingly fraught with challenges, aggressions, and perceived threats under the polarization of power and resultant nuclear arms race between the US and the Soviet Union. And the results had dramatic effects on the Latinx community. The long Cold War Period (1947–1991) essentially began with the military reorganization that resulted from the National Security Act (1947), which merged the War and Navy Departments into the new Department of Defense. This move facilitated a fuller strategy to prevent the US's total involvement in wars by executing covert military interventions that undermined socialist or communist governments throughout the world, even regimes that were installed by free and open democratic elections. The Cold War Period entered a phase known to some historians as the Second Cold War (1979–1985), most remarkable (to our purposes) for the foreign affairs policies of President Ronald Reagan (1911–2004) and the effects they had on Central America. Soon after he assumed office in 1980, Reagan adopted a philosophy that from 1985 onwards would be known as the Reagan Doctrine: to provide funding, organization, training, and arms to guerillas fighting to overthrow communist-leaning governments in Africa, Asia, the Middle East, and Latin America.

Applying the Reagan Doctrine throughout the American hemisphere exacerbated the Central American Crisis (1979–1996) and comparable strife in Latin America as far as the Strait of Magellan. In 1970, Salvador Allende (1908–1973) assumed the presidency of Chile as the first Marxist president of a country ever elected to office in a liberal democracy. His policies to redistribute wealth to the poor and working classes were widely supported but unpopular with Chile's entrepreneurial and affluent classes, who welcomed US intervention. A CIA-backed coup d'état ensued in 1973 and General Augusto Pinochet (1915–2006) rose to power, ruling Chile until 1990 and collaborating with US military intelligence to carry out assassinations of political opponents through Operation Condor (1975–1989). In Nicaragua, and after its occupation by the US military from 1912 to 1933, the Somoza Dynasty held power as a family dictatorship for forty-six years. In 1979, loyalists to the beloved and anti-US rebel Augusto Sandino (1898–1934) formed the *Frente Sandinista de Liberación Nacional* (Sandinista National Liberation Front) and overthrew the dictatorship. But the US disapproved of the *Sandinistas'* socialist sentiments and, beginning in the early 1980s, the CIA applied the Reagan Doctrine to invest in a new oppositional force, the *Contras*. In El Salvador, five left-wing militias who denounced their US-supported government formed the Farabundo Martí National Liberation Front and waged the Salvadoran Civil War (1979–1990) in spite of the US channeling several billions of dollars to the cause of the military dictatorship the Front opposed. The Guatemalan Civil War, which lasted from 1960 to 1996 and caused hundreds of thousands of casualties, was waged largely by poor Mayan and *Ladino* rebels against a military regime installed by US armed forces and defended by Green Berets. Honduras became a key geographical location for US Special Forces to train Nicaraguan Contras, ignoring Honduran sovereignty and safety in the Reagan government's pursuit of winning the worldwide Cold War against the USSR.

The sum of US military intervention in South and Central America during this time constituted a *proxy war* against the Soviet Union, but the harm was suffered by Latin Americans. Ubiquitous violence coupled with the passage of the Refugee Act (1980), which raised the yearly limit for accepting refugees from 17,400 to 50,000, sent unrelenting waves of exiles to the US in search of asylum. Overall immigration from Central America rose steeply, tripling from 1980 to 1990. The US also received Cuban refugees from the Mariel Boatlift (1980), when approximately 125,000 Cuban exiles arrived in Florida over the span of just five months. Latinx scholars sometimes refer to the 1980s as the "Decade of the Hispanic" with a heavy dose of sarcasm, because the ways that US public discourse increasingly espoused inclusive rhetoric regarding Latinxs were factually undermined by the realities of US proxy wars decimating Latin America, a federal reduction in social spending under "Reaganomics," and an intentional retaliation against prior social movements and radicalisms of the recent past.

As Latin American immigration soared through the 1980s, US policy evolved. The Immigration Reform and Control Act (1986), sometimes called "*la amnistia*" ("the amnesty"), implemented two divergent measures. On the one hand, it forgave most undocumented immigrants who had arrived before 1982; but on the other, it raised penalties for employers who hired undocumented immigrants as workers, resulting in stricter border patrol and a higher frequency of law enforcement raids on job sites. Combining the effects of the Central American Crisis, the authority of Reagan's "amnesty law," and stateside births, the Latinx population in the US increased from 9.6 million in 1970 to 22.4 million in 1990. Although to this day, undocumented immigration under federal law is a misdemeanor offense with minor penalties ($50–$250 in fines, zero to six months in jail), Anglo-American public opinion increasingly equated undocumented immigration by Latinxs with an affront to American values threatening US social and economic stability that called for harsher consequences. In California, Proposition 187 (1994) was passed by an overwhelming majority of voters, making it illegal for undocumented immigrants to use public services of any kind—from receiving welfare benefits to riding a bus. The 1990s saw closer interaction between criminal law enforcement and immigration law via the reforms brought on by President Bill Clinton (b.1946). In 1996, Clinton signed the Illegal Immigration Reform and Immigrant Responsibility Act (IIRAIRA) that erected what journalists and policy analysts often refer to as the "Clinton deportation machine" and many consider "the most diverse, divisive and draconian immigration law enacted since the Chinese Exclusion Act of 1882."[89] The IIRAIRA (pronounced "Ira Ira") extended the reach of government authority to deport not only undocumented residents but green card holders, too, by expanding the list of crimes that would make immigrants eligible for deportation. Immigrants, legal or otherwise, who were convicted of crimes were no longer allowed to testify on their own behalf before a judge. The IIRAIRA allowed "an individual immigration inspector to make an unreviewable, unappealable determination on an alien's admissibility" and "to use that unreviewable, unappealable removal order as a basis for a criminal prosecution"[90] in spite of the fact that the due process protections afforded in the US Constitution apply to all "persons," not solely "citizens." Clinton's legislation increased border enforcement operations through its corollary initiative, Operation Gatekeeper. Between 1994 and 1997, the annual budget for the Immigration and Naturalization Service (INS) almost doubled, to $800 million, thanks largely to the IIRAIRA's requirements to hold more classes of apprehended immigrants in detention centers before deportation.

While Clinton's policies drastically recriminalized the border for immigrants, his North American Free Trade Agreement (NAFTA, 1994), a trade deal between Canada, Mexico, and the US, made the border far easier to cross for US corporations. It reduced or eliminated taxes, tariffs, duties, and penalties for businesses that processed raw materials into finished goods in the "export zone" of the US-Mexico border— leading to a sharp increase in the opening of *maquiladoras*: Mexican factories controlled by foreign corporations that would receive the goods without having to pay import tariffs or fees. NAFTA allowed US-based corporations to rely on Mexican and other Central American laborers paid far less than the US minimum wage, spurring the growth of *multinational corporations*. NAFTA also required the Mexican government to allow for the privatization of communally held lands. Latinx critics, analysts, politicians, activists, and even artists responded to NAFTA with a wide range of opinion, from hopefulness to cynicism to sheer outrage. On the twentieth anniversary of NAFTA, the US poet Hugo García Manríquez published a small book titled *Anti-Humboldt: A Reading of the North American Free Trade Agreement* (2014), which takes the text of the NAFTA document and turns it into an *erasure poem*: lightening some parts of the text while darkening others to suggestively produce a text-within-a-text. García Manríquez's experimental book consistently evokes a disembodied, brooding, almost haunted feeling sown into NAFTA's postmodern, late-capital borderland, one of countless twenty-first-century examples from Latinx arts invested with the spirit of political consciousness and social critique.

By the 2000s, a growing undocumented population with undocumented youth brought here as children had become impatient with the prolonged inability to regularize their precarious legal status. In 2001, a bipartisan proposal called the Development, Relief, and Education for Alien Minors Act, officially referred to as the DREAM Act, drew attention to the conditions and safety of undocumented children under the age of sixteen, labeling them "Dreamers." But as of today, the DREAM Act has not passed in Congress, and widespread frustration over the federal government's refusal to protect the most vulnerable members of our society billowed into public demonstrations such as the mega-marches of 2006 and subsequent Dreamer movements of recent years. This public activism alongside private lobbying culminated in the implementation of the Deferred Action for Childhood Arrivals (DACA) policy, an executive memorandum signed by President Barack Obama (b.1961) in 2012. DACA provides temporary relief from deportation for undocumented immigrants who arrived to the US when still minors, but Obama's successor, President Donald Trump (b.1946) pursued the retrenchment and outright voidance of this policy, giving rise to emergent family separation policies and immigration bans still under development and judicial review. A major change in precedent that empowered Trump to expand the federal government's control over immigration law enforcement came in the aftermath of the terrorist attacks on the World Trade Center and the Pentagon (2001). After 9/11, President George W. Bush (b.1946) signed into law the Patriot Act (2001), which ultimately cleared the path to establishing the Department of Homeland Security (2003) as well as Immigration and Customs Enforcement (2003).

Despite its outsize coverage in news media and public debate by elected officials, immigration has not been the only significant social issue at play in Latinx communities in the twenty-first century. What is growing now in the US into a multilayered movement to publicly vilify—if not criminalize—Latinxs a group by blurring the distinctions between *cultural citizenship*, *ethnic citizenship*, and *legal citizenship* has resulted in increasingly disheartening sentiments within Latinx communities regarding our relationship with the US government and its voting citizenry. Anglo-centric *nativist movements* that have recently spread in reaction to the steady rise of the US Latinx population (now our largest non-Anglo ethnic group) have, on routine occasion, called for the deportation of Puerto Ricans, too, even though such action would be impossible since all Puerto Ricans are still inherently US citizens by birthright. The emergent shifts and contemporary issues facing the Puerto Rican community have therefore had different legal and political contexts, even if related to Central American immigrants' condition by means of shared language, culture, and ethnicity. In 1976, the Internal Revenue Service (IRS) adopted Section 936 of the US Tax Code, which provided US corporations that conducted at least 75 percent of their operations on the island of Puerto Rico full income tax rebates exactly equal to their income tax burdens. But under pressure by fellow politicians seeking to reform "corporate welfare," Bill Clinton announced in 1996 that a ten-year plan to gradually yet completely phase out the corporate benefits of Section 936 would be implemented. Coupled with the effects of the 2007-2008 Global Financial Crisis that strained corporate investment potential, the phase-out of Section 936 had catastrophic effects on Puerto Rico's economy. The damage to Puerto Rico's economy was exacerbated further with the subsequent government-debt crisis that peaked in 2014, when Standard & Poor's downgraded Puerto Rico's *triple-tax exempt municipal bonds* to "junk status." Because of its political status as an unincorporated territory of the US, Puerto Rico is not eligible to file for bankruptcy under Chapter 9 Title 11 of the US Bankruptcy Code (the way Detroit did in 2013), and thus the island's debt burden has exceeded $74 billion. *Austerity* proposals for Puerto Rico have proliferated in recent years, including the introduction in 2016 of House Resolution 4900, which has proposed, among other measures, to reduce the legal minimum wage in Puerto Rico from the federal minimum of $7.25 per hour to $4.25 per hour. To make matters worse, Hurricane Maria struck the island in 2017, destroying about 80 percent of the island's agriculture and inflicting an estimated $90 billion in damage. As a result of such misfortunes both recent and historical, Puerto Rico suffers from inordinate poverty. The most recent data collected by the US Census Bureau reports that the current poverty rate in Puerto Rico is 44.4 percent—more than double that of the poorest state in the country (Mississippi, 19.8 percent). While the national average of US median household income is $59,039, in Puerto Rico the figure is only $19,775.

To this day, Puerto Ricans on the island are not permitted to vote in any US federal elections. Puerto Rico is still represented in US Congress solely by a Resident Commissioner in the House of Representatives. Since 1900, when the Foraker Act was passed, until January 2019, the Resident Commissioner could not cast a vote on any congressional matter. Beginning with the 116th US Congress, new House Rules now allow the Resident Commissioner to cast a *symbolic vote*, i.e. only if that vote is not a tiebreaker and thereby not decisive of a legislative outcome. The Puerto Rico Oversight Management and Economic Stability Act (PROMESA) of 2016, which established an oversight board to manage Puerto Rico's debt crisis, explicitly states that eligibility to serve on this commission requires that the considered "individual is not an officer, elected official, or employee of the territorial government, a candidate for elected office of the territorial government, or a former elected official of the territorial government." In other words, PROMESA is explicit and intentional in denying the opportunity for Puerto Rico's democratically elected representatives to participate in developing the economic recovery strategy of their own commonwealth.

Nevertheless, the will of the Puerto Rican people to assert their fundamental human right to cultural (if not political) sovereignty has remained strong. Migration to the US mainland has seen a dramatic resurgence since Hurricane Maria, on a scale not witnessed since Operation Bootstrap in the 1950s. On March 27, 2019, Puerto Rico's Governor Ricardo Roselló (b.1979) signed an executive order that immediately banned the practice of "gay conversion therapy" throughout the island, a major victory for the Puerto Rican LGBT community and an exemplar for improving social tolerance and inclusion to the world. In January of 2019, Representative Alexandria Ocasio-Cortez (b.1989), a Nuyorican from the Bronx, was sworn in to office and, at twenty-nine years old, became the youngest woman ever to serve in the US Congress. Ocasio-Cortez, along with Supreme Court Justice Sonia Sotomayor (b.1954), are the leading Latina voices in mainstream US government, and both are fervent supporters of liberal policies and interpretations of law. Their progressive sociopolitical purview is shared by most US Latinxs who are continually in the process of self-determinism. This process within the realm of identity politics is one grounded in a richly complex and keenly self-aware cultural discourse that not only pervades political action, but also reaches to the most fundamental element of our being: language. Today, the politics of Latinx self-representation continue to be negotiated, and a thoughtful, ongoing conversation in the national community has been on the matter of terminology. "Latino" and "Chicano" have long since been supplemented (if not replaced) with "Latinx" and "Chicano/a" thanks to the intervention of outspoken English-speaking feminists, but the debate still continues on the matter of terminology in referring to ourselves. Since Spanish is a romance language and hence its nouns are inherently gendered, the "-o/a" or "-a/o" option has become customary in Latinx expression. But as our community becomes more informed and respectful of the spectrum of gender identities we inhabit, the masculine/feminine dichotomy does not suit individuals who are either transgender or non-binary gender, and thus new terms have been introduced in Latinx cultural studies. The most salient third option proposed by intellectuals and activists has recently become the term *Latinx* (pronounced 'lah-TEEN-ecks'), and a fourth choice with modest but growing popularity is *Latine* (preserving the vowel suffix but avoiding a conventional signal of feminine or masculine). "Latinx" is endorsed principally by US Latinxs whose dominant language is English, for many of us who are native speakers of Spanish not only find "Latinx" odd-looking and a bit more cumbersome to say, but also do not necessarily see the *–o* and *–a* endings as unequivocally definitive of the gender of all nouns (e.g. *la mano*, "the hand" is a feminine noun; *el problema* "the problem" is a masculine one). The issue of self-identity, self-representation, inclusivity and respect, and the language we use to express who we are and what we value is a thought-provoking area of Latinx culture that evinces how healthy and vibrant our cultural communities are.

Latinx vitality can be seen in myriad aspects of our lives. Our cultural and ideological diversity as a broadly defined people in this country run the gamut of possibilities. Some of the most well-known political conservatives in the US are Latinxs, such as Florida Senator Marco Rubio (b.1971); Texas's own Ted Cruz (b.1970) and George Prescott Bush (b.1976); and Susana Martinez (b.1959), who recently ended her term as governor of New Mexico. The Congressional Hispanic Caucus (f.1976) and the Congressional Hispanic Conference (f.2003) represent, respectively, the Democratic and Republican cohorts of Latinx officials in the federal legislature. Nevertheless, Latinxs as a whole have historically tended to vote more often for liberal-leaning candidates than conservative ones in elections; in 2016, Latinx voters cast 66 percent of their ballots for Hillary Clinton and only 28 percent for President Trump. There are a host of reasons for this tendency, chief among them the respective platforms of the Democratic and Republican parties: raising the minimum wage, progressive income tax scales, and single-payer healthcare for Democrats; punitive anti-immigration measures, deregulating corporate oversight, and expanding military spending for Republicans. But depending on a range of factors (e.g. geographical, financial, religious), how Latinxs as a voting bloc will express themselves in political elections is becoming increasingly difficult to predict, and many political scientists reject the idea that there is such a thing as "the Latinx vote." The heritage religion of the vast majority of Latinxs is Roman Catholicism, and hence those Latinxs who self-identify as doctrinaire, faithful, practicing Catholics would be more inclined to support the restriction or outright prohibition of abortion, or a ban on same-sex marriage, as espoused by most Republican candidates. Latinxs far removed from the migrant generation of their family background and who have deeply assimilated into mainstream Anglo-American culture may be more inclined to support strict immigration policies, and even systematic deportations. Latinx veterans are often strongly in favor of increased military spending. Depending on a variety of factors—some easy to see, others less so—Latinxs are surely a political force to be reckoned with, but the final say of such a reckoning is more complicated than non-Latinxs might think.

Conclusion: Responsible Americans
Of the myriad challenges facing the Latinx community today, perhaps the most daunting is the reality of the *racial wealth gap*. As this essay has tried to illustrate in detail, from the Taíno-Spanish War five centuries ago to children in detention centers five years ago, the history of Latinxs has been colored by an undeniable legacy of exploitation. This is not to be pessimistic, or melodramatic, or angry: it is not to suggest we have no happy occasions, golden opportunities, or moments of peace and joy. It is simply a reasonable conclusion to draw from the record of historical events, as well as from the results of the American colonial experiment that, in the present, can be measured empirically. Recent data reveals that the total GDP of all Latin American countries combined totals a sum of roughly $4.3 trillion dollars. In comparison, the total GDP of the US, on its own, is approximately $22.7 trillion. While one might be inclined to believe that this gross discrepancy in favor of the US has resulted from benign factors (e.g. robust population, financial

intelligence, work ethic, responsible governance, sheer luck), one has to pause and consider the extent to which an ideology of *American exceptionalism* has informed such an optimistic and self-serving view. But to come full circle here, and to return to the era of the founding of our country, let us consider what really mattered to the civic-minded people who envisioned it. In the years between the signing of the Treaty of Paris in 1783 and the ratification of the Constitution of the United States of America in 1790, the leaders of the original thirteen colonies understood that a new, comprehensive political order needed to enumerate a code of civil regulations to replace the default authority of British Common Law. In his *Notes on the State of Virgina* (1787), "Thomas Jefferson ranked reform of the law of inheritance even above the statute on religious freedom in his list of the 'most remarkable alterations' needed in the common law."[91] The reason was that British Common Law modelled the financial inheritance of private property on two key practices: *primogenture* and *entail*. Primogenture was the legal requirement applied to situations when an individual died and left behind an estate but did not have a living will that articulated exactly how and onto whom the estate would be passed. In such a case, primogeniture assured that the entire estate would be inherited solely by one's firstborn child: and in the feudal tradition, particularly one's firstborn son. *Entail* applied to the event of a deceased person leaving behind privately owned land: in this scenario, if the deceased did not have any direct decendants who would be the rightful inheritors of the land, the land would revert back to the grantor from whom he acquired it. Jefferson and many other leading American colonists believed that this aristocratic system, fundamentally engineered to allow wealth to perpetually remain in the hands of the wealthy, was amoral. Inspired by his contemporary, the economist Adam Smith, Jefferson famously wrote: "A power to dispose of estates for ever is manifestly absurd. The earth and the fulness of it belongs to every generation, and the preceding one can have no right to bind it up from posterity. Such extension of property is quite unnatural." Jefferson's fellow patriots, including James Madison and George Washington, agreed. They were more sympathetic to *wealth redistribution* than untaxed direct inheritance. Primogeniture had already been abolished in all of the New England colonies except for Rhode Island by as early as 1700, and Georgia, Virgina, and North Carolina all followed suit before the US Constitution was ratified.[92] That private property could be hoarded by a relative few who then would effectively comprise a new aristocracy—this time with entitlements derived from capital instead of tradition—was considered by the founding fathers as among the greatest dangers to the Republic.

The current state of private wealth in the US is a situation trending not towards Jefferson's and Smith's dream but rather their nightmare. Financial inheritance in the US, while not systematized as narrowly as it was under British Common Law, is so firmly based on the premise that property ought to pass from parent to child that many of us believe it to be the only fair way to circulate money across generations. But when we study the long history of our nation, careful to include the stories of *all* of our diverse ancestries, we realize that not all communities had equal opportunity to amass capital. Not all communities had equal opportunity to even receive wages for their labor. Or even to shelter in the rights and protections enumerated in the Constitution. The centuries-long history of our country reveals that most of it unfolded in a paradigm that clearly privileged certain demographics of people solely for their inherent membership in a privileged class. And the circumstances of law, politics, education, ambition, and talent notwithstanding, our system of the familial inheritance of estates has preserved the legacy of inequity in America. In recent years, economists and statisticians have begun to rigorously examine the long-term consequences of financial inheritance, and as they do, their findings paint a picture that illustrates how deep and lasting the effects of systemic exploitation have been on our society. Time and again, scholarly research shows that the history of *institutional racism* in the America—and the mechanisms of our economy that, by design, extract profit from disenfranchised underclasses to ensure the prosperity of ruling classes—have led to stark divisions of wealth along racial boundaries.

In 2018, four scholars from Stanford, Harvard, and the US Census Bureau published a paper titled "Race and Economic Opportunity in the United States: An Intergenerational Perspective" that tabulates, among many other things, the differences in average wages between different ethnicities in the US. They found that per capita median annual income for white people was $33,620; for Latinxs, $27,140; for African Americans, $19,550.[93] Put another way, white Americans on (median) average earn wages 23.8 percent higher than those of Latinxs, and 71.9 percent higher than those of African Americans. However, when researchers shift their focus of attention from per capita wages to household net worth, the findings are remarkably different. Whether considering averages in either median or mean terms, the average white family has a household net worth approximately *500 percent higher* than that of either Latinxs or African Americans: an extreme socioeconomic divide that has existed for as long as such data has been collected, and in recent decades has only grown wider. The consensus opinion of expert research analysts is that our country's system of the financial inheritance of private property, coupled with tax rates on investment returns lower than income tax rates, has *over generations* resulted in a severely racialized stratification of socioeconomic classes that reflects the histories of the social conditions these respective groups have experienced over the course of our nation's existence.

This Latinx Studies curriculum has many purposes. It is certainly intended to provide content and resources for teachers and students in pursuit of more accurate portrayals of US history and culture than extant Social Studies K-12 curricula have heretofore provided. Yet as inherently valuable as such an intention might be, the underpinning of it is not purely intellectual. It is not solely a matter of percepts and concepts, exposure to new information, and formation of skills for students pursuing academic rigor. At the heart of this curriculum is a more expansive objective: *empowerment*. To learn more about the history of US Latinxs, our ancestries and our present conditions, has value insofar as we commit ourselves to employ the information and skills toward improving the Fort Worth community. FWISD is a remarkably diverse school district that over the past generation has experienced a demographic renewal. This transformation is the byproduct of a vast web of social and economic forces—and whether they were imposed on us or we are their cause or some combination thereof, in the end we all share responsibility for doing the right thing. This country was not founded on preserving comforts and privileges bestowed by birthright or inheritance. In fact, our country was founded on the idea that this is precisely what the Old World had wrong. For Latinx students and teachers who recognize their own experience and heritage in these pages, one hopes that knowledge of self will strengthen their confidence and resolve as they envision their ambitions. Many of us can personally relate to the disheartening realities of the racial wealth gap but know that education is our best opportunity to do our part and reverse the trend. For students and teachers of other backgrounds, there is ample room in this curriculum to discover hidden truths and new understandings that breed patience and empathy, and to gain vital critical and social skills in the process. One hopes that this curriculum will provide enough of a resource to make greater sense of a rapidly changing world. And maybe even provide—*ojalá*—something you never imagined you would love.

Notes

1. Trickey, "The Little-Remembered Ally."
2. Moreno, "Latinos Could Fuel."
3. Potter and Hoque, "Texas Population Projections," 4.
4. Frederick, "Honoring Arturo Schomburg's Legacy."
5. Williams, *In the American Grain*, 73.
6. Dugger, "Integration Hero."
7. Escobar, "How 50 Years."
8. Mariscal, *Brown-Eyed Children of the Sun*, 213.
9. Mariscal, *Brown-Eyed Children of the Sun*, 213.
10. Balter, "Mysterious link emerges."
11. Russell, *The History of Mexico*, 2.
12. Haas and Creamer, "Crucible of Andean Civilization," 745–46.
13. Diehl, *The Olmecs*, 11–12; Haas and Creamer, "Crucible of Andean Civilization," 745; Rosenwig, *The Beginnings of Mesoamerican Civilization*, 3; Russell, *The History of Mexico*, 4.

14. Hooper, "New insight into ancient Americans."

15. Haas et al., "Gourd Lord," 9.

16. Brotherston, *Book of the Fourth World*, 17.

17. Russell, *The History of Mexico*, 4.

18. Haslip-Viera et al., "Robbing Native American Cultures."

19. Silberman et al., "Writing: Introduction."

20. Magni, "Olmec Writing the Cascajal 'Block' – New Perspectives," 69.

21. Rosenswig, *The Beginnings of Mesoamerican Civilization*, 43.

22. Ochoa et al., *Lengua y cultura mayas*, 170.

23. Houston and Inomata, *The Classic Maya*, 34, 30–31, 32.

24. Mann, *1491*, 324.

25. Phillips and Phillips, *A Concise History of Spain*, 11–12.

26. Learn, "Origin of Mysterious 2,700-Year-Old Gold."

27. Phillips and Phillips, *A Concise History of Spain*, 36, 30.

28. Feros, *Speaking of Spain*, 79.

29. Phillips and Phillips, *A Concise History of Spain*, 3–4.

30. Phillips and Phillips, *A Concise History of Spain*, 17.

31. Brotherston, *Image of the New World*, 14.

32. Denevan, *The Native Population*.

33. Keys, "Details of horrific first voyages."

34. Russell, *The History of Mexico*, 32.

35. Peck, "Lucas Vázquez de Ayllón's Doomed Colony," 184.

36. Peck, "Lucas Vázquez de Ayllón's Doomed Colony," 190.

37. Feros, *Speaking of Spain*, 217.

38. Russell, *The History of Mexico*, 49.

39. Price, Introduction, In *Maroon Societies*, 3.

40. Russell, *The History of Mexico*, 49.

41. Feros, *Speaking of Spain*, 50.

42. Romero, "Indian Slavery Once Thrived in New Mexico."

43. Coronado, *A World Not to Come*, 142–43 and passim.

44. O'Sullivan, "Annexation," 5.

45. Stewart and de León, *Not Room Enough*, 5.

46. Cantrell, *Stephen F. Austin*, 94; Bradley, "*We Never Retreat*," 172.

47. Cantrell, *Stephen F. Austin*, 99.

48. Stewart and de León, *Not Room Enough*, 7.

49. Cantrell, *Stephen F. Austin*, 45.

50. Cantrell, *Stephen F. Austin*, 44.

51. Santa Fe Trail Association.

52. Chipman and Joseph, *Spanish Texas, 1519–1821*, 222–23.

53. Augenbraum and Fernández-Olmos, *The Latino Reader*, 80–81.

54. Paredes, "The United States, Mexico, and *Machismo*," 26, 36.

55. Cortina, "Documents on the Brownsville Uprising."

56. De León, *They Called Them Greasers*, 84.

57. Ponce, *Kansas's War*, 2.

58. "Las Gorras Blancas Announce Their Platform, 1890" qtd. in Vargas, *Major Problems in Mexican American History*, 182.

59. Martí and Gómez, "Manifesto Montecristi."

60. Thompson, *Filipino English and Taglish*, 61.

61. Pérez y González, *Puerto Ricans in the United States*, 29.

62. Daniels, *Coming to America*, 97.

63. Stewart and de León, *Not Room Enough*, 9.

64. Daniels, *Coming to America*, 307.

65. Stewart and de León, *Not Room Enough*, 27, 33.

66. Cuéllar, *Stories from the Barrio*, 2, 8, 11.

67. Coerver, "Plan of San Diego."

68. Morán González, "The History of Racial Violence."

69. John Morán González qtd. in Benavides, "The Texas Rangers Killed Hundreds."

70. "Mexico Faces Ruin," *International Herald Tribune*, 1917.

71. Maroney, "Oilfield Strike of 1917."

72. Sánchez, *Becoming Mexican American*, 91, 92.

73. Sánchez, *Becoming Mexican American*, 93–95.

74. Hoffman, *Unwanted Mexican Americans in the Great Depression*, 2.

75. Brilliant, *The Color of America Has Changed*, 5–9 and passim.

76. Acosta-Belén and Santiago, *Puerto Ricans in the United States*, 79.

77. Mass, "Puerto Rico," 66.

78. Mass, "Puerto Rico," 72, 78.

79. Acosta-Belén and Santiago, *Puerto Ricans in the United States*, 96.

80. Sánchez, *Becoming Mexican American*, 254.

81. Márquez, *LULAC*, 2–4.

82. Sánchez, *Becoming Mexican American*, 245.

83. García, *Operation Wetback*, 70.

84. Márquez, *LULAC*, 54.

85. Delaney, "Dorothy Height."

86. Blackwell, ¡Chicana *Power!*, 161–64.

87. Leon, "La Hermandad and Chicanas Organizing," 1–5 and passim.

88. Vento, *Mestizo*, 198.

89. Danilov, "US Courts Offer No Protection," A19.

90. Grable, "Personhood under the Due Process Clause," 821–22.

91. Orth, "After the Revolution," 33.

92. Orth, "After the Revolution," 35, 36.

93. Chetty, Hendren, Jones, and Porter, "Race and Economic Opportunity in the United States," 56.

III. Bibliography

Contents:

1. Works Cited

2. Works Consulted

1. Works Cited

Acosta-Belén, Edna, and Carlos E. Santiago. *Puerto Ricans in the United States: A Contemporary Portrait.* 2nd ed. Boulder: Lynne Rienner Publishers, 2018.

Augenbraum, Harold, and Margarite Fernández-Olmos, eds. *The Latino Reader: An American Literary Tradition from 1542 to the Present.* New York: Houghton Mifflin Company, 1997.

Balter, Michael. "Mysterious link emerges between Native Americans and people half a globe away." *Science.* July 21, 2015. Accessed September 22, 2018. http://www.sciencemag.org/news/2015/07/mysterious-link-emerges-between-native-americans-and-people-half-globe-away.

Benavides, Lucía. "The Texas Rangers Killed Hundreds of Hispanic Americans During the Mexican Revolution." *Texas Standard.* January 22, 2016. Accessed June 7, 2019. https://www.texasstandard.org/stories/texas-exhibit-refuses-to-forget-one-of-the-worst-periods-of-state-sanctioned-violence/.

Blackwell, Maylei. ¡Chicana *Power!: Contested Histories of Feminism in the Chicano Movement.* Austin: University of Texas Press, 2016.

Bradley, Ed. *"We Never Retreat": Filibustering Expeditions in Spanish Texas, 1812–1822.* College Station: Texas A&M University Press, 2015.

Brilliant, Mark. *The Color of America Has Changed: How Racial Diversity Shaped Civil Rights Reform in California, 1941–1978.* New York and Oxford: Oxford University Press, 2010.

Brotherston, Gordon. *Book of the Fourth World: Reading the Native Americas Through Their Literature.* Cambridge: Cambridge University Press, 1992.

———. *Image of the New World: The American Continent Portrayed in Native Texts.* London: Thames & Hudson, 1979.

Cantrell, Gregg. *Stephen F. Austin: Empresario of Texas.* New Haven: Yale University Press, 1999.

Chetty, Raj, Nathaniel Hendren, Maggie R. Jones, and Sonya R. Porter. "Race and Economic Opportunity in the United States: An Intergenerational Perspective." March 2018. Accessed June 26, 2019. http://www.equality-of-opportunity.org/assets/documents/race_paper.pdf.

Chipman, Donald E., and Harriett Denise Joseph. *Spanish Texas, 1519–1821.* Austin: University of Texas Press, 2010.

Coerver, Don M. "Plan of San Diego." *Handbook of Texas Online.* October 5, 2015. Accessed June 7, 2019. http://www.tshaonline.org/handbook/online/articles/ngp04.

Coronado, Raúl. *A World Not to Come: A History of Latino Writing and Print Culture.* Cambridge, MA: Harvard University Press, 2013.

Cortina, Juan Nepomuceno. "Documents on the Brownsville Uprising of Juan Cortina." *New Perspectives on the West.* PBS. Sep/Nov 1859. Accessed May 28, 2019. http://www.pbs.org/weta/thewest/ resources/archives/four/cortinas.htm#0959.

Cuéllar, Carlos E. *Stories from the Barrio: A History of Mexican Fort Worth.* Fort Worth: TCU Press, 2003.

Danilov, Dan P. "US Courts Offer No Protection from Latest Immigration Law." *Seattle Post-Intelligencer.* December 17, 1996.

De León, Arnoldo. *They Called Them Greasers: Anglo Attitudes Toward Mexicans in Texas, 1821–1900.* Austin: University of Texas Press, 1983.

Delaney, Paul. "Dorothy Height and the Sexism of the Civil Rights Movement." *The Root.* May 12, 2010. Accessed June 22, 2019. https://www.theroot.com/dorothy-height-and-the-sexism-of-the-civil-rights-movem-1790879502.

Daniels, Roger. *Coming to America: A History of Immigration and Ethnicity in American Life.* 2nd ed. New York: Harper Perennial, 2002.

Denevan, William M., ed. *The Native Population of the Americas in 1492.* 2nd ed. Madison: University of Wisconsin Press, 1992.

Diehl, Richard A. *The Olmecs: America's First Civilization.* London: Thames & Hudson, 2004.

Dugger, Ronnie. "Integration Hero and Education Legend George I. Sanchez Gets a New Biography." *Texas Observer.* March 18, 2015. Accessed January 23, 2019. https://www.texasobserver.org/george-i-sanchez-biography/.

Escobar, Natalie. "How 50 Years of Latino Studies Shaped History Education." *The Atlantic.* September 7, 2018. Accessed October 7, 2018. https://www.theatlantic.com/education/archive/2018/09/how-50-years-of-latino-studies-shaped-history-education/569623/.

Feros, Antonio. *Speaking of Spain: The Evolution of Race and Nation in the Hispanic World.* Cambridge, MA: Harvard University Press, 2017.

Frederick, Candace. "Honoring Arturo Schomburg's Afro-Latino Legacy." *New York Public Library* (blog). July 1, 2016. Accessed October 6, 2018. https://www.nypl.org/blog/2016/07/01/honoring-schomburg-afro-latino-legacy.

García, Juan Ramón. *Operation Wetback: The Mass Deportation of Mexican Undocumented Workers in 1954.* Westport and London: Greenwood Press, 1980.

Grable, David M. "Personhood Under the Due Process Clause: A Constitutional Analysis of the Illegal Immigration Reform and Immigrant Responsibility Act of 1996." *Cornell Law Review* 83.820 (1998): 820–65.

Haas, Jonathan, and Winifred Creamer. "Crucible of Andean Civilization: The Peruvian Coast from 3000 to 1800 BC." *Current Anthropology* 47.5 (October 2006): 745–75.

Haas, Jonathan, Winifred Creamer, Alvaro Ruiz, and Roberto Bartoloni. "Gourd Lord." *Archaeology* 56.3 (May/June 2003): 9.

Haslip-Viera, Gabriel, Bernard Ortiz de Montellano, and Warren Barbour. "Robbing Native American Cultures: Van Sertima's Afrocentricity and the Olmecs." *Current Anthropology* 38.3 (June 1997): 419–41.

Hoffman, Abraham. *Unwanted Mexican Americans in the Great Depression: Repatriation Pressures, 1929–1939.* Tuscon: University of Arizona Press, 1974.

Hooper, Simon. "New insight into ancient Americans." CNN. January 4, 2005. Accessed September 26, 2018. http://www.cnn.com/2005/TECH/science/01/04/norte.chico/.

Houston, Stephen D., and Takeshi Inomata. *The Classic Maya.* Cambridge: Cambridge University Press, 2009.

Keys, David. "Details of horrific first voyages in transatlantic slave trade revealed." *Independent*. August 17, 2018. Accessed October 1, 2018. https://www.independent.co.uk/news/world/americas/transatlantic-slave-trade-voyages-ships-log-details-africa-america-atlantic-ocean-deaths-disease-a8494546.html.

Learn, Joshua Rapp. "Origin of Mysterious 2,700-Year-Old Gold Treasure Revealed." *National Geographic*. April 10, 2018. Accessed September 30, 2018. https://news.nationalgeographic.com/2018/04/carambolo-treasure-tartessos-gold-atlantis-spain-archaeology/.

Leon, Kendall M. "La Hermandad and Chicanas Organizing: The Community Rhetoric of the Comisión Femenil Mexicana Nacional." *Community Literacy Journal* 7.2 (2013): 1–20.

Magni, Caterina. "Olmec Writing The Cascajal 'Block' - New Perspectives." *Arts & Cultures* 9 (2008): 64–81.

Mann, Charles C. *1491: New Revelations of the Americas Before Columbus*. New York: Vintage, 2006.

Mariscal, George. *Brown-Eyed Children of the Sun: Lessons from the Chicano Movement, 1965–1975*. Albuquerque: University of New Mexico Press, 2005.

Maroney, James C. "Oilfield Strike of 1917." *Handbook of Texas Online*. June 15, 2010. Accessed June 7, 2019. http://www.tshaonline.org/handbook/online/articles/doott.

Márquez, Benjamin. *LULAC: The Evolution of a Mexican American Political Organization*. Austin: University of Texas Press, 1993.

Martí, José, and Máximo Gómez. "Manifesto Montecristi." March 25, 1895. Accessed May 29, 2019. http://www.historyofcuba.com/history/marti/Manifesto.htm.

Martínez, María del Carmen Rodríguez, Ponciano Ortíz Ceballos, Michael D. Coe, Richard A. Diehl, Stephen D. Houston, Karl A. Taube, and Alfredo Delgado Calderón. "Oldest Writing in the New World." *Science* 313.5793 (September 15, 2006): 1610–14.

Mass, Bonnie. "Puerto Rico: A Case Study of Population Control." *Latin American Perspectives* 4.4 (Autumn 1977): 66–81.

"Mexico Faces Ruin as Strikes Spread." *International Herald Tribune*. May 23, 1917. Accessed June 7, 2019. https://iht-retrospective.blogs.nytimes.com/2017/05/23/1917-mexico-faces-ruin-as-strikes-spread/?partner=bloomberg.

Morán González, John. "The History of Racial Violence on the Mexico-Texas Border." *Refusing to Forget*. 2019. Accessed Jun 7, 2019. https://refusingtoforget.org/the-history/.

Moreno, Carolina. "Latinos Could Fuel Nearly A Quarter Of The US Economy By 2020: Study." *Huffington Post*. March 15, 2018. Accessed November 12, 2018. https://www.huffingtonpost.com/entry/latinos-will-fuel-nearly-a-quarter-of-the-us-economy-by-2020-study_us_595d381fe4b02e9bdb09de8e.

Ochoa, Lorenzo, and Patricia Martel, eds. *Lengua y cultura mayas*. Mexico City: UNAM, Institute for Anthropological Investigations, 2002.

O'Sullivan, John L. "Annexation." *The United States Magazine and Democratic Review* 17 (1845): 5–6, 9–10.

Orth, John V. "After the Revolution: 'Reform' of the Law of Inheritance." *Law and History Review* 10.1 (Spring 1992): 33–44.

Paredes, Américo. "The United States, Mexico, and *Machismo*." *Journal of the Folklore Institute* 8.1 (1971): 17–37.

Peck, Douglas T. "Lucas Vázquez de Ayllón's Doomed Colony of San Miguel de Guadalupe." *Georgia Historical Quarterly* 85.2 (2001): 183–98.

Pérez y González, María E. *Puerto Ricans in the United States*. Westport: Greenwood Press, 2000.

Phillips, William D., and Carla Rahn Phillips. *A Concise History of Spain*. Cambridge: Cambridge University Press, 2010.

Ponce, Pearl T., ed. *Kansas's War: The Civil War in Documents*. Columbus: Ohio State University Press, 2011.

Potter, Lloyd B., and Nazrul Hoque. "Texas Population Projections, 2010 to 2050." Office of the State Demographer of Texas. November 2014. Accessed January 24, 2019. http://osd.texas.gov/Data/TPEPP/Projections/.

Price, Richard. "Introduction." In *Maroon Societies: Rebel Slave Communities in the Americas*, edited by Richard Price, 1–32. Baltimore: Johns Hopkins University Press, 1996.

Romero, Simon. "Indian Slavery Once Thrived in New Mexico. Latinos Are Finding Family Ties to It." *New York Times*. January 28, 2018. Accessed October 20, 2018. https://www.nytimes.com/2018/01/28/us/ indian-slaves-genizaros.html.

Rosenswig, Robert M. *The Beginnings of Mesoamerican Civilization: Inter-Regional Interaction and the Olmec*. Cambridge: Cambridge University Press, 2010.

Russell, Philip L. *The History of Mexico: From Pre-Conquest to Present*. New York: Routledge, 2010.

Sánchez, George J. *Becoming Mexican American: Ethnicity, Culture, and Identity in Chicano Los Angeles, 1900–1945*. New York and Oxford: Oxford University Press, 1993.

Santa Fe Trail Association. 2019. Accessed May 28, 2019. https://santafetrail.org/.

Silberman, Neil Ascher, et al. "Writing: Introduction." In *The Oxford Companion to Archaeology*, 2nd ed. edited by Neil Ascher Silberman. Oxford: Oxford University Press, 2012.

Stewart, Kenneth L., and Arnoldo de León. *Not Room Enough: Mexicans, Anglos, and Socio-Economic Change in Texas, 1850–1900*. Albuquerque: University of New Mexico Press, 1993.

Thompson, Roger M. *Filipino English and Taglish: Language Switching from Multiple Perspectives*. Amsterdam and Philadelphia: John Benjamins Publishing Company, 2003.

Trickey, Erick. "The Little-Remembered Ally Who Helped America Win the Revolution." *Smithsonian Magazine*. Jan 13, 2017. Accessed November 12, 2018. https://www.smithsonianmag.com/history/little-remembered-ally-who-helped-america-win-revolution-180961782/.

Vargas, Zaragosa, ed. *Major Problems in Mexican American History*. Belmont, CA: Wadsworth, Cengage Learning, 1999.

Vento, Arnoldo C. *Mestizo: The History, Culture, and Politics of the Mexican and the Chicano*. Lanham, MD: University Press of America, 1998.

Williams, William Carlos. *In The American Grain*. New York: New Directions, 1925.

2. Works Consulted

Anzaldúa, Gloria. *Borderlands/La Frontera: The New Mestiza*. San Francisco: Aunt Lute Books, 1987.

Armbruster-Sandoval, Ralph. *Starving for Justice: Hunger Strikes, Spectacular Speech, and the Struggle for Dignity*. Tuscon: University of Arizona Press, 2017.

Barreto, Matt A., and Gary M. Segura. *Latino America: How America's Most Dynamic Population Is Poised to Transform the Politics of the Nation*. New York: Public Affairs, 2014.

Beltrán, Cristina. *The Trouble with Unity: Latino Politics and the Creation of Identity*. New York: Oxford University Press, 2010.

Burger, Richard L. *Chavin and the Origins of Andean Civilization*. New York: Thames & Hudson, 1992.

Casillas, Dolores I. *Sounds of Belonging: US Spanish-Language Radio and Public Advocacy*. New York: NYU Press, 2014.

Conklin, William J., and Jeffrey Quilter, eds. *Chavín: Art, Architecture and Culture*. Los Angeles: UCLA Cotsen Institute of Archaeology, 2008.

Chávez, Leo R. *The Latino Threat: Constructing Immigrants, Citizens, and the Nation*. Stanford: Stanford University Press, 2008.

Cockcroft, Eva S., and Holly Barnet-Sánchez. *Signs from the Heart: California Chicano Murals*. Venice, CA: Social and Public Art Resource Center, 1990.

Dávila, Arlene. *Latino Spin: Public Image and the Whitewashing of Race*. New York: NYU Press, 2008.

De la Teja, Jesús F., ed. *Tejano Leadership in Mexican and Revolutionary Texas*. College Station: Texas A&M University Press, 2010.

DeSipio, Louis, and Rodolfo O. de la Garza. *US Immigration in the Twenty-First Century: Making Americans, Remaking America*. Boulder: Westview Press, 2015.

Flores, William V., and Rina Benmayor. *Latino Cultural Citizenship: Claiming Identity, Space, and Rights*. Boston: Beacon Press, 1997.

García Bedolla, Lisa. *Latino Politics*. Cambridge, UK: Polity, 2014.

García, John A. *Latino Politics in America: Community, Culture, and Interests*. Lanham: Rowman & Littlefield, 2011.

Gonzales, Roberto G. *Lives in Limbo: Undocumented and Coming of Age in America*. Oakland: University of California Press, 2015.

González, Juan. *Harvest of Empire: A History of Latinos in America*. New York: Penguin Books, 2011.

Grande, Reyna. *The Distance between Us*. New York: Washington Square Press, 2013.

Jackson, Carlos F. *Chicana and Chicano Art: Protest Arte*. Tuscon: University of Arizona Press, 2009.

Krochmal, Max. *Blue Texas: The Making of a Multiracial Democratic Coalition in the Civil Rights Era*. Chapel Hill: University of North Carolina Press, 2016.

Krochmal, Max, and J. Todd Moye, eds. *Civil Rights in Black and Brown: Histories of Resistance and Liberation in Texas*. Austin: University of Texas Press, 2021.

Minian, Ana Raquel. *Undocumented Lives: The Untold Story of Mexican Migration*. Cambridge, MA: Harvard University Press, 2018.

Mohamed, Heather S. *The New Americans?: Immigration, Protest, and the Politics of Latino Identity*. Lawrence: University Press of Kansas, 2017.

Moraga, Cherríe, and Gloria Anzaldúa. *This Bridge Called My Back: Writings by Radical Women of Color*. New York: Kitchen Table/Women of Color Press, 1983.

Parédez, Deborah. *Selenidad: Selena, Latinos, and the Performance of Memory*. Durham: Duke University Press, 2009.

Sandoval, Denise M. *"White" Washing American Education: The New Culture Wars in Ethnic Studies*. Santa Barbara: Praeger, an imprint of ABC-CLIO, 2016.

Trigger, Bruce G. "Writing systems: a case study in cultural evolution." In *The First Writing: Script Invention as History and Process*, edited by Stephen D. Houston, 39–70. Cambridge: Cambridge University Press, 2004.

Urrea, Luis A. *The Devil's Highway: A True Story*. New York: Little, Brown, 2004.

Valenzuela, Angela. *Subtractive Schooling: US-Mexican Youth and the Politics of Caring*. Albany: SUNY Press, 1999.

Vargas, José Antonio. *Dear America: Notes of an Undocumented Citizen*. New York: HarperCollins Publishers, 2018.

Velásquez, Janeta. *The Woman in Battle: A Narrative of the Exploits, Adventures, and Travels of Madame Loreta Janeta Velazquez, Otherwise Known as Lieutenant Harry T. Buford, Confederate States Army*, edited by C. J. Worthington. Chapel Hill: University of North Carolina at Chapel Hill Library, 2017. First edition, 1876.

Wides-Muñoz, Laura. *The Making of a Dream: How a Group of Young Undocumented Immigrants Helped Change What it Means to be American*. New York: HarperCollins Publishers, 2018.

Zamora, Javier. *Unaccompanied*. Port Townsend: Copper Canyon Press, 2017.

3. Overarching Enduring Understandings and Essential Questions

Overarching understandings and questions organize the curriculum infusion at a macro-level. They serve both an aspirational purpose and as a guide for how the content themes are infused. They represent conceptual takeaways students will have as a result of their K-12 social studies experience in FWISD schools.

Enduring Understandings

Students will understand that...

- Studying the long history and cultures of Latinxs, and the heritage of others, can serve as a source of individual pride, self-confidence, and respect for the dignity of people from all racial and ethnic backgrounds;

- The historical origins and emergence of Latinxs have roots in peoples, ethnicities, and cultures from all over the world, in varying degrees depending on geographies and migrations, but we are united as an ethnic group in the US through our shared cultural heritage of the Hispanophone Americas;

- The pursuit of Latinx political sovereignty and cultural autonomy has been an ongoing historical process that extends to the present day and into the future;

- The cultural, social, political, artistic, agricultural, and economic contributions that Latinx people have made and continue to make to local communities, the State of Texas, the US, and global civilization are enjoyed by all peoples every day; and,

- Single narratives of history are incomplete and often lead to misconceptions. Challenging them with accurate and well-substantiated claims can be a powerful means of contributing to a healthier democracy.

Essential Questions

Students will consider...

- Why study Latinx history and culture?

- How can I remain authentic in my own cultural identity while I learn about cultures that are different from mine?

- How do I use my ability to critically think when learning to understand cultures different from my own?

- How is each of us connected to the past? How has history influenced who each of us is today?

- How have the contributions of Latinxs throughout history improved the political, economic, and social development of humanity?

- Why have the history of Latinxs and our contributions to the world been underrepresented in the mainstream narratives of world and US history?

- How will I utilize an education in Latinx Studies to make positive change in my communities and my personal ambitions as I prepare myself for taking on adult responsibilities and living life as an adult?

- How will the narrative of Latinx history and culture change in the future?

4. Guiding Themes of the Latinx Studies Curriculum

Latinxs of all nations across the Americas study and celebrate their national history as a modern heritage with roots both diverse and ancient. But Latinxs in the US are in a country with an overlapping Anglo history. For many centuries, Latinxs have made significant social contributions to America, and to the world—on our margins, in our centers, and everywhere in between. Nevertheless, social studies curricula in the US have traditionally overemphasized the achievements and value of Anglo-Americans at the expense of proportional attention to Latinx contributions and issues.

This curriculum for FWISD will incorporate more Latinx content into social studies instruction to recover that omission. In doing so, it will also demonstrate how understanding Latinxs, our cultures, and our histories can provide vital information, skills, and vocabulary necessary for all Americans of all ethnicities to understand and reconcile their own place in present-day society. Latinxs and our ancestors have been an integral part of history, both here and abroad. The themes are intended to provide students in the FWISD an overall curriculum that infuses the experience of Latinxs throughout the district's curricula.

1. Pre-Colonial Indigenous American Civilizations and Iberian History

This theme addresses the worlds of America and Spain prior to Spanish arrival over five centuries ago. It addresses the diverse ancestry of Latinxs and the historical influences—from ancient times to antiquity—on our cultures, identities, and values. This theme includes the study of civilizations such as the Norte Chico, Chavín, Olmec, Aztec, Maya, Carib, and Taíno. It also considers Spain prior to 1492, including the Moorish Empire's control for over seven centuries, emphasizing the diverse nature of Spanish culture that influenced social order throughout Latin America.

In a spirit of partnership with the African American and African Studies (AAAS) Curriculum, this theme ends by opening further pathways for pointed inquiry into African ancestries in the Americas (e.g. Afro-Latinxs, Antilleans, Afro-Mexicans, the Garifuna of Central America, and deeply integrated Latinx communities), which will be explored further under subsequent themes.

Broad topics:

1. Early Indigenous Civilizations of Present-Day Latin America
2. Indigenous American Histories and Archeological Findings
3. Indigenous American Cultures and Religions
4. Ancient American Cities
5. Prehistoric Iberia
6. Iberia Under Carthaginian, Roman, and Germanic Rule
7. Medieval Iberia, the Umayyad Caliphate of Mecca, and the Moorish Empire
8. Spain in 1492
9. The Diverse Origins of Modern Latinx Peoples

Enduring Understandings

Students will understand that...

■ Individuals have history, and this history combines ancestry, context, and experience;

■ Many modern customs, languages, foods, and religious practices have roots in ancient traditions;

■ Agriculture has existed in present-day Latin America for at least 10,000 years;

■ Over 50 million indigenous people inhabited the Americas in 1492;

■ The earliest known civilization in present-day Latin America is as old as Ancient Egypt;

■ Ancient Peru is considered one of the world's six "pristine civilizations";

■ The Olmec civilization is one of the three civilizations of the world where writing first emerged and developed independently;

■ Before 1492, Spain itself was repeatedly colonized by numerous tribes and empires;

■ The Moorish Empire of Arabia and Northern Africa, which was Islamic, ruled Spain for over seven hundred years;

■ The Islamic influence of the Moors in Spain is still evident in the architecture, language, arts, politics, and religions of Spain and Latin America to this day;

■ Latinxs have diverse origins and ancestries.

Essential Questions

Students will consider...

■ Why is ancient history important?

■ How does studying ancient history increase my knowledge of myself?

■ How does studying ancient history increase my confidence in myself?

■ How does studying ancient history increase my appreciation and respect for different people and cultures?

■ How does ancient history affect what it means to be Latinx today?

■ Were ancient ethics and values compatible with those of today?

■ What was "modern" about the ancient civilizations of present-day Latin America?

■ How does the study of ancient societies and belief systems help us be better judges of the ways we can succeed as a society today and in the future?

■ What is progress?

Resources Recommended by the TCU CRES Curriculum Consultants:

Library of Congress. "What Came To Be Called 'America.'" *1492: An Ongoing Voyage*. Exhibition catalog. Accessed May 30, 2022. http://loc.gov/exhibits/1492/america.html.

"Native Americans Prior to 1492." *History Central*. Accessed May 30, 2022. https://www.historycentral.com/Indians/Before.html.

"Muslim Spain (711-1492)." *BBC*. Accessed May 30, 2022. http://www.bbc.co.uk/religion/religions/islam/history/spain_1.shtml.

"Aztec, Inca, Maya." *Lesson Planet*. Accessed May 30, 2022. https://www.lessonplanet.com/teachers/aztec-inca-maya.

For further reading about this theme:

Balter, Michael. "Mysterious link emerges between Native Americans and people half a globe away." *Science*. July 21, 2015. Accessed September 22, 2018. http://www.sciencemag.org/news/2015/07/mysterious-link-emerges-between-native-americans-and-people-half-globe-away.

Brotherston, Gordon. *Book of the Fourth World: Reading the Native Americas Through Their Literature.* Cambridge: Cambridge University Press, 1992.

Burger, Richard L. *Chavín and the Origins of Andean Civilization.* New York: Thames & Hudson, 1992.

Conklin, William J., and Jeffrey Quilter, eds. *Chavín: Art, Architecture and Culture.* Los Angeles: UCLA Cotsen Institute of Archaeology, 2008.

Denevan, William M., ed. *The Native Population of the Americas in 1492.* 2nd ed. Madison: University of Wisconsin Press, 1992.

Diehl, Richard A. *The Olmecs: America's First Civilization.* London: Thames & Hudson, 2004.

Haas, Jonathan, and Winifred Creamer. "Crucible of Andean Civilization: The Peruvian Coast from 3000 to 1800 BC." *Current Anthropology* 47.5 (October 2006): 745–75.

Haas, Jonathan, Winifred Creamer, Alvaro Ruiz, and Roberto Bartoloni. "Gourd Lord." *Archaeology* 56.3 (May/June 2003): 9.

Haslip-Viera, Gabriel, Bernard Ortiz de Montellano, and Warren Barbour. "Robbing Native American Cultures: Van Sertima's Afrocentricity and the Olmecs." *Current Anthropology* 38.3 (June 1997): 419–41.

Hooper, Simon. "New insight into ancient Americans." CNN. January 4, 2005. Accessed September 26, 2018. http://www.cnn.com/2005/TECH/science/01/04/norte.chico/.

Houston, Stephen D., and Takeshi Inomata. *The Classic Maya.* Cambridge: Cambridge University Press, 2009.

Learn, Joshua Rapp. "Origin of Mysterious 2,700-Year-Old Gold Treasure Revealed." *National Geographic.* April 10, 2018. Accessed September 30, 2018. https://news.nationalgeographic.com/2018/04/carambolo-treasure-tartessos-gold-atlantis-spain-archaeology/.

Magni, Caterina. "Olmec Writing: The Cascajal 'Block' - New Perspectives." *Arts & Cultures* 9 (2008): 64-81.

Mann, Charles C. *1491: New Revelations of the Americas Before Columbus.* New York: Vintage, 2006.

Martínez, María del Carmen Rodríguez, Ponciano Ortíz Ceballos, Michael D. Coe, Richard A. Diehl, Stephen D. Houston, Karl A. Taube, and Alfredo Delgado Calderón. "Oldest Writing in the New World." *Science* 313.5793 (September 15, 2006): 1610–14.

Phillips, William D., and Carla Rahn Phillips. *A Concise History of Spain.* Cambridge: Cambridge University Press, 2010.

Rosenswig, Robert M. *The Beginnings of Mesoamerican Civilization: Inter-Regional Interaction and the Olmec.* Cambridge: Cambridge University Press, 2010.

Russell, Philip L. *The History of Mexico: From Pre-Conquest to Present.* New York: Routledge, 2010.

Silberman, Neil Ascher, et al. "Writing: Introduction." In *The Oxford Companion to Archaeology*, 2nd ed., edited by Neil Ascher Silberman. Oxford: Oxford University Press, 2012.

Trigger, Bruce G. "Writing systems: a case study in cultural evolution." In *The First Writing: Script Invention as History and Process*, edited by Stephen D. Houston. Cambridge: Cambridge University Press, 2004. 39–70.

2. Spanish America and the Colonial Era

This theme addresses the history and development of societies during the era of Iberian colonization in the Americas and the Caribbean. It considers the effects of Spanish influence on social order, including the spread of Spanish language and Catholicism, as well as the impositions of slavery, large-scale war, and infectious diseases that were crucial to Spain's success in establishing sustainable colonies in the New World. It also addresses the survival and sovereignty of non-European communities, such as indigenous nations and maroon societies founded by rebellion. This theme also explores events that contributed to the emergence of peoples unique to the Americas, e.g. *mestizos*, Afro-Latinxs (including Afro-Mexicans), the Garifuna of Central America, and other Latinx populations that, by the measure of race and ethnicity, are deeply integrated.

The historical span of this theme begins around 1492 and ends around 1821, the year when many Latin American countries won their independence, marking the collapse of the Spanish Empire in the Americas.

Broad topics:

1) Spanish Influence in the Americas

2) The Spread of Catholicism through Missionaries

3) Legacies of the African Diaspora in Greater Latin America

4) Maroon Societies, Sovereignty, and Micro-Societies

5) Indigenous Peoples in the Spanish Empire

6) Rebellions and the Emergence of Modern Latin American Nations

Enduring Understandings

Students will understand that...

■ Christopher Columbus did not "discover" America, because over 50 million indigenous inhabitants of the Americas already knew of their lands' existence;

■ Spanish colonization of the Americas was a process that lasted centuries;

■ Spanish colonization had vast effects on peoples in the Americas, empowering some while persecuting many others;

■ The success of Spanish colonization was fundamentally dependent on the free labor of enslaved African and indigenous American peoples;

■ Spaniards succeeded in colonizing the Americas largely because of infectious diseases they introduced and spread, which decimated tens of millions of indigenous Americans;

(Continues)

Essential Questions

Students will consider...

■ What is the legacy of Spanish American colonization?

■ How has colonization affected our contemporary culture?

■ How do we have control in the present over the effects of past events that cannot ever be changed?

■ How and why have the narratives of colonial history changed so much over time?

■ To what extent was the fate of peoples in the Americas, through colonization and the establishment of European authorities, dependent on events that were essentially random or haphazard?

(Continues)

- The longstanding Spanish system of manumission (coartación) freed more people from enslavement than did the outright abolition of slavery;

- Spanish colonizers did not have absolute, uniform control over every region, community, or population that they occupied within the Americas;

- There were many communities of people in the Americas who were independent of colonial rule, and many of these communities thrived on their own for years if not decades or even generations;

- Legally recognized and documented maroon societies existed in what is now Brazil, Colombia, Cuba, Ecuador, Surinam, Jamaica, Mexico, Haiti, and the Dominican Republic;

- Spanish colonization involved officials of both the Spanish government and the Catholic Church;

- In the colonial period, the authority of the Catholic Church superseded the authority of the Spanish Crown;

- The Catholic Church's Patron Saint of the Americas is La Virgen de Guadalupe.

- What are the dangers and harms of a cultural or racial group claiming inherent superiority over others?

- What are the surprising, unintended, beautiful things that have come out of the tragedies and injustices of colonization?

- Have we overcome colonization?

- What role did the Catholic Church and missionaries play in colonization?

- What was the experience of Africans and African Americans in colonial Spanish America?

- What was the experience of indigenous Americans in colonial Spanish America?

- What was the experience of creoles in Spanish America?

- What is sovereignty?

Resources Recommended by the TCU CRES Curriculum Consultants:

"Spanish Colonial Central America Teacher Resources." *Lesson Planet*. Accessed May 30, 2022. https://www.lessonplanet.com/lesson-plans/spanish-colonial-central-america/all.

"Latin America: the Colonial Era." *TimeMaps*. Accessed May 30, 2022. https://www.timemaps.com/civilizations/latin-america-the-colonial-era/.

"Spanish colonization." *Khan Academy*. Accessed May 30, 2022. https://www.khanacademy.org/humanities/us-history/precontact-and-early-colonial-era/spanish-colonization/v/spanish-colonization.

For further reading about this theme:

Brotherston, Gordon. *Image of the New World: The American Continent Portrayed in Native Texts*. London: Thames & Hudson, 1979.

Feros, Antonio. *Speaking of Spain: The Evolution of Race and Nation in the Hispanic World*. Cambridge, MA: Harvard University Press, 2017.

Keys, David. "Details of horrific first voyages in transatlantic slave trade revealed." *Independent*. August 17, 2018. Accessed October 1, 2018. https://www.independent.co.uk/news/world/americas/transatlantic-slave-trade-voyages-ships-log-details-africa-america-atlantic-ocean-deaths-disease-a8494546.html.

McKnight, Kathryn Joy, and Leo J. Garofalo, eds. *Afro-Latino Voices: Narratives from the Early Modern Ibero-Atlantic World, 1550–1812*. Indianapolis: Hackett Publishing Company, 2009.

Peck, Douglas T. "Lucas Vázquez de Ayllón's Doomed Colony of San Miguel de Guadalupe." *Georgia Historical Quarterly* 85.2 (2001): 183–98.

Price, Richard. "Introduction." In *Maroon Societies: Rebel Slave Communities in the Americas*, edited by Richard Price. Baltimore: Johns Hopkins University Press, 1996. 1–32.

Romero, Simon. "Indian Slavery Once Thrived in New Mexico. Latinos Are Finding Family Ties to It." *New York Times*. January 28, 2018. Accessed October 20, 2018. https://www.nytimes.com/2018/01/28/us/ indian-slaves-genizaros.html.

Russell, Philip L. *The History of Mexico: From Pre-Conquest to Present*. New York: Routledge, 2010.

3. US Imperialism and Latin American Nationalisms

This theme addresses the emergence and growth of Latin American national identities, from Mexican Independence to Puerto Rican annexation. It also considers the effects of US expansionism on territories and peoples, especially the results of the Treaty of Guadalupe Hidalgo (1848) and the Treaty of Paris (1898)—i.e. the US usurping most of Mexico's land mass as well as Guam and the Philippines in the Western Pacific and Puerto Rico in the Caribbean. It covers the history of the transformation of *Tejas* as a Mexican territory to Texas the twenty-eighth state of the Union from the perspective of Latinxs, much like the history of filibusters in greater Latin America and squatters in California right after the Mexican Cession. Latinx involvement in the US Civil War and the motivations, means, and outcomes of borderland rebellions such as the Cortina Wars and *Las Gorras Blancas* are also examined here, as well as the distinctly opposed positions on slavery that Mexico and the Southern US had in the mid-nineteenth century, a difference crucial to the dynamism of political development of the time.

The historical span of this theme begins around 1821 with Mexican Independence and ends in 1898, when the US won the Spanish-American War and took possession of Puerto Rico, Guam, and the Philippines at the height of US neo-imperialist expansion.

Broad topics:

1) The Emergence of Sovereign Nations in Greater Latin America

2) The Monroe Doctrine, Manifest Destiny, and US Neo-Imperialism in Latin America

3) The Empresarial System and the Anglo-American Settlement of Mexico

4) The Treaty of Guadalupe Hidalgo and the Transformation of *Tejas* into Texas

5) Latinxs in the US Civil War

6) Latinx Rebellions in the Borderlands

7) The Spanish-American War and US Neo-Imperialism in the Caribbean

Enduring Understandings

Students will understand that...

■ Mexico gained its independence from Spain in 1821, as did many other Latin American nations;

■ The Monroe Doctrine and manifest destiny were philosophies that motivated and attempted to justify the US colonizing Latin America;

■ Empresarios were foreigners granted contracts for free lands by the Mexican government in exchange for arranging hundreds of families to establish farming and ranching settlements in scarcely populated regions;

■ Slavery was abolished in Mexico in 1829 by President Vicente Guerrero, an Afro-Mexican;

■ Anglo-American empresarial settlers in the Mexican state of Coahuila y Tejas (Texas) violated laws requiring Mexican allegiance, speaking Spanish, and practicing the Catholic faith, as well as prohibiting slaveholding and keeping guns, which led to conflict with the Mexican government;

■ The Bustamante Act (1830) prohibited immigration into Mexico from the US;

■ Filibusters were US citizens who acted as mercenaries to overthrow Latin American governments and take power for their own profit;

■ The All Mexico Movement was a failed initiative to annex the entirety of Mexico as a territory of the US;

■ Empresarial settlers of Tejas waged the Texas Revolution and established the Republic of Texas to assume authority over Mexican territory and thereby maintain their slave plantation economy;

■ The Mexican-American War ended with the Treaty of Guadalupe Hidalgo (1848), which ceded Arizona, California, Nevada, New Mexico, Utah, and portions of Colorado and Wyoming to the US as spoils of war;

■ Squatters were US citizens who migrated into the Southwest after the Mexican Cession and schemed with US lawmakers and land purveyors to occupy and claim lands and property owned by Mexican Americans;

(Continues)

Essential Questions

Students will consider...

■ What were the motivations of Latin Americans in pursuing independence from Spain? What did they hope for themselves?

■ What effects of the US colonization of Latin America—through settler-colonialism, squatting, filibustering, financing, and waging war—still linger today?

■ What is neo-imperialism?

■ Considering the history of political interaction between Latin America and the US, what has been the price of US prosperity?

■ How did sociopolitical values differ between the US and Mexican governments in the early to mid-nineteenth century?

■ What do you think is meant by the phrase, "we didn't cross the border: the border crossed us"?

■ Is it more or less rare today for a country to invade, take over, and own another country than it was in the nineteenth century? Why do you think that is?

■ Considering relations between the US and Mexico, how does the immigration issue in the 1820s compare to the immigration issue in the present day?

■ How does one reconcile a history of violence and injustice in one's ancestral heritage? How can understanding it be positive, or even empowering?

■ What does postcolonial mean?

■ What is autonomy?

- Latinxs served in significant numbers in the US Civil War and were instrumental in defending the Southwest from advancing Confederate forces;

- Numerous Mexican rebellions occurred after the US Civil War throughout the borderlands in resistance to Anglo-American governance and economic exploitation;

- The Spanish-American War (1898) liberated Cuba from Spain and ceded Guam, the Philippines, and Puerto Rico to the US.

Resources Recommended by the TCU CRES Curriculum Consultants:

Official Spanish Trail Association. Accessed May 30, 2022. https://santafetrail.org/.

Stern, Alexandra. "The Civil War and the Far West: Classroom Suggestions." *U.S. History Scene.* Accessed May 30, 2022. http://ushistoryscene.com/article/the-civil-war-and-the-far-west/.

"The Treaty of Guadalupe Hidalgo." *National Archives.* Accessed May 30, 2022. https://www.archives.gov/education/lessons/guadalupe-hidalgo.

"Lares Flag." *El Boricua: Un Poquito de Todo.* Accessed May 30, 2022. http://elboricua.com/lares.html.

"Crucible of Empire: The Spanish-American War." *PBS.* Accessed May 30, 2022. http://www.pbs.org/crucible/.

For further reading about this theme:

Augenbraum, Harold, and Margarite Fernández-Olmos, eds. *The Latino Reader: An American Literary Tradition from 1542 to the Present.* New York: Houghton Mifflin Company, 1997.

Bradley, Ed. *"We Never Retreat": Filibustering Expeditions in Spanish Texas, 1812–1822.* College Station: Texas A&M University Press, 2015.

Cantrell, Gregg. *Stephen F. Austin: Empresario of Texas.* New Haven: Yale University Press, 1999.

Chipman, Donald E., and Harriett Denise Joseph. *Spanish Texas, 1519–1821.* Austin: University of Texas Press, 2010.

Coronado, Raúl. *A World Not to Come: A History of Latino Writing and Print Culture.* Cambridge, MA: Harvard University Press, 2013.

Cortina, Juan Nepomuceno. "Documents on the Brownsville Uprising of Juan Cortina." US Cong., H., Difficulties on the Southwestern Frontier, 36th Cong.; 1st Sess., 1860, H.Exec. Doc. 52, 70–82. *In New Perspectives on the West.* PBS. 2001. http://www.shoppbs.pbs.org/weta/thewest/resources/archives/four/cortinas.htm

De la Teja, Jesús F., ed. *Tejano Leadership in Mexican and Revolutionary Texas.* College Station: Texas A&M University Press, 2010.

De León, Arnoldo. *They Called Them Greasers: Anglo Attitudes Toward Mexicans in Texas, 1821–1900.* Austin: University of Texas Press, 1983.

Martí, José, and Máximo Gómez. "Manifesto Montecristi." March 25, 1895. Accessed May 29, 2019. http://www.historyofcuba.com/history/marti/Manifesto.htm.

O'Sullivan, John L. "Annexation." *United States Magazine and Democratic Review* 17 (1845): 5–6, 9–10.

Paredes, Américo. "The United States, Mexico, and *Machismo*." *Journal of the Folklore Institute* 8.1 (1971): 17–37.

Pérez y González, María E. *Puerto Ricans in the United States*. Westport: Greenwood Press, 2000.

Ponce, Pearl T., ed. *Kansas's War: The Civil War in Documents*. Columbus: Ohio State University Press, 2011.

Stewart, Kenneth L., and Arnoldo de León. *Not Room Enough: Mexicans, Anglos, and Socio-Economic Change in Texas, 1850–1900*. Albuquerque: University of New Mexico Press, 1993.

Vargas, Zaragosa, ed. *Major Problems in Mexican American History*. Belmont, CA: Wadsworth, Cengage Learning, 1999.

Velásquez, Janeta. *The Woman in Battle: A Narrative of the Exploits, Adventures, and Travels of Madame Loreta Janeta Velazquez, Otherwise Known as Lieutenant Harry T. Buford, Confederate States Army*, edited by C.J. Worthington. Chapel Hill: University of North Carolina at Chapel Hill Library, 2017. First edition, 1876.

4. Migration and the Making of Latinx Communities

This theme addresses the changing geographic, migratory, cultural, and political patterns of Latinxs who populated the US after US colonization reached its fullest extent. It examines how ordinary people, despite long odds, moved to new places, survived, and thrived in the changed political and economic environment they faced. Enduring US neo-imperialism, Latinxs responded by building vibrant communities as a powerful defense against white supremacy, which was ascendant in the period. Latinxs developed hybrid cultures celebrating their indigenous roots and countries of origin while also adapting and incorporating elements of the US mainstream. Some resisted efforts at assimilation while others did not. Most toiled as low-wage industrial and agricultural workers, performing undesirable and dangerous jobs while also facing nativist threats from Anglo/European Americans. They organized mutual aid associations, unions, and political clubs to assert their civil and human rights in the US. Successive waves of new immigrants from the Americas consistently forced US-born Latinxs to reconsider their status, race/ethnicity, culture, and national loyalties—and to redefine their families, communities, and ethnic allegiances.

The historical span of this theme begins in 1898 with the Spanish-American War and the annexation of Puerto Rico; and it ends loosely around the 1930s, when Latinxs had established themselves as a key labor force and had planted roots in neighborhoods (*barrios*).

Broad topics:

1) Filipinos and the Latinx Global South

2) Puerto Rico, Citizenship, and Revolving-Door Migration

3) The Growth of Population and Industry in the Southwest

4) *Barrios*: Early Latinx Neighborhoods

5) The Texas Rangers, Mexican Americans, and *La Matanza*

6) Early Labor Union Organizing

7) The Emergence of Latinx Media

Enduring Understandings

Students will understand that...

■ The Spanish-American War (1898) resulted in the US annexing Guam, the Philippines, and Puerto Rico;

■ In 1917, Puerto Ricans were made US citizens, but while they can travel freely back and forth between Puerto Rico and the mainland US, voting rights in Puerto Rico and representation in federal government is significantly limited;

■ Latinxs already in the US Southwest were joined by more recent immigrants fleeing economic dislocation, political persecution, and colonial exploitation;

■ In Mexico, the Porfiriato (1876–1910) and Revolution (1910–1920) led hundreds of thousands of people to migrate to the US;

■ The recent arrivals brought new life to old Latinx communities, and together they created large enclaves or barrios to facilitate mutual aid, self-help, and cultural fluorescence. Mutualistas (mutual-aid societies) represented the key manner of organizing communities, along with Latino-owned businesses, Spanish-language media, and labor unions;

■ Latinxs created the ranching culture of the US West and served as the earliest vaqueros, or cowboys. Their knowledge and experience became the bedrock of commercial ranching as it moved north and became consolidated as big business;

■ Latinxs built the basic infrastructure of the Southwest's economy, including railroads and the expansion of commercial agriculture and industrial mining;

■ Latinxs faced new incursions from Anglo settlers, resulting in economic suffering and the loss of hereditary lands;

■ Anglos imposed a new system of "Juan Crow" race relations that disfranchised Latinxs, relegated them to low-wage labor, denigrated Latinx culture, denied them educational opportunities, and imposed an unequal justice system;

■ State-sanctioned violence against Latinxs was common, including (but not limited to) the Texas Rangers' murderous campaigns to dispossess and disempower Latinxs in South Texas;

Essential Questions

Students will consider...

■ How did the lives of Latinxs change after US colonization?

■ Why and how were Latinxs largely confined to low-wage labor?

■ What was "Juan Crow"?

■ Why did Latinxs migrate to the US? Where did they settle?

■ How did Latinxs help themselves by building communities in the US?

■ When did my family/ancestors come to the US and why? What kinds of jobs did they do on arrival? What kind of neighborhood did they live in?

■ How did "progressive reformers" impose their world view via eugenics and Americanization campaigns? How did Latinxs respond?

■ What role did the state play in creating Juan Crow and enacting violence against Latinxs?

■ How did Latinxs organize themselves to survive and thrive amidst Juan Crow?

■ Why did Nativists want to restrict immigration? Why did growers seek to keep the doors open? Who won?

■ What has been the nature of the relationship between the US and Puerto Rico? Is this relationship fair? Is this relationship sustainable?

■ How did Latinx cultures change over time? What is meant by hybridity?

- Latinxs served the US military during World War I, but they were also victimized by the war effort in the service and on the homefront;

- Anglos used eugenics and forced sterilization campaigns aimed at reducing the future population of Latinxs in Puerto Rico and the US Southwest;

- Self-described "progressive" Anglos attempted to erase Latinx culture through forced "Americanization" and assimilation campaigns;

- Life in the barrios and at work led Latinxs to develop new hybrid cultures that blended US and Latin American influences. These were reflected in new familial and gender practices as well as new religious, cultural, and residential preferences;

- Latinas gained new independence from their husbands and fathers, engaging in wage work, consuming mass culture (going to dances, riding in cars, listening to new radio stations), and developing new religious rituals in the home. Latinas served their communities, helped others, and organized politically;

- Latinxs formed labor unions that fought for both civil rights and workers' rights, and they did so often with workers of other races/ethnicities;

- Latinxs encountered rising hostility and Nativism from other US Americans as well as growing surveillance by the government.

Resources Recommended by the TCU CRES Curriculum Consultants:

"Life and Death on the Border, 1910–1920." Bob Bullock Museum of Texas History. Online exhibition. Accessed May 30, 2022. https://www.thestoryoftexas.com/visit/exhibits/life-and-death-on-the-border-1910-1920.

Teresa Carey. "The Jones Act, explained (and what waiving it means for Puerto Rico)." *PBS News Hour*. Accessed May 30, 2022. https://www.pbs.org/newshour/nation/jones-act-explained-waiving-means-puerto-rico.

"Researching, Preserving & Sharing the Puerto Rican Experience." Centro, the Center for Puerto Rican Studies, Hunter College, City University of New York. Accessed May 30, 2022. https://centropr.hunter.cuny.edu/.

United States Army. "Hispanic Americans: Shaping the Bright Future of America." *Hispanics in the U.S. Army*. Accessed May 30, 2022. https://www.army.mil/hispanics/.

For further reading about this theme:

Benavides, Lucía. "The Texas Rangers Killed Hundreds of Hispanic Americans During the Mexican Revolution." *Texas Standard.* January 22, 2016. Accessed June 7, 2019. https://www.texasstandard.org/stories/texas-exhibit-refuses-to-forget-one-of-the-worst-periods-of-state-sanctioned-violence/.

Coerver, Don M. "Plan of San Diego." *Handbook of Texas Online.* October 5, 2015. Accessed June 7, 2019. http://www.tshaonline.org/handbook/online/articles/ngp04.

Cuéllar, Carlos E. *Stories From the Barrio: A History of Mexican Fort Worth.* Fort Worth: TCU Press, 2003.

Daniels, Roger. *Coming to America: A History of Immigration and Ethnicity in American Life.* 2nd ed. NewYork: Harper Perennial, 2002.

Maroney, James C. "Oilfield Strike of 1917." *Handbook of Texas Online.* June 15, 2010. Accessed June 7, 2019. http://www.tshaonline.org/handbook/online/articles/doott.

"Mexico Faces Ruin as Strikes Spread." *International Herald Tribune.* May 23, 1917. Accessed June 7, 2019. https://iht-retrospective.blogs.nytimes.com/2017/05/23/1917-mexico-faces-ruin-as-strikes-spread/?partner=bloomberg.

Morán González, John. "The History of Racial Violence on the Mexico-Texas Border." *Refusing to Forget.* 2019. Accessed June 7, 2019. https://refusingtoforget.org/the-history/.

Thompson, Roger M. *Filipino English and Taglish: Language Switching from Multiple Perspectives.* Amsterdam and Philadelphia: John Benjamins Publishing Company, 2003.

5. The Long and Wide Civil Rights Movement

This theme addresses the struggles among Latinx peoples for personal freedom, community power, inclusion, fair treatment, protection, and recognition in mainstream US society. These struggles were ever present but accelerated during the Great Depression, World War II, and the Cold War. The economic crisis forced myriad transformations in the nation's *barrios,* with forced repatriation driving out many immigrants and those who remained behind redoubling their efforts to survive and thrive. Many communities across the US supported vibrant civil rights and labor movements that at times connected immigrant and settled Latinx communities, and at other times emphasized acculturation as hybrid Americans in US politics and society. Activists created new local and national organizations—including the League of United Latin American Citizens (LULAC) and the American GI Forum—and participated in multiethnic movements such as the Congress of Industrial Organizations (CIO). Latinxs created their own civil rights movement that ran parallel to the African American freedom struggle and also intersected in various productive ways.

The historical span of this theme is the 1930s to the 1960s, including the Great Depression, World War II, and the Cold War periods.

Broad topics:

1) Established Latinx Communities in the US
2) Progressives, Social Reformers, and Americanization
3) LULAC, the American GI Forum, and Fighting Anti-Latinx Racism
4) Operation Bootstrap, the Puerto Rican Commonwealth, and Puerto Rican Nationalism
5) The Bracero Program, Operation Wetback, and Unionizing Farm Workers

6) Latinas, Women's Causes, and Activism

7) The Young Lords, Sleepy Lagoon, the Zoot Suit Riots, and Urban Civil Rights

Enduring Understandings

Students will understand that...

■ During the Great Depression, state and local governments repatriated almost 500,000 Mexicans residing in the US;

■ Endorsing democracy and free-market capitalism but opposing racism, the influential League of United Latin American Citizens (LULAC) was founded in 1929 in San Antonio, Texas;

■ Numerous labor organizations fought against Depression-era repatriation and advocated for bilingual education and better housing;

■ Worker rights for minorities were expanded in the early 1940s by action of the federal government under President Franklin D. Roosevelt;

■ The Bracero Program (1942–1964) brought millions of farm laborers from Mexico to the US;

■ Operation Bootstrap (1947) intended to industrialize Puerto Rico's economy but resulted in massive migration from the island to the US mainland;

■ *Méndez v. Westminster* (1947) was the first legal decision stating that segregated schools violated the Fourteenth Amendment to the US Constitution, laying important groundwork for the landmark *Brown v. Board of Education* decision seven years later;

■ *Hernández v. Texas* (1954) decided that Mexican Americans were treated "as a class apart" and denied Fourteenth Amendment protections, setting precedent for successful challenges in other discrimination cases;

■ "Operation Wetback" (1954) deported over a million Mexican residents of the US, many here legally or even US citizens;

■ A new era of radical Latinx activism emerged in the 1965 to early 1970s period;

(Continues)

Essential Questions

Students will consider...

■ What role did the Great Depression play in the forced and voluntary migrations of large numbers of Mexicans?

■ What were some of the key civil rights cases LULAC took up in its early development? What is meant by the idea that Mexicans are "a class apart?"

■ How did World War II shape a new generation of Mexican Americans?

■ Who were the Zoot Suiters? What was the connection between the Sleepy Lagoon case and the Zoot Suit Riot of 1943?

■ How did the political and governmental status of Puerto Rico shift and yet its people still persist in a dependent and often contested relationship with the US government?

■ What were some of the consequences and controversies concerning the Bracero Program?

■ Who was Lolita LeBrón, and what were the key aims of Puerto Rican Nationalism?

■ In what ways did the Cold War inform American neo-imperialism in Latin America, particularly in Guatemala and the Dominican Republic?

■ What was "Operation Wetback?" How did its scope and impact compare with earlier examples of deportation and forced repatriation?

■ Who were some of the key early twentieth-century Latino political leaders in the US Congress and Senate? What were some of their notable legislative accomplishments?

- Several major Latinx political leaders emerged in the 1960s, especially in Texas, California, and New York;

- The civil rights movement was long and wide, involving a huge range of efforts and lasting much longer than a single decade.

Resources Recommended by the TCU CRES Curriculum Consultants:

United States Congress. H.Con.Res. 253. 110th Cong. (2007–2008). Accessed May 30, 2022. https://www.congress.gov/bill/110th-congress/house-concurrent-resolution/253/text.

"About." *Bracero History Archive*. Accessed May 30, 2022. http://braceroarchive.org/about.

For further reading about this theme:

Acosta-Belén, Edna, and Carlos E. Santiago. *Puerto Ricans in the United States: A Contemporary Portrait*. 2nd ed. Boulder: Lynne Rienner Publishers, 2018.

Brilliant, Mark. *The Color of America Has Changed: How Racial Diversity Shaped Civil Rights Reform in California, 1941–1978*. New York and Oxford: Oxford University Press, 2010.

García, Juan Ramón. *Operation Wetback: The Mass Deportation of Mexican Undocumented Workers in 1954*. Westport and London: Greenwood Press, 1980.

Hoffman, Abraham. *Unwanted Mexican Americans in the Great Depression: Repatriation Pressures, 1929–1939*. Tuscon: University of Arizona Press, 1974.

Márquez, Benjamin. *LULAC: The Evolution of a Mexican American Political Organization*. Austin: University of Texas Press, 1993.

Mass, Bonnie. "Puerto Rico: A Case Study of Population Control." *Latin American Perspectives* 4.4 (Autumn 1977): 66–81.

Sánchez, George J. *Becoming Mexican American: Ethnicity, Culture, and Identity in Chicano Los Angeles, 1900–1945*. New York and Oxford: Oxford University Press, 1993.

6. Radical Movements, Critiques, and Legacies

This theme addresses a new style of Latinx politics and culture, from the mid-1960s to early 1980s, that emerged out of prior civil rights movements and was marked by growing collective agency; the use of confrontational tactics; and the embracing of indigenous origins, bilingualism/biculturalism, anti-imperialism, and at times non-white racial identities like "Brown," "Chicano/a," and *"boricua."* Activists transformed old organizations and created new ones that more clearly demanded self-determination, power, and resources—not just access or rights. These included the Brown Berets, the Mexican American Youth Organization (MAYO), the Puerto Rican Alliance, the Young Lords, and to some extent, the United Farm Workers. Youth and student activists led many of these "Brown Power" movements, including school walk-outs and campaigns for the creation of Chicano Studies, Mexican American Studies, Puerto Rican Studies, etc. These movements also engendered stringent critiques from within and without, including discussions of the limits of cultural nationalism, the need to better address gender and sexuality, and the ongoing need for incorporation and acceptance in the dominant society. Chicanas and Puerto Rican feminists challenged their male *compañeros* (comrades) to reexamine race and ethnicity through the lenses of multiple inter-secting oppressions, while more liberal and conservative Hispanic activists charted different courses to-ward inclusion. At the same time, legal openings in the mid-1960s contributed to massive immigration, demographic shifts, cultural regeneration, and a renewed nativist movement.

The historical span of this theme is from roughly 1965, after the Civil Rights Act, to 1980 and the Reagan Era.

Broad topics:

1) Migrant Labor and the United Farm Workers (UFW)

2) The Chicano/a Movement and its Legacies

3) MAYO, La Raza Unida Party, Crystal City, and the Movement in Texas

4) Chicano/a and Puerto Rican Youth Movements

5) Radicalisms in Latin America

6) Chicana Activism and Third-Wave Feminism

7) The Triumph of "Hispanic" and Political Incorporation

8) Liberal Immigration Reform & Demographic Shifts

Enduring Understandings

Students will understand that...

■ Latinxs embraced a new style of community organizing in the late 1960s and 1970s, replacing rights with power and self-determination;

■ The myth of "whiteness" gave way among many Latinxs to a new identity rooted in being "Brown";

■ Students and youth led the larger social move-ments, walking out of schools, issuing manifestos, and forming new organizations;

■ Cultural nationalism brought activists together, but it wasn't enough to erase internal differences of class, gender, race, sexuality, and ideology;

■ A cultural renaissance among Latinx muralists and other artists took great pride in their mixed origins, celebrating indigenous ancestry;

(Continues)

Essential Questions

Students will consider...

■ How and why did Latinxs find new ways to chal-lenge Juan Crow?

■ In what ways was their activism a departure (or not) from earlier civil rights efforts?

■ What/who were some of the key organizations and leaders in the Chicano/a movement—nation-wide and in Texas specifically?

■ How did the changing identities of Latinxs con-tribute to their changing politics regarding foreign policy and immigration?

■ How did the violence of the US (police brutality, imperialism/militarism, systemic racialized pov-erty) compare with and relate to violence in Latin America?

(Continues)

- Texas was a critical site of the Chicano Movement, a forgotten civil rights movement that transformed the US;

- Women activists confronted multiple forms of oppression simultaneously, challenging the sexism of their male comrades and the racism of Anglo-American culture;

- Latinos formed militant organizations that used armed self-defense to defend their barrios and serve working-class Latino communities;

- Latinx "Brown Power" activists formed tight coalitions with African American "Black Power" activists;

- Student movements also rocked much of Latin America and the Caribbean;

- Youth movements spawned a host of "second-generation" civil rights and educational organizations that still exist today;

- In 1965, Congress passed immigration reform that remade the nation's demographics;

- Chicano movement activists embraced their immigrant brethren as never before, creating today's political alignment on the issue.

- What were some of the key areas of activism in the movement? What did activists hope to change or improve?

- What was the role of women Chicanas in the movement? Who are some notable Chicana activists?

- How did Latinx activists in this era relate to African Americans and Native Americans and their own Black and indigenous roots?

- Why did US Latinxs become supporters of immigrant rights?

- How did conservative and liberal "Hispanics" and other Latinxs gain new stature in the wake of more radical youth-led movements? What are some of their concrete accomplishments?

- How did the US government and schools count Latinxs, and how did this change over time?

Resources Recommended by the TCU CRES Curriculum Consultants:

"Stolen Education." *Video Project*. Accessed May 30, 2022. https://www.videoproject.com/Stolen-Education.html.

The Carnalismo National Brown Berets Website. Accessed May 30, 2022. http://nationalbrownberets.org/.

Estrada, Josue. "MEChA and Chicano Student Organizations 1967-2012." *Mapping American Social Movements Project*. University of Washington. Accessed May 30, 2022. https://depts.washington.edu/moves/MEChA_map.shtml.

¡Viva La Raza! Documenting Tarrant County's Mexicano Activism. Accessed May 30, 2022. https://fortworthmexicanoactivism.wordpress.com/.

Civil Rights in Black and Brown Interview Database. Accessed May 30, 2022. http://crbb.tcu.edu/.

Chicana por mi Raza Digital Memory Project. Accessed May 30, 2022. https://chicanapormiraza.org/.

For further reading about this theme:

Anzaldúa, Gloria. *Borderlands/La Frontera: The New Mestiza.* San Francisco: Aunt Lute Books, 1987.

Armbruster-Sandoval, Ralph. *Starving for Justice: Hunger Strikes, Spectacular Speech, and the Struggle for Dignity.* Tuscon: University of Arizona Press, 2017.

Blackwell, Maylei. *¡Chicana Power!: Contested Histories of Feminism in the Chicano Movement.* Austin: University of Texas Press, 2016.

Casillas, Dolores I. *Sounds of Belonging: US Spanish-Language Radio and Public Advocacy.* New York: NYU Press, 2014.

Cockcroft, Eva S., and Holly Barnet-Sánchez. *Signs from the Heart: California Chicano Murals.* Venice, CA: Social and Public Art Resource Center, 1990.

García, Alma M., ed. *Chicana Feminist Thought: The Basic Historical Writings.* New York: Routledge, 1997.

González, Juan. *Harvest of Empire: A History of Latinos in America.* New York: Penguin Books, 2011.

Jackson, Carlos F. *Chicana and Chicano Art: Protest Arte.* Tuscon: University of Arizona Press, 2009.

Leon, Kendall M. "La Hermandad and Chicanas Organizing: The Community Rhetoric of the *Comisión Femenil Mexicana Nacional.*" *Community Literacy Journal* 7.2 (2013): 1–20.

Minian, Ana Raquel. *Undocumented Lives: The Untold Story of Mexican Migration.* Cambridge, MA: Harvard University Press, 2018.

Moraga, Cherríe, and Gloria Anzaldúa, eds. *This Bridge Called My Back: Writings by Radical Women of Color.* Watertown: Persephone Press, 1981.

Vento, Arnoldo C. *Mestizo: The History, Culture, and Politics of the Mexican and the Chicano.* Lanham, MD: University Press of America, 1998.

7. Emergent Shifts and Contemporary Issues

This theme addresses the key social, political, and cultural transformations that Latinx people and communities have experienced since the 1980s. Sometimes referred to pejoratively as the "Decade of the Hispanic" for the broken promises of mainstream inclusion associated with that decade, the 1980s saw a federal reduction in social spending and a crackdown on the social movements of the previous decades. At the same time, economic fluctuations in Latin America, including Mexico, and US intervention in Central America spurred an increase in migration levels to the US. This theme continues with examining how the 1990s saw a tighter interaction between criminal law enforcement and immigration law via sweeping reforms. By the 2000s, a growing undocumented population, with undocumented youth brought here as children, began to grow impatient with a prolonged inability to regularize their status. This frustration exploded in the mega-marches of 2006 and the "Dreamer" movements of the late 2000s, which culminated in the implementation of DACA in 2012. This theme considers how, through these transformations, art and culture continued to both reflect and shape the key issues of the times, often serving as a harbinger of the issues that would become central to the larger Latinx community in later times. This was powerfully true in the area of gender politics, with queer Chicanas and Chicanos especially calling into question lingering patriarchal structures in Latinx families, communities, and even organizations. Today, such politics of self-representation continue to be negotiated, finding perhaps their greatest intensity in the debate over the inclusion of Mexican-American Studies (MAS) in public schools; and within the Latinx community, over the use of the spectrum-inclusive—but still largely Eurocentric—term *Latinx*. This theme encourages students to see their family and personal histories reflected in the content, perhaps most well-represented by the social and cultural transformations of the 1980s and 2010s, making this final theme a rich space for students to situate their life histories in a historical context.

The historical period of this theme spans the mid-1970s to the present day.

Broad topics:

1) Effects of US Neo-Imperialism in Latin America, 1970–1990
2) Immigration Reforms, Citizenships, and Complexities
3) Puerto Rico, Oversight Economics, and Recovery
4) Latinx Politics and Representation in US Government
5) Socio-Economics and Living Conditions of Latinxs
6) Latino/a, Latinx, Latine: Emergent Identities
7) Latinx Fort Worth

Enduring Understandings

Students will understand that...

■ The Latinx community includes an increasingly diverse mix of over twenty nations, with Mexicans, Puerto Ricans, Cubans, and Salvadorans representing the largest groups;

■ Latinx individuals have named and defined themselves in a variety of ways, including by national origin, pan-ethnic terms, and more recently as Latinx;

■ Levels of immigration have changed over time depending in part on the relationship between the US and other countries in Latin, Central, and South America;

■ Latinx communities have accessed citizenship and belonging through a variety of cultural and political processes;

■ Since the 1980s, US immigration policies have increasingly emphasized enforcement and illegality;

■ Electoral politics and community organizing/ protest are ways that Latinx communities have asserted their rights in American politics;

■ Despite gains in the number of Latinx elected officials, Latinx representation still lags behind;

(Continues)

Essential Questions

Students will consider...

■ How do identities intersect? And how does the intersection of identities produce complexity, both as new experiences to celebrate and as challenges to solving social problems?

■ Why does the fight for cultural and political recognition and access continue today, and why does it matter to students and their families?

■ How do political, economic, and legal factors influence family history?

■ What are ways students can participate in politics?

■ What issues, including immigration, do Latinx communities care about?

■ How will immigration continue to shape the Latinx experience in the US and beyond?

■ How do Latinxs represent their culture and experiences?

■ How do the arts impact the construction and representation of identity? Why do groups' identities shift over time?

■ Latinx students have fought a long struggle for recognition and inclusion in schools and continue to face curricular, economic, and legal barriers to education access and equity;

■ Key debates and social identities in the Latinx community are negotiated through multiple genres in the arts, including outlets like film, literature, and theatre, and other media.

Resources Recommended by the TCU CRES Curriculum Consultants:

Migration Policy Institute. Accessed May 30, 2022. https://www.migrationpolicy.org/.

Pew Research Center. Accessed May 30, 2022. https://www.pewresearch.org.

NBC News Latino. Accessed May 30, 2022. https://www.nbcnews.com/latino.

Latino Decisions. Accessed May 30, 2022. http://www.latinodecisions.com.

"The Graduates - The Girls." *Independent Lens.* Accessed May 30, 2022. https://www.pbs.org/video/independent-lens-graduates-girls/.

"Immigrant High." *Independent Lens.* Accessed May 30, 2022. https://www.pbs.org/video/independent-lens-immigrant-high/.

"Chicano Park Murals." *The History of Chicano Park, San Diego, California.* Accessed May 30, 2022. http://www.chicanoparksandiego.com/murals/.

Latinopia.com. Accessed May 30, 2022. http://latinopia.com/.

Center for Cultural Power. Accessed May 30, 2022. https://www.culturalpower.org/.

Hemispheric Institute. Accessed May 30, 2022. https://hemisphericinstitute.org/en/.

For further reading about this theme:

Barreto, Matt A., and Gary M. Segura. *Latino America: How America's Most Dynamic Population is Poised to Transform the Politics of the Nation.* New York: Public Affairs, 2014.

Beltrán, Cristina. *The Trouble with Unity: Latino Politics and the Creation of Identity.* New York: Oxford University Press, 2010.

Parédez, Deborah. *Selenidad: Selena, Latinos, and the Performance of Memory.* Durham: Duke University Press, 2009.

Chávez, Leo R. *The Latino Threat: Constructing Immigrants, Citizens, and the Nation.* Stanford: Stanford University Press, 2008.

Chetty, Raj, Nathaniel Hendren, Maggie R. Jones, and Sonya R. Porter. "Race and Economic Opportunity in the United States: An Intergenerational Perspective." March 2018. Accessed June 26, 2019. http://www.equality-of-opportunity.org/assets/documents/race_paper.pdf.

Dávila, Arlene. *Latino Spin: Public Image and the Whitewashing of Race.* New York: NYU Press, 2008.

DeSipio, Louis, and Rodolfo O. de la Garza. *US Immigration in the Twenty-First Century: Making Americans, Remaking America.* Boulder: Westview Press, 2015.

Flores, William V., and Rina Benmayor. *Latino Cultural Citizenship: Claiming Identity, Space, and Rights.* Boston: Beacon Press, 1997.

García Bedolla, Lisa. *Latino Politics.* Cambridge, UK: Polity, 2014.

García, John A. *Latino Politics in America: Community, Culture, and Interests.* Lanham: Rowman & Littlefield, 2011.

Gonzales, Roberto G. *Lives in Limbo: Undocumented and Coming of Age in America.* Oakland: University of California Press, 2015.

Grable, David M. "Personhood Under the Due Process Clause: A Constitutional Analysis of the Illegal Immigration Reform and Immigrant Responsibility Act of 1996." *Cornell Law Review* 83.820 (1998): 820–65.

Grande, Reyna. *The Distance between Us.* New York: Washington Square Press, 2013.

Mohamed, Heather S. *The New Americans?: Immigration, Protest, and the Politics of Latino Identity.* Lawrence: University Press of Kansas, 2017.

Sandoval, Denise M. *"White" Washing American Education: The New Culture Wars in Ethnic Studies.* Santa Barbara: Praeger, an imprint of ABC-CLIO, 2016.

Urrea, Luis A. *The Devil's Highway: A True Story.* New York: Little, Brown, 2004.

Valenzuela, Angela. *Subtractive Schooling: US-Mexican Youth and the Politics of Caring.* Albany: SUNY Press, 1999.

Vargas, José Antonio. *Dear America: Notes of an Undocumented Citizen.* New York: HarperCollins Publishers, 2018.

Wides-Muñoz, Laura. *The Making of a Dream: How a Group of Young Undocumented Immigrants Helped Change What it Means to be American.* New York: HarperCollins Publishers, 2018.

Zamora, Javier. *Unaccompanied.* Port Townsend: Copper Canyon Press, 2017.

5. K-12 Classroom Implementation

Annotated Bibliography: Implementing a Latinx Studies Curriculum

1. Coppersmith, Sarah A., and Kim H. Song. "Integrating Primary Sources, Artifacts, and Museum Visits into the Primary Years Program Inquiry Curriculum in an International Baccalaureate Elementary Setting." *Journal of Social Studies Education Research* 8.3 (2017): 24–49.

> Questions remain about inquiry instruction, while research confirms that using primary sources can aid students' inquiry learning processes. This study questioned: "How do second-grade teachers at an International Baccalaureate Organization/IBO language immersion setting incorporate inquiry methods in instructional practices?"; "How does training in the use of primary sources, artifacts, and museum visits shape second-grade teachers' instructional practice?" A Library of Congress Teaching with Primary Sources grant supported this university-school social studies partnership, which accessed artifacts, primary sources, and a national archives and museum. Data sources in this mixed methods study were from the SAMPI Inquiry Observation Instrument, interviews, and observations in French and Spanish language settings. Analysis revealed teachers incorporating inquiry learning via museum/archives visits and using primary sources in a study of the history and geography of the French and Spanish Colonial fur trade era. Results revealed a subsequent integration of primary sources and learning kits in the immersion school network's ongoing inquiry curriculum design process.

2. Drossopoulos, Arianna, and Danielle King-Watkins. "Creating an Understanding of an Unfamiliar Culture (Islam) through Young Adult Literature." *English Journal* 107.6 (July 1, 2018). https://library.ncte.org/journals/ej/issues/v107-6/29708.

> This article focuses on the implementation of one unit and ways educators might consider using YA literature featuring Muslim characters to foster meaningful discussions about society as a whole. These implementation strategies and techniques can inform comparable or parallel activities with Latinx Studies content.

3. Ehst, E. Suzanne, and Lewis Caskey. "Writing toward Democracy: Scaffolding Civic Engagement with Historically Marginalized Students." *English Journal* 107.6 (July 1, 2018). https://library.ncte.org/journals/EJ/issues/v107-6/29709.

> This article describes the implementation of a persuasive writing unit with mostly Latinx students in a "focused track" at a Midwestern high school. The authors scaffold not only writing skills but also the experience of engaging policy issues and power structures.

4. Enríquez-Loya, Aydé, and Kendall Leon. "Chicanx/Latinx Rhetorics as Methodology for Writing Program Design at HSIs." *Composition Studies* 45.2 (October 1, 2017). https://www.jstor.org/stable/26402792.

> This article discusses the introduction of Chicanx and Latinx rhetorics in the writing program design at Hispanic-Serving Institution (HSI). It mentions the argument of Iris Ruiz in "Reclaiming Composition for Chicanos/as and Other Ethnic Minorities" that examine the histories of rhetoric and composition. It notes that the Chicanx and Latinx rhetoric and writing must take place in designing programs and institutions.

5. Evans, Luna N., William P. Evans, and Bret Davis. "Indigenous Mexican culture, identity and academic aspirations: results from a community-based curriculum project for Latina/Latino students." *Race Ethnicity and Education* 18.3 (2015): 341–62. http://dx.doi.org/10.1080/13613324.2012.759922.

> The Latina/Latino population is the largest minority group in the United States and has the highest high school dropout rate of any ethnic group. Nationally, just over one-half of Latina/Latino students

graduate on time with a regular diploma, compared to nearly 80 percent of Whites. Because of the growing population and the wide achievement gap, there is utility in understanding factors, strategies, and programs that facilitate the academic performance of Latina/Latino students in order to address a serious social justice issue in education. This study examines a community-based cultural program about indigenous Mesoamerican traditions and heritage. Results of the mixed-method evaluation study include quantitative and qualitative data for 225 high school students who were primarily Latina/Latino. Students participated in a program based on Mesoamerican ancestry that sought to enhance academic aspirations and reduce the appeal of dropping out of high school. Survey results indicated positive changes in ethnic identity and improvements in academic aspirations. Interviews revealed enhanced attachment to ethnic identity and higher academic aspirations, in addition to ideas about how the program could be improved for future participants. Implications of this culturally relevant curriculum as a strategy to enhance student academic motivation and aspirations are discussed.

6. Misco, Thomas, and Martha E. Castaneda. "'Now, What Should I Do for English Language Learners?': Reconceptualizing Social Studies Curriculum Design for ELLs." *Educational Horizons* 87.3 (Spring 2009): 182–89. https://eric.ed.gov/?id=EJ849018.

One of the main professional-development challenges social studies teachers face involves adjusting content and instruction to accommodate the surging population of English Language Learners (ELLs). Between the 1993–1994 and 2004–2005 school years, ELL school populations increased 68 percent to more than 5.1 million, compared to a 7.8 percent increase among non-ELL students (NCELA 2008). Because most ELLs are "mainstreamed" into content-area classrooms, the burgeoning population of non-native speakers makes instructional adaptation legally and morally imperative to provide all students with meaningful learning experiences. Providing such learning experiences is still very much an issue, even when an English for Speakers of Other Languages (ESOL) program is available to students. A short taxonomy can articulate what social studies teachers actually need to accomplish—some precise guidance on what they should be doing for ELLs, easily juxtaposed with content standards, instructional strategies, key skill domains, and dispositional objectives when crafting unit and lesson plans. This article focuses on a particular example of reconceptualizing social studies curricula through reverse-chronological history instruction, an exercise applicable to secondary ELL pull-out classes and mainstream social studies classrooms alike.

7. Virtue, David C., Anne Buchanan, and Kenneth E. Vogler. "Digging Postholes Adds Depth and Authenticity to a Shallow Curriculum." *Social Studies* 103.6 (2012): 247–51. DOI: 10.1080/00377996.2011.630699.

In the current era of high-stakes testing and accountability, many social studies teachers struggle to find creative ways to add depth and authenticity to a broad, shallow curriculum. Teachers can use the time after tests are administered for students to reflect back on the social studies curriculum and select topics they want to study more deeply by digging "postholes," or inquiries into questions, persons, processes, or events of their choosing. This article describes one teacher's efforts to implement an inquiry project in which she conferred with her students individually to formulate research questions and a research strategy and gave them opportunities to publicly and authentically share their work.

Sources Focused on the Need for Program Change

8. Alim, H. S. "Critical language awareness in the United States: Revisiting issues and revising pedagogies in a resegregated society." *Educational Researcher* 34.7 (2005): 24–31.

As scholars examine the successes and failures of more than fifty years of court-ordered desegregation since *Brown v. Board of Education of Topeka, Kansas*, and twenty-five years of language education of Black youth since *Martin Luther King Elementary School Children v. Ann Arbor School District Board*, this article revisits the key issues involved in those cases and urges educators and sociolinguists to work together to revise pedagogies. After reviewing what scholars have contributed, the author suggests the need for critical language awareness programs in the United States as one important way in which we can revise our pedagogies, not only to take the students' language into account but also to account for the interconnectedness of language with the larger sociopolitical and sociohistorical phenomena that help to maintain unequal power relations in a still-segregated society.

9. Alim, H. S. "Critical hip-hop language pedagogies: Combat, consciousness and the cultural politics of communication." *Journal of Language, Identity, and Education* 6.2 (2007): 161–176.

This article addresses two long-standing tensions in the education of linguistically marginalized youth: (a) the cultural tension, or cultural combat, that such students engage in as they form their linguistic identities, and (b) the tensions between the development of critical language pedagogies and the lack of their broader implementation due to disinterested and discriminatory teachers. This article presents critical Hip-hop language pedagogies (CHHLPs) as a holistic approach aimed at both students and teachers, incorporating theory and practice, so that innovative approaches might be implemented. After situating CHHLPs within critical language studies, the article argues that educators are obligated to present the current sociolinguistic reality to students who are subjugated in mainstream institutions. To this end, several pedagogical approaches are presented and discussed. The article concludes with a vision for critical, reflexive pedagogies and a call to mobilize the full body of language, social, and cultural theory to produce consciousness-raising pedagogies.

10. Baker-Bell, A. "I never really knew the history behind African American Language: Critical language pedagogy in an advanced placement English language arts class." *Equity & Excellence in Education* 46.3 (2013): 355–70.

This article responds to two long-standing dilemmas that limit the effectiveness of language education for students who speak and write in African American Language (AAL): (1) the gap between theory and research on AAL and classroom practice, and (2) the need for critical language pedagogies. This article presents the effectiveness of a critical language pedagogy used in one eleventh grade advanced placement English Language Arts (ELA) class. Findings show that students held negative attitudes toward AAL before the implementation of the critical language pedagogy, and that the critical language pedagogy helped students to interrogate dominant notions of language and to express an appreciation of AAL.

11. Busey, Christopher L., and William B. Russell III. "'We Want to Learn': Middle School Latinx Students Discuss Social Studies Curriculum and Pedagogy." *RMLE Online* 39.4 (2016): 1–20. DOI: 10.1080/19404476.2016.1155921.

This qualitative study examines the perceptions that Latino students have of middle school social studies. Twelve Latinx middle school students provided written narratives recounting their experiences in social studies and participated in two semi-structured phenomenological interviews. Findings indicate that social studies teachers rely heavily upon "banking" pedagogy and the curriculum lacks cultural diversity. Students also perceived social studies as the ideal subject area in middle school to engage in global learning opportunities as well as discussion about current events. Latinx students' experiences and subsequent perceptions of middle school social studies are consistent with theory and research pertaining to adolescent identity, cognitive, and psychosocial development. Findings from this investigation add to the extant canon of literature on students' perceptions of social studies and further emphasize the significance of social studies in meeting the needs of twenty-first century diverse learners. Lastly, the authors offer suggestions for practice and issue a call for research in the field of social studies education that is middle-level specific with implications as to how culturally responsive social studies fosters identity and psychosocial adolescent development for culturally and ethnically diverse students.

12. Callahan, Rebecca, and Kathryn Obenchain. "Finding a Civic Voice: Latino Immigrant Youths' Experiences in High School Social Studies." *High School Journal* 96 (2012): 20–32. DOI: 10.1353/hsj.2012.0013.

Socialization into the dominant civic and political discourse lies at the heart of social studies. As they become proficient in the discourse of home and school, Latino immigrant youth could uniquely benefit from this socialization. This qualitative study explores ten Latino immigrant young adults' perceptions of how their social studies experiences shaped their young adult civic selves. Participants internalized not only their parents' high expectations for them, but also those of their teachers, highlighting the potentially instrumental role of schools in the civic fabric of the nation. In addition, the Latino young adults felt empowered by their social studies teachers via civic expectations and academic encouragement, and perceived this empowerment to have facilitated the skill development necessary for later civic leadership. The authors reflect on immigrant students' incorporation of the discourse of the dominant culture with that of the home to develop their own civic voices.

13. Cherry-McDaniel, Monique. "#WOKE: Employing Black Textualities to Create Critically Conscious Classrooms." *English Journal* 106.4 (2017): 41–46. http://www.ncte.org/library/NCTEFiles/Resources/Journals/EJ/1064-mar17/EJ1064WOKE.pdf.

This article employs the use of black textualities to reimagine an English classroom designed to cultivate critically conscious students. The author argues that a critically conscious classroom engages students in self-determination, citizenship formation, and strategic activism, and further argues that black textualities are perfect for supporting this work.

14. Lyiscott, Jamila. "Racial Identity and Liberation Literacies in the Classroom." *English Journal* 106.4 (2017): 47–53.

The author explores the racial and cultural ideologies that inform what it means to be Black in the US and how this mainstream framing of Blackness intersects with teacher preparedness to engage Black textual expressions in the classroom. As Black lives and, subsequently, Black cultural productions continue to be stigmatized and devalued within and beyond classrooms, practical approaches are needed for English teachers to do this work of engaging Black textual expressions and the sociocultural contexts they were forged within. These Black textual expressions serve as cultural artifacts for better understanding the interwoven racial and literate identities of Black students. To center them in the classroom is to center the issues, questions, cultural practices, and cognitive skills they evoke.

15. Martínez, Danny. "Imagining a Language of Solidarity for Black and Latinx Youth in English Language Arts Classrooms." *English Education* 49.2 (January 1, 2017). https://library.ncte.org/journals/EE/issues/v49-2/28920.

English educators must interrogate acts of physical and linguistic violence against Black and Latinx youth and take them into consideration when shaping curricula. English teachers can provide a space for youth to make sense of their racialized experiences. The author highlights the marginal treatment of Black and Latinx languages in English classrooms and shows the relationship between the racialized physical violence against Black and Latinx communities and the linguistic violence many Black and Latinx youth face in English classrooms, then presents examples of emerging solidarity movements between Black and Latinx activists and communities and illustrates how this renewed sense of solidarity can be leveraged to incite transformative learning experiences. I conclude with recommendations for how a language of solidarity framework can take place in all English classrooms.

16. Paris, Django. "Culturally sustaining pedagogy: A needed change in stance, terminology, and practice." *Educational Researcher* 41.3 (2012): 93–97. https://web.stanford.edu/class/linguist159/restricted/readings/Paris2012.pdf.

Seventeen years ago Gloria Ladson-Billings (1995) published the landmark article "Toward a Theory of Culturally Relevant Pedagogy," giving a coherent theoretical statement for resource pedagogies that had been building throughout the 1970s and 1980s. The author, like countless teachers and university-based researchers, has been inspired by what it means to make teaching and learning relevant and responsive to the languages, literacies, and cultural practices of students across categories of difference and (in)equality. Recently, however, the author has begun to question if the terms "relevant" and "responsive" are really descriptive of much of the teaching and research founded upon them and, more importantly, if they go far enough in their orientation to the languages and literacies and other cultural practices of communities marginalized by systemic inequalities to ensure the valuing and maintenance of our multiethnic and multilingual society. In this essay, the author offers the term and stance of culturally sustaining pedagogy as an alternative that embodies some of the best research and practice in the resource pedagogy tradition and as a term that supports the value of our multiethnic and multilingual present and future. Culturally sustaining pedagogy seeks to perpetuate and foster—to sustain—linguistic, literate, and cultural pluralism as part of the democratic project of schooling. In the face of current policies and practices that have the explicit goal of creating a monocultural and monolingual society, research and practice need equally explicit resistances that embrace cultural pluralism and cultural equality.

17. Storm, Scott, and Emily C. Rainey. "Striving Toward Woke English Teaching and Learning." *English Journal* 107.6 (July 1, 2018). https://library.ncte.org/journals/ej/issues/v107-6/29718.

The authors offer an illustration of a pedagogical routine designed to support students' critical consciousness and literacy learning through the collective examination of shared texts.

Sample Syllabus for College-Level Introductory Course

Introduction to Latinx Studies - LTNX 20003 - Texas Christian University
Instructor Name: Dr. Santiago Piñón

Course Description
US Latinxs are the fastest ethnic/racialized/minoritized group in the United States. This course is an introduction to the study of characteristics and experiences of the Latinx community in the United Sates. As we review the historical, social, political, religious, and anthropological aspects, among others, we will evaluate the diversity within the community in order to locate this group within the United States society. In this sense, it is important to look beyond the misconceptions, generalizations, and stereotypes, in order to understand the main characteristics of this group.

Learning Outcomes

- develop an understanding of the major issues within the field of Latinx studies

- develop a critical, analytical and creative reflection of the different issues and topics regarding Latinx groups in the United States (eg. identity, cultures)

- develop a personal engagement with different stories and perspectives that allow them the opportunity to develop their own perceptions regarding the Latinx community in the United States

Required Texts / Materials
Gutierrrez, Ramon A., and Tomas Almaguer, eds. *The New Latino Studies Reader: A Twenty-First Century Perspective*. Oakland, CA: University of California Press, 2016. (NLSR)

Course Policies and Requirements

Grading

Table 6.1 – Grading Overview

Percent / Point Value	Item
15%/15	Exam #1
15%/15	Exam #2
15%/15/1 pt each	Discussions
20%/20	Final Exam
15%/10	Group Project – MMIW March 2
15%/15	– Campus Tour April 7
10%/10	Borderlands Institute Forum on Immigration and Social Justice at Brite Divinity School, April 18, 2020 9:00am-3:45pm

Courtesy of Santiago Piñón.

There will be two in-class exams throughout the course of the semester, which are meant to allow students to demonstrate their understanding of the major issues within the field of Latinx studies.

The Final Exam is meant to allow students to demonstrate their critical, analytical, and creative reflection of the different issues and topics regarding Latinx groups in the US.

Weekly Threaded Discussions are designed for students to personally engage with different stories and perspectives that allow for the development of their own perceptions regarding Latinx community in the US. Students are expected to post their response to the posed question and reflect on one other comment by classmates.

Students are expected to participate in the Missing and Murdered Indigenous Women project during the week of March 2. More details will be provided in class.

Students will also lead a campus tour for fifteen local middle school students and their parents on the evening of April 7 5:00, and have dinner at the BLUU with the families. This will give students the opportunity to develop a personal engagement with different stories and perspectives that allow them the opportunity to develop their own perception, regarding the Latinx community in the US.

Students are expected to attend the Borderlands Institute Forum on Immigration and Social Justice at Brite Divinity School, April 18, 2020 9:00am–3:45pm, either the morning or afternoon session. A 500 word reflection on the event will be due on April 21 in class.

Table 6.2 - Final Numerical/Letter Grade Calculation (+/-)

Grade	Score
A	94-100
A-	90-93
B+	87-89
B	84-86
B-	80-83
C+	77-79
C	74-76
C-	70-73
F	0-69

Courtesy of Santiago Piñón.

Course Schedule

Table 6.3 - Course Schedule

Day	Date	Topic	Reading	Assignment / Class Activity
1	Jan 14	Intro	NLSR 1-18	Discussion 1
2	Jan 16	What's in a Name	NLSR 19-53	
3	Jan 21	Know Thyself	NLSR 54-82	Discussion 2
4	Jan 23	The Colonial Aztlan	NLSR 85-107	
5	Jan 28	Latino Immigration: An Oxymoron?	NLSR 108-125	Discussion 3
6	Jan 30	The Latino Threat?	NLSR 126-149	
7	Feb 4	You Are Different	NLSR 153-184	Discussion 4
8	Feb 6	Is Beauty Skin Deep?	NLSR 185-209	
9	Feb 11	Race, Raza, & Others	NLSR 210-227	Discussion 5
10	Feb 13	Latinos & Chinese Buffets	NLSR 231-265	Discussion 6
11	Feb 18	From the Schoolyard to the Yard	NLSR 288-312; 571-592	
12	Feb 20	Exam #1		
13	Feb 25	El Traspatio**		

Courtesy of Santiago Piñón.

(Continues)

**Trigger warning due to domestic violence, rape, and murder of women

Table 6.3 - Course Schedule (Continued from previous page)

Day	Date	Topic	Reading	Assignment / Class Activity
14	Feb 27	El Traspatio**		Discussion 7
15	Mar 3	The Myth of Assimilation	NLSR 313-339	
16	Mar 5	When Affirmative Action was White	NLSR 340-371	Discussion 8
17	Mar 10	Spring Break		
18	Mar 12	Spring Break		
19	Mar 17	Where you From?	NLSR 372-408	Discussion 9
20	Mar 19	Sharon Herrera		Discussion 10
21	Mar 24	Spicy Latinas/os	NLSR 415-442	
22	Mar 26	Holy Thursday	No Class	
23	Mar 31	Exam #2		
24	Apr 2	Trans-Latino	NLSR 443-471	Discussion 11
25	Apr 7	Respeto/Respect	NLSR 472-509	Campus Tour
26	Apr 9	He's Guapo/Cute	NLSR 510-534	Discussion 12
27	Apr 14			
28	Apr 16	Politicos	NLSR 535-560	Discussion 13
29	Apr 21	Youth of Latinas/os	NLSR 561-570	
30	Apr 23		NLSR 593-608	Discussion 14
31	Apr 28		NLSR 609-624	Discussion 15
32	May 5		11:00-1:30pm	

Courtesy of Santiago Piñón.

*Trigger warning due to domestic violence, rape, and murder of women

Adding Depth through K-12 Secondary Electives

Cultural Studies

Provide a framework for students in grades six through eight to become culturally competent by exploring the complex nature of culture and learning skills to create inclusive communities. During the course, students learn how to:
• Examine the meaning of culture, and the various ways in which variables such as race, class, and gender influence a society's beliefs, attitudes, and ways of life;
• Recognize and challenge discrimination and racism;
• Investigate and create opportunities for people to identify common ground, respect differences, and appreciate strengths; and
• Become an ally through supporting and empowering people in a diverse community.

Latinx Studies

Students explore Latinx and Chicano/Chicana experiences from the pre-Columbian era to the present day. Topics of study include an examination of the historical, economic, social, and cultural contributions of people and descendants of Mexico, Central and South America, and the Caribbean. Through their exploration of these topics, students will investigate the diversity of Latino(a)/Chicano(a) culture, ponder the various factors that have come to form their identities, and analyze how their experiences have shaped American society today. This course provides authentic academic experiences and is designed to prepare students for success in college and in their chosen careers. Students are expected to conduct in-depth research, prepare a product of professional quality, and make presentations to appropriate audiences.

Secondary Latinx Studies Elective - Scope and Sequence and Unit Guides

Table 6.4 - Secondary Latinx Studies Elective - Scope and Sequence and Unit Guides

Ongoing Process Standards: SPTSS.3ABCDEF		
Unit 1: Latino Identity	Unit 2: Pre-Colonial Indigenous American Civilizations and Iberian History	Unit 3: Spanish America and the Colonial Era
Fall Number of Days: 5 A/B Days Fall Dates: September 8 – September 21 (10 Days) Spring Number of Days: 5.5 A/B Days Spring Dates: February 2 – February 17 (11 Days) **Concepts/Topics:** The Need for Ethnic Studies (.5 Day) Who are Latinos (1.5 Days) Stereotypes and Demographics of Latinos (1.5 Days) Summative: Latino Community in Fort Worth (1.5 / 2 Days) Celebrate Freedom Resources **Assessment(s):** 1.5 / 2 Days	Fall Number of Days: 3 A/B Days Fall Dates: September 22 – September 29 (6 Days) Spring Number of Days: 3.5 A/B Days Spring Dates: February 18 – February 26 (7 Days) **Concepts/Topics:** Pre Colonial Indigenous American Civilizations (1.5 Days) Spain Pre-1492 (1 Days) Summative: Latino Origins (.5 Day / 1 Day) SY 20-21 Election/Voting Resources **Assessment(s):** .5 / 1 Day	Fall Number of Days: 4.5 A/B Days Fall Dates: September 30 – October 13 (9 Days) Spring Number of Days: 5 A/B Days Spring Dates: March 1 – March 12 (10 Days) **Concepts/Topics:** 1492 (.5 Day) Cortés' Destruction of the Aztec Empire Through Paintings (1 Day) Spanish Influence (2 Days) Maroon Societies (.5 Day) Summative: Resistance, Independence, and Latino Identity (.5 /1 Day) **Assessment(s):** .5 / 1 Day

Secondary Latino/a Studies Elective – Scope and Sequence and Unit Guides. Courtesy of FWISD Department of Social Studies.

Unit 4: US Imperialism and Latin American Nationalisms	Unit 5: Migration and the Making of Latinx Communities	Unit 6: The Long and Wide Civil Rights Movement
Fall Number of Days: 5.5 A/B Days Fall Dates: October 14 – October 28 (11 Days) Spring Number of Days: 6 A/B Days Spring Dates: March 22 – April 8 (12 Days) **Concepts/Topics:** Independence in Latin America (1.5 Days) Foreigners in Their Own Land (2.5 / 3 Days) Spanish American War (1 Day) Summative: Perceptions of Mexico (.5 Day) **Assessment(s):** .5 Day	Fall Number of Days: 6.5 A/B Days Fall Dates: October 29 – November 16 (13 Days) Spring Number of Days: 7 A/B Days Spring Dates: April 9 – April 29 (14 Days) **Concepts/Topics:** Puerto Rico (1.5 Days) Migration and Contributions (1.5 Days) Summative: Juan Crow and Latino Voice (3.5 /4 Days) **Assessment(s):** 3.5 Days / 4 Days	Fall Number of Days: 6 A/B Days Fall Dates: November 17 – December 9 (12 Days) Spring Number of Days: 6 A/B Days Spring Dates: April 30 – May 17 (12 Days) **Concepts/Topics:** Mexican Repatriation and the Bracero Program (1.5 Days) Latino Activism (1.5 Days) Summative: Long and Wide Civil Rights Movement (3 Days) **Assessment(s):** 3 Days

Unit 7: Radical Movements, Critiques, and Legacies	Unit 8: Emergent Shift, and Contemporary Issues	
Fall Number of Days: 7 A/B Days Fall Dates: December 10 – January 14 (14 Days) Spring Number of Days: 7.5 A/B Days Spring Dates: May 18 – June 8 (15 Days) **Concepts/Topics:** The Chicano Movement (3 /4 Days) Student Activism (3 Days) Summative: Counterculture becomes Culture (1 Day) **Assessment(s):** 1 Day	Fall Number of Days: 4 A/B Days Fall Dates: January 15 – January 29 (10 Days) Spring Number of Days: 5 A/B Days Spring Dates: June 9 – June 18 (8 Days) **Concepts/Topics:** Effects of Neo-Imperialism (1 / 2 Days) Immigration Reforms, Citizenships, and Complexities (1 Day) Latino/a Politics and Representation in US Government (1 Day) Summative: Who Are Latinos? (.5 Day) Holocaust Remembrance Week Resources **Assessment(s):** .5 Day	

Unit	Unit 1: Latino/a Identity	Designated Marking Period	MP:1 September 8 - October 16 MP:4 February 2 – March 12
Instructional Days	Fall Number of Days: 5 A/B Days Fall Dates: September 8 – September 21 (10 Days) Spring Number of Days: 5.5 A/B Days Spring Dates: February 2 – February 17 (11 Days) Scope and Sequence Instructional Calendar	Assessment Dates	N/A
Content Contact	FWISD Curriculum Coordinator Xavier Pantoja xavier.pantoja@fwisd.org	Assessment/ Assessment Blueprint	Unit 1 Summative Activity

Unit Overview

This unit of instruction explores identity and diversity in the Latino American community. Students will explore the need/purpose for ethnic studies, and how they will play a role in active participation of social justice.

Infusion Curriculum Connections:

African and African-American History and Culture Infusion Curriculum

Latino(a) History and Culture Infusion Curriculum

LA
Theme 1: Pre-Colonial Indigenous American Civilizations and Iberian History
Theme 2: Spanish America and the Colonial Era
Theme 3: US Imperialism and Latin American Nationalisms
Theme 4: Migration and the Making of Latinx Communities
Theme 5: The Long and Wide Civil Rights Movement
Theme 6: Radical Movements, Critiques, and Legacies
Theme 7: Emergent Shifts and Contemporary Issues

Transfer Goals	<ul><li>Recognize and value the interconnectivity and diversity found in humanity.</li><li>Evaluate the relationships between people, places, and environments to interpret the past and present and plan for the future.</li><li>Use scientific and technological innovations to change the present and shape the future.</li><li>Gather and use evidence to discover multiple narratives of the past, present, and future.</li><li>Understand the dynamic nature of how people use systems to address their needs.</li></ul>	
Essential Questions	<ul><li>Who are Latinos?</li><li>Where do Latinos live?</li><li>How has history influenced the diversity of Latinos?</li><li>How has the Latino language and culture influenced mainstream culture of the United States?</li></ul>	

Unit Understandings	Overarching & Unit Concepts	Demonstration of Learning
Understanding of Latino History is crucial to the understanding of United States History	Community Ethnicity Empathy Identity	DOL 1 – Research the benefits of Ethnic Studies to complete a reflection that prompts students to set learning goals for their learning.
Latinos are diverse in location, color, and cultural makeup.	Culture Location Diffusion	DOL 2 – Create a web that describes all elements of Latino people and culture and categorize them into the course themes. Students will reflect on their learning by composing a response using the stem: I used to think, but now I know …
Latinos are diverse in location, color, and cultural makeup. Understanding of Latino History is crucial to the understanding of United States History Perception of Latinos has changed over time and affects the Latino Experience.	Migration Demographics	DOL 3 – Write a fact–checking blog responding to an anti-Latino politician speech that uses stereotypical language rather than facts

Latino/Latina Americans are diverse, are perceived in many ways, have a rich and varied history.		
Latinos are diverse in location, color, and cultural makeup. Understanding of Latino History is crucial to the understanding of United States History	Community Ethnicity Empathy Identity	DOL 4 - Summative: Create a Latino Fort Worth Instagram that answer questions about where Latinos live in Fort Worth, why Latinos migrated to Fort Worth, economic activities of Latinos in Fort Worth, and contributions of Latinos to the political landscape of Fort Worth. Compose a written reflection about the identity and diversity of the Latino American community using the stem "I used to think, but now I know."

Demonstration of Learning

DOL 1: The Need for Ethnic Studies (.5 Day)

Research the benefits of Ethnic Studies to complete a reflection that prompts students to set learning goals for their learning.

EL differentiation

SPED differentiation-Refer to student's IEP and accommodations first

Standards: SPTSS.1ABCDEFG, SPTSS.2ABCDEFGH

DOL 2: Who are Latinos? (1.5 Days)

Create a web that describes all elements of Latino people and culture and categorize them into the course themes. Students will reflect on their learning by composing a response using the stem: I used to think, but now I know …

EL differentiation

SPED differentiation-Refer to student's IEP and accommodations first

Standards: SPTSS.1ABCDEFG, SPTSS.2ABCDEFGH

DOL 3: Stereotypes and Demographics of Latinos (1.5 Days)

Write a fact-checking blog responding to an anti-Latino politician speech that uses stereotypical language rather than facts

EL differentiation

SPED differentiation-Refer to student's IEP and accommodations first

Standards: SPTSS.1ABCDEFG, SPTSS.2ABCDEFGH

	DOL 4: Summative: Latino Community in Fort Worth (1.5 / 2 Days)

Create a Latino Fort Worth Instagram that answers questions about where Latinos live in Fort Worth, why Latinos migrated to Fort Worth, economic activities of Latinos in Fort Worth, and contributions of Latinos to the political landscape of Fort Worth. Compose a written reflection about the identity and diversity of the Latino American community using the stem "I used to think, but now I know."

EL differentiation

SPED differentiation-Refer to student's IEP and accommodations first

Standards: SPTSS.1ABCDEFG, SPTSS.2ABCDEFGH, SPTSS.3ABCDEF |
| **Academic Vocabulary** | Ethnic Identity – an affiliative construct, where an individual is viewed by themselves and by others as belonging to a particular ethnic or cultural group

Diversity – An understanding that each individual is unique, and recognizing our individual differences. These can be along the dimensions of race, ethnicity, gender, sexual orientation, socio-economic status, age, physical abilities, religious beliefs, political beliefs, or other ideologies.

Gilbert C. Garcia- Early leader of the Latina/o community of Fort Worth, WWII veteran, established a local chapter of the American GI Forum and many other organizations with goals of increasing the upward mobility of Latina/os in Fort Worth

Louis Zapata-first Latino city councilman of Fort Worth (1977-1991) |
| **Prerequisite Skills** | <ul><li>identify and explain the geographic factors responsible for the location of economic activities in places and regions; (6.5A)</li><li>identify geographic factors such as location, physical features, transportation corridors and barriers, and distribution of natural resources that influence a society's ability to control territory (6.5B)</li><li>analyze the effects of physical and human geographic patterns and processes on the past and describe their impact on the present, including significant physical features and environmental conditions that influenced migration patterns and shaped the distribution of culture groups today (9.1.A)</li><li>trace the historical development of the civil rights movement in the 19th, 20th, and 21st centuries, including the 13th, 14th, 15th, and 19th amendments (US.9A)</li><li>describe the roles of political organizations that promoted civil rights, including ones from African American, Chicano, American Indian, women's, and other civil rights movements (US.9B)</li></ul> |
| **Misconceptions** | Latinos all look a certain way.
All Latinos are from Mexico. |

	Best Practices for All, Essential for English Learners (ELs)
Instructional Strategies	Adaptations for All, Essential for Specially Designed Instruction (SDI)
	Social Studies Instructional Framework and Best Practices
	Engaged Literacy Strategy
	Engaged Literacy Strategy chart
	4 Rs of Culturally Responsive Instruction
	Social Emotional Learning Sample Activities
	FWISD Learning Model
	Cultural Relevant Instruction and Coaching

High Leverage Standards in the Unit

TEKS	Example – Unit Level Taught Directly	Unit Level Specificity
SPTSS.1D	examine the role of diverse communities in the context of the selected topic;	Students will examine the relationship between Latin American Countries and the United States in various contexts.
SPTSS.1E	analyze ethical issues raised by the selected topic in historic, cultural, and social contexts;	Throughout each unit, students will examine the social, economic, geographic, and historical factors that inform the question "Who are Latinos?"
SPTSS.2C	read narrative texts critically and identify points of view from the historical context surrounding an event and the frame of reference that influenced the participants;	Students will use primary and secondary sources to examine narratives and counter narratives to understand that Latino/a history is American history.
Process Standards	SPTSS.3ABCDEF	

NOTE

Resources

DOL resources as indicated:

DOL 1: The Need for Ethnic Studies (.5 Day)
DOL 2: Who are Latinos (1.5 Days)
DOL 3: Stereotypes and Demographics of Latinos (1.5 Days)
DOL 4: Summative - Latino Community in Fort Worth (1.5 / 2 Days)

Harvest of Empire – Juan Gonzalez

ConnectEd Online Resources – MY.FWISD.ORG
African and African-American History and Culture Infusion Curriculum

Latino(a) History and Culture Infusion Curriculum
SB30 Resources

Harvest of Empire. Juan Gonzalez trailer
Pew Research Center: Hispanic Trends, data sets
PBS Latino Americans Digital Resources

Best Practices for All, Essential for English Learners (ELs)
Adaptations for All, Essential for Specially Designed Instruction (SDI)
Social Studies Instructional Framework and Best Practices
Engaged Literacy Strategy
Engaged Literacy Strategy chart
4 R's of Culturally Responsive Instruction
Social Emotional Learning Sample Activities
FWISD Learning Model
Cultural Relevant Instruction and Coaching

High Leverage Standards in the Unit

TEKS	Example – Unit Level Taught Directly	Unit Level Specificity
SPTSS.1D	examine the role of diverse communities in the context of the selected topic;	Students will examine the relationship between Latin American Countries and the United States in various contexts.
SPTSS.1E	analyze ethical issues raised by the selected topic in historic, cultural, and social contexts;	Throughout each unit, students will examine the social, economic, geographic, and historical factors that inform the question "Who are Latinos?"
SPTSS.2C	read narrative texts critically and identify points of view from the historical context surrounding an event and the frame of reference that influenced the participants;	Students will use primary and secondary sources to examine narratives and counter narratives to understand that Latino/a history is American history.
Process Standards	SPTSS.3ABCDEF	

NOTE

DOL resources as indicated:

DOL 1: The Need for Ethnic Studies (.5 Day)
DOL 2: Who are Latinos (1.5 Days)
DOL 3: Stereotypes and Demographics of Latinos (1.5 Days)
DOL 4: Summative - Latino Community in Fort Worth (1.5 / 2 Days)

Harvest of Empire – Juan Gonzalez

ConnectEd Online Resources – MY.FWISD.ORG
African and African-American History and Culture Infusion Curriculum

Latino(a) History and Culture Infusion Curriculum
SB30 Resources

Harvest of Empire. Juan Gonzalez trailer
Pew Research Center: Hispanic Trends, data sets
PBS Latino Americans Digital Resources

Digital Monitoring	N/A
Critical Components	19 TAC Chapter 113. Texas Essential Knowledge and Skills for Social Studies Texas College and Career Readiness Standards National Council for the Social Studies Wineburg, Sam. Thinking Like a Historian: Historical Thinking: Memorizing Facts and Stuff? Wineburg, S.S., Martin, D. & Monte-Sano, C. (2011) Reading like a historian: Teaching literacy in middle and high school history classrooms. Adams, Caralee. (July 1, 2013). Reviving History Instruction: What's Old is New Again, Education Week. Lesh, Bruce A., (2011) "Why Won't You Just Tell Us the Answer? "Teaching Historical Thinking Grades 7-12. Steinhouse Publishers

Sample Assessment Items

Formative Assessment Examples

Written responses
Four Corners
Stop and Jot
3-2-1
Get the Gist
Socratic discussion
Collect information using a graphic organizer
Conduct research using primary and secondary sources.
Use maps to understand the spatial organization of the world
Employ Think-Pair-Share strategies to facilitate class discussions

Summative Examples

Unit 1 Summative Activity

Instructional Standards

Process TEKS	TEKS	TECH	CCR
SPTSS.3ABCDEF	SPTSS.1ABCDEFG, SPTSS.2ABCDEFGH	1D, 4ACE	1.C.1a, II.B4a. I.A.6b (IB3) IIB6 (IIIA1)

English Language Proficiency Standards

In order for ELLS to be successful, they must acquire both social and academic language proficiency in English. Effective instruction in second language acquisition involves giving ELLs opportunities to listen, speak, read, and write at their current English development while gradually increasing the linguistic complexity of the English they read and hear, and are expected to speak and write.

Learning Strategies - 1.A, 1.E, 1.G, 1.H

Listening - 2.C, 2.E, 2.H

Speaking - 3.B, 3.E, 3.H

Reading - 4.D, 4.G, 4.J, 4.K

Proficiency Level Descriptors

SPTSS Latino/a Studies
Unit 1: Latino Identity

DOL 1 — The Need for Ethnic Studies

Research the benefits of Ethnic Studies to complete a reflection that prompts students to set learning goals for their learning.

Resources:
- *The Value of Ethnic Studies — For All Students Article*
- *Graphic Organizer*
- *Compass*
- *Linked Articles*

TEKS: SPTSS.1ABCDEFG, SPTSS.2ABCDEFGH
ELPS: 1C, 2E, 3EH
Process skills: SPTSS.3ABCDEF

Social Studies DOL Criteria Rubric	
Advanced Understanding - 4 • The idea is perceptive and reflects an awareness of the complexities of the text. • The text evidence used to support the idea is specific and well chosen. • The combination of the idea/text evidence demonstrates a deep understanding of the text.	**Emerging Understanding - 2** • The idea is reasonable, but does not contain text evidence. • The idea is reasonable, but the text evidence is flawed. • The idea needs more explanation or specificity. • The idea represents only a literal reading of the text, with or without text evidence.
Proficient Understanding - 3 • The idea is reasonable and goes beyond a literal reading of the text. • The text evidence used to support the idea is accurate and relevant. • The idea/text evidence used to support it are clearly linked. • The combination of the idea/text evidence demonstrates a good understanding of the text.	**Beginner Understanding - 1** • The idea is not an answer to the question asked. • The idea is incorrect because it is not based on the text. • The idea is too general vague or unclear to determine whether it is reasonable. • No idea is present …because it merely repeats verbatim, or "echoes" the text evidence.

Preview

Students will create a timeline of the events leading to them taking the ethnic studies course. Have students compare their timeline events. Make note of the different types of answers spanning from logistic to more consciously motivated answers.

Engage

Have students create a document titled "My Why" that they can keep throughout the year. Have them write for 5 minutes regarding the reasons they have chosen to take the course and/or the concerns they may have.

Read the article titled "The Value of Ethnic Studies — For All Students" where the author explains the journey of ethnic studies in Arizona, including challenges and victories. Have students cite text that supports what the students believe the main idea of the article is using the graphic organizer.

Debrief the article using the compass. Note that the compass can be used throughout the year as a vehicle to discuss complex and/or sensitive topics. (Compass Explanation)

Below are supplemental resources to further explore the importance of ethnic studies.

Ethnic studies supports Academic Performance

Tucson Revives Mexican-American Studies Program

LAUSD requiring ethnic studies for graduation.

If time allows, consider watching The Danger of a Single Story, and give time to revisit the "My Why" document.

Introduce students to the following classroom resources: Harvest of Empire book + Video, and PBS Latino Americans Digital Resources.

Process

Review some of the prevalent ideas that have arisen during the day's conversation. Have students create a set of learning goals for their study of ethnic studies.

Why ethnic studies matters

If time allows, consider watching The Danger of a Single Story, and give time to revisit the "My Why" document.

Introduce students to the following classroom resources: Harvest of Empire book + Video, and PBS Latino Americans Digital Resources.

Process

Review some of the prevalent ideas that have arisen during the day's conversation. Have students create a set of learning goals for their study of ethnic studies.

SPTSS Latino/a Studies
Unit 1: Latino Identity

DOL 2 –Who are Latinos?

Create a web that describes all elements of Latino people and culture and categorize them into the course themes. Students will reflect on their learning by composing a response using the stem: I used to think but now I know ...

Resources:
- *Harvest of Empire* book
- *Theme Organizer*
- *PBS Latino Americans Digital Resources*

TEKS: SPTSS.1ABCDEFG, SPTSS.2ABCDEFGH
ELPS: 1C, 2E, 3EH
Process skills: SPTSS.3ABCDEF

Social Studies DOL Criteria Rubric	
Advanced Understanding - 4	**Emerging Understanding - 2**
• The idea is perceptive and reflects an awareness of the complexities of the text. • The text evidence used to support the idea is specific and well chosen. • The combination of the idea/text evidence demonstrates a deep understanding of the text.	• The idea is reasonable, but does not contain text evidence. • The idea is reasonable, but the text evidence is flawed. • The idea needs more explanation or specificity. • The idea represents only a literal reading of the text, with or without text evidence.
Proficient Understanding - 3	**Beginner Understanding - 1**
• The idea is reasonable and goes beyond a literal reading of the text. • The text evidence used to support the idea is accurate and relevant. • The idea/text evidence used to support it are clearly linked. • The combination of the idea/text evidence demonstrates a good understanding of the text.	• The idea is not an answer to the question asked. • The idea is incorrect because it is not based on the text. • The idea is too general vague or unclear to determine whether it is reasonable. • No idea is present ...because it merely repeats verbatim, or "echoes" the text evidence.

Preview

Have students review the Themes Organizer handout and discuss the terms on the organizer. Share out ideas and discuss what context may be needed to explain some of the themes. Explain that students will interact with this organizer throughout the course to organizer their findings into these broader categories.

Engage

Part 1- Who Are Latinos
https://www.pbs.org/latino-americans/en/education/
PBS Activity – "Who Are Latinos?"
Materials -
Video Trailer
Activity PDF with Organizer
Survey the class about what they know about Latinos, follow up with the discussion questions below.

* Who are Latinos?
• Where do Latinos live?
• When did Latinos arrive in the United States?
• Where do Latinos come from?
• What issues are important when we talk about Latino Americans?
• Is there such thing as a typical Latino? If so, who?
• What have Latinos contributed to the United States?

View the video trailer for PBS Latino Americans and debrief how the video confirms or challenge their expectations. Develop questions from the learning to be applied to the rest of the course.

Pt 2 – Web
Preview the videos below and ask students to take notes on new learning that will be applied in future steps.

Defining Latino - https://www.youtube.com/watch?v=QePAmImu2wA
Latino or Hispanic https://www.youtube.com/watch?v=5RN9DQMrgSg

Present students with the ideas below.
- Latinos are diverse in location, color, and cultural makeup.
- Perception of Latinos has changed over time and impacts the Latino Experience.
- Latinos shaped North American over the last 500 years.
- Understanding of Latino History is crucial to the understanding of United States History.

Using these ideas to work in small groups, students will gauge prior knowledge and news findings by categorizing their ideas into the theme organizer. Students will explain what they know about Latinos in terms of each theme, as well as what information is needed to supplement any gaps. Provide an opportunity to supplement their organizer by researching video, images, and online articles that explain how Latino culture has influenced life in the United States. A guide to support student conversation provided below.

Process

Facilitate a class discussion to create a web as a class that describes elements of Latino people and culture and categorize them into the course themes. Students may use their organizer. Note that students will have more opportunities to explore cultural elements in future learning. Students will reflect on their learning by composing a response using the stem: I used to think, but now I know ...

Unit Themes:
Identity
- Who are Latinos? Where do Latinos live? What language(s) do Latinos speak? What kinds of jobs do Latinos have? What belief systems do Latinos practice?
- Culture makeup of a people group

Land
- How is land ownership defined? Why is land important? How are boundaries defined? How is land connected to history? How does geography impact lifestyles?
- A territory

Movement
- Where have Latinos come from? What are push and pull factors influencing Latino migration? Where do Latinos migrate? What factors influence settlement patterns?
- The act of changing location

Diversity
- The arts and other manifestations of human intellectual achievement regarded collectively

Citizenship
- How do you earn citizenship? Who are citizens? What are the rights and responsibilities of citizenship? What are the benefits of citizenship? What are the perceptions of non-citizens?
- A legally recognized subject or national of a state or commonwealth, either native or naturalized

Representation
- How are Latinos represented in the political landscape, both past and present? How do people make their voice heard?
- The activity of making citizens' voices, opinions, and perspectives present in the public policy-making processes.

Interdependence
- How is the United States dependent on Latin American nations? How has the United States benefitted from the relationship with Latin America? How has Latin America benefitted from the relationship with the United States?
- Mutual dependence.

Contributions
- How have Latinos contributed to the success at the local, state, and national level? How have Latinos contributed to mainstream culture?
- Adding value

DOL 3 –Stereotypes and Demographic of Latinos

Write a fact-checking blog responding to an anti-Latino politician speech that uses stereotypical language rather than facts.

Resources:
- *Harvest of Empire book*
- *PBS Latino Americans Digital Resources*

TEKS: SPTSS.1ABCDEFG, SPTSS.2ABCDEFGH
ELPS: 1C, 2E, 3EH
Process skills: SPTSS.3ABCDEF

Social Studies DOL Criteria Rubric	
Advanced Understanding - 4	**Emerging Understanding - 2**
• The idea is perceptive and reflects an awareness of the complexities of the text. • The text evidence used to support the idea is specific and well chosen. • The combination of the idea/text evidence demonstrates a deep understanding of the text.	• The idea is reasonable, but does not contain text evidence. • The idea is reasonable, but the text evidence is flawed. • The idea needs more explanation or specificity. • The idea represents only a literal reading of the text, with or without text evidence.
Proficient Understanding - 3	**Beginner Understanding - 1**
• The idea is reasonable and goes beyond a literal reading of the text. • The text evidence used to support the idea is accurate and relevant. • The idea/text evidence used to support it are clearly linked. • The combination of the idea/text evidence demonstrates a good understanding of the text.	• The idea is not an answer to the question asked. • The idea is incorrect because it is not based on the text. • The idea is too general vague or unclear to determine whether it is reasonable. • No idea is present …because it merely repeats verbatim, or "echoes" the text evidence.

Preview

Students respond to the following – Have you ever been judged unfairly because of how you look, the way you speak, or the type of name you have? How does it feel? Is it fair or unfair? Has anyone ever made assumptions about you because of your age, your ethnicity, or your gender? Write your responses to these questions and share them in small groups. Discuss and define the term "stereotype."

Preview this clip - https://www.youtube.com/watch?v=jH8kxD9oA5c

Engage

Part 1 – Representation in Media
Ask students to identify 5 different representations of Latinos in the media: film, tv, news, music, and sports. Generate a list of individuals for the assigned category, and compose a spectrum that labels each individual as positively portrayed to negatively portrayed. Based on their findings, ask students to respond to the questions "Are Latinos represented more favorably or less favorably in today's media? Is there a difference according to gender, age, nationality, or socioeconomic status?"

Watch 4 Hs of Latinos in Hollywood and debrief with students how their responses reconcile with the stereotypes discussed in the video

View the following trailer from HBO Latin Explosion: A New America.

Latin Explosion: A New America

Ask Students:

- How are Latinos represented in the trailer?
- What is the perception of Latinos in the United States, according to trailer?
- How does media define success and achievement in Latino culture?

Compose a reflection describing how media has personally influenced the student's perception of Latinos. Extend the writing by commenting on what needs to change.

Part 2- Stereotypes versus Statistics

PBS Latino American – Stereotypes versus Statistics

Organizer Map Pew and Latino Decision Links (Live Links)

Students will use the resources linked above to -

1- Examine Stereotypes
2- Conduct a Jigsaw to research Hispanic Origin Groups/ Graduation Data, population, economic trends, healthcare
3- Use a graphic organizer to compare and contrast myths and realities about Latinos.

Extension Opportunity - Consider using the activity below as an extension to understanding the geography and demographics of Latinos

Examine the geography and demographics of Latinos

- Teachers will share a map of the world to ask students where they are most likely to find Latinos living in the United States. Thinks Pair Share to compile a list of places where students think Latinos are located. Transition to the Pew Data Sets.
  - http://www.pewhispanic.org/2012/06/27 /country-of-origin-profiles/
  - Explain to students that they will use the data to construct a map that represents the diversity and distribution of Latinos in the United States according to county with the highest population.
    - Share a google map where students can plot the locations
    - Or print a Mega Map to accomplish the same goal
  - Debrief the geographic distribution using the following questions
    - What do you notice about the geographic distribution? (Answers might include – proximity to the home country, large concentration of groups in specific regions/cities/states)
    - Why do you think certain groups migrated to these specific locations? (Answers might include – pull factors that might include jobs, family connections)
    - How might the migration of these groups to these locations change the place? (Answers might include – predominant language, cultural traditions and celebrations, and access to authentic goods)
- After completing the geographic distribution of Latinos, instruct students to browse the rest of the demographic data and respond to the following:
  - Who would benefit from this type of data?
  - What do you notice about the data?
  - Select and share one data set you found most interesting, with a list of questions about the data. Are there any connections that can be made across data sets?

Process

As a blogger for a prominent news site, you receive a call from your editor early one morning: a well-known politician was on national TV the night before describing Latinos with a lot of stereotypical language. Your editor wants you to write a piece sorting out Latino stereotypes from actual statistics. You can present your write-up in paragraph form (as if it were a blog), through a PowerPoint, or using prezi.com. (PBS Latino Americans Digital Resources)

DOL 4 – Latino Community in Fort Worth

Create a Latino Fort Worth Instagram that answer questions about where Latinos live in Fort Worth, why Latinos migrated to Fort Worth, economic activities of Latinos in Fort Worth, and contributions of Latinos to the political landscape of Fort Worth. Compose a written reflection about the identity and diversity of the Latino American community using the stem "I used to think, but now I know."

Resources:
- *Harvest of Empire* book
- *Black and Brown Oral History Project*

TEKS: SPTSS.1ABCDEFG, SPTSS.2ABCDEFGH
ELPS: 1C, 2E, 3EH
Process skills: SPTSS.3ABCDEF

Social Studies DOL Criteria Rubric	
Advanced Understanding - 4 • The idea is perceptive and reflects an awareness of the complexities of the text. • The text evidence used to support the idea is specific and well chosen. • The combination of the idea/text evidence demonstrates a deep understanding of the text.	**Emerging Understanding - 2** • The idea is reasonable, but does not contain text evidence. • The idea is reasonable, but the text evidence is flawed. • The idea needs more explanation or specificity. • The idea represents only a literal reading of the text, with or without text evidence.
Proficient Understanding - 3 • The idea is reasonable and goes beyond a literal reading of the text. • The text evidence used to support the idea is accurate and relevant. • The idea/text evidence used to support it are clearly linked. • The combination of the idea/text evidence demonstrates a good understanding of the text.	**Beginner Understanding - 1** • The idea is not an answer to the question asked. • The idea is incorrect because it is not based on the text. • The idea is too general vague or unclear to determine whether it is reasonable. • No idea is present …because it merely repeats verbatim, or "echoes" the text evidence.

Preview

Have student groups develop a list of examples of Latino Identity (Culture, Economics, Political, etc) found in Fort Worth. Watch the Video below and have students compare their list with the examples from the video. Give an opportunity to revisit and develop the list.

Snapshot of Fort Worth - https://www.youtube.com/watch?v=nZkXrrPc--w&t=60s

Engage

Students will examine Local Latino history through research, oral histories, and other archives to develop a photo collage of Latino influences on local history with text descriptions. A few starting points are listed below. Please note that these ideas will be revisited in future units.

- The first Latina/o to migrate to Fort Worth came to work on the railroad, meatpacking plants in Northside, and steel mills in Southside.
- Prior to World War II, Latina/o in Fort Worth developed their own small entrepreneurial class of restaurants, grocery stores, barbershops, and social clubs.
- Beginning in the late 1940s, Fort Worth has had an active group of Latina/o leaders working for equality in all aspects of society and political inclusion for their community.
- In the 1960s and 1970s a generation of Latina/os, frustrated by persistent discrimination and poverty, found a new way forward, through social action and the building of a new "Chicano" identity.

Research Sources:

Black and Brown Oral History Project

https://crbb.tcu.edu/

Hispanic Heritage Sites

https://assets.simpleviewinc.com/simpleview/image/upload/v1/clients/fortworth/Hispanic_Heritage_1sheet_167f2c1c-1d87-4bfa-8245-7a28a8c128a5.pdf

The Early Development of the Hispanic Community In Fort Worth and Tarrant County 1849- 1948

https://scholarworks.sfasu.edu/cgi/viewcontent.cgi?article=2303&context=ethj

Latino Fort Worth YouTube channel

https://www.youtube.com/channel/UCqHWktgiyP_szeR8K71cCTw

Viva La Raza: Documenting Tarrant County's Mexicano Activism website

https://fortworthmexicanoactivism.wordpress.com/

Fort Worth Library Digital Archives: Latino Americans

http://www.fortworthtexasarchives.org/cdm/landingpage/collection/p16084coll25

Extension: Students will analyze up to six Latino oral histories from the TCU Black and Brown Oral History Project and document their findings. Students will then write short essay tracing the impact of Latinos on local history.

Process

Create a Latino Fort Worth Instagram that answers questions about where Latinos live in Fort Worth, why Latinos migrated to Fort Worth, economic activities of Latinos in Fort Worth, and contributions of Latinos to the political landscape of Fort Worth. Compose a written reflection about the identity and diversity of the Latino American community using the stem "I used to think, but now I know."

Teacher note – This project should a collection of photos and captions in the fashion of Instagram. Each photograph should help answer one of the questions below. If a campus is considering using an actual Instagram account, please see local guidelines regarding social media.

Questions to consider

- o   Where do Latinos live in Fort Worth, Texas?
- o   Why did Latinos migrate to Fort Worth, Texas? (Meatpacking industry, railroad, steel manufacturing)
- o   How have Latinos influenced the economic activities of Fort Worth, Texas? (grocery stores, restaurants, barbershops, entrepreneurship, housing construction)?
- o   How have Latinos contributed to the political landscape of Fort Worth, Texas? (judges, city council, superintendents, school board, community activism, military)?

Optional Extension-
Students will choose an element of Latina/o culture (for example: economics, social, political, religion, sports, or education) to research and compose a narrative essay about the history of that element in Fort Worth according to the standards of a rubric with a score of 85% or better.

Unit	Unit 2: Pre-Colonial Indigenous American Civilizations and Iberian History	Designated Marking Period	MP:1 September 8 - October 16 MP:4 February 2 – March 12
Instructional Days	Fall Number of Days: 3 A/B Days Fall Dates: September 22 – September 29 (6 Days) Spring Number of Days: 3.5 A/B Days Spring Dates: February 18 – February 26 (7 Days) Scope and Sequence Instructional Calendar	Assessment Dates	N/A
Content Contact	FWISD Curriculum Coordinator Xavier Pantoja xavier.pantoja@fwisd.org	Assessment/ Assessment Blueprint	Unit 2 Summative Activity

Unit Overview

This unit addresses the worlds of America and Spain prior to Spanish arrival over five centuries ago. It addresses the diverse ancestry of Latinos/as and the historical influences—from ancient times to antiquity—on our cultures, identities, and values. This theme regards civilizations such as the Norte Chico, Chavín, Olmec, Aztec, Maya, Carib, and Taíno. It also considers Spain prior to 1492, including the Moorish Empire's control for over seven centuries, emphasizing the diverse nature of Spanish culture that influenced social order throughout Latin America.

Infusion Curriculum Connections:

Latino(a) History and Culture Infusion Curriculum

LA

Theme 1: Pre-Colonial Indigenous American Civilizations and Iberian History

Theme 2: Spanish America and the Colonial Era

Theme 3: US Imperialism and Latin American Nationalisms

Theme 4: Migration and the Making of Latinx Communities

Theme 5: The Long and Wide Civil Rights Movement

Theme 6: Radical Movements, Critiques, and Legacies

Theme 7: Emergent Shifts and Contemporary Issues

- Recognize and value the interconnectivity and diversity found in humanity.
- Evaluate the relationships between people, places, and environments to interpret the past and present and plan for the future.
- Use scientific and technological innovations to change the present and shape the future.
- Gather and use evidence to discover multiple narratives of the past, present, and future.
- Understand the dynamic nature of how people use systems to address their needs.

Essential Questions

- Why is ancient history important?
- How does studying ancient history increase knowledge of myself?
- How does studying ancient history increase confidence in myself?
- How does studying ancient history increase my appreciation and respect for different people and cultures?
- How does ancient history affect what it means to be Latino/a today?
- Were ancient ethics and values compatible with those of today?
- What was "modern" about the ancient civilizations of present-day Latin America?
- How does the study of ancient societies and belief systems help us be better judges of the ways we can succeed as a society today and in the future?
- What is progress?

Unit Understandings	Overarching & Unit Concepts	Demonstration of Learning
Agriculture has existed in present-day Latin America for at least 10,000 years; Over 50 million indigenous people inhabited the Americas in 1492; The earliest known civilization in present-day Latin America is as old as Ancient Egypt; Ancient Peru is considered one of the world's six "pristine civilizations" the Olmec civilization is one of the three civilizations of the world where writing first emerged and developed independently;	Migration Ideas/Innovation Custom/Traditions Human-Environment Interaction	DOL 1 – Research and create an annotated map demonstrating the development of Indigenous civilizations to develop a "welcome to our city" introduction guide for each civilization.
Before 1492, Spain itself was repeatedly colonized by numerous tribes and empires; The Moorish Empire of Arabia and Northern Africa, which was Islamic, ruled Spain for over 700 years; The Islamic influence of the Moors in Spain is still evident in the architecture, language, arts, politics, and religions of Spain and Latin America to this day;	Culture Language Community Diffusion	DOL 2- Cite modern examples of the remnants of cultural diffusion stemming from Spain prior to 1492 and create a reflection of diverse origins of Latinos
Latinos/as have diverse origins and ancestries; Individuals have history, and this history combines ancestry, context, and experience; Many modern customs, languages, foods, and religious practices have roots in ancient traditions;	Ideologies Culture Diffusion	DOL 3 – Summative: Create a semantic map to organize findings and respond to an "I used to think, but now I know" prompt regarding the origins of Latino Peoples

Demonstration of Learning

DOL 1: Pre–Colonial Indigenous American Civilizations (1.5 Days)

Research and create an annotated map demonstrating the development of Indigenous Civilizations to develop a "welcome to our city" introduction guide for each civilization.

EL differentiation

SPED differentiation-Refer to student's IEP and accommodations first

Standards: SPTSS.1ABCDEFG, SPTSS.2ABCDEFGH

DOL 2: Spain Pre-1492 (1 Day)

Cite modern examples of the remnants of cultural diffusion stemming from Spain prior to 1492 and create a reflection of diverse origins of Latinos.

EL differentiation

SPED differentiation-Refer to student's IEP and accommodations first

Standards: SPTSS.1ABCDEFG, SPTSS.2ABCDEFGH

DOL 3: Summative – Latino Origins (.5 / 1 Day)

Create a semantic map to organize findings and respond to an "I used to think, but now I know" prompt regarding the origins of Latino Peoples

EL differentiation

SPED differentiation-Refer to student's IEP and accommodations first

Standards: SPTSS.1ABCDEFG, SPTSS.2ABCDEFGH

Academic Vocabulary	Indigenous - originating or occurring naturally in a particular place; native. Iberian - relating to or denoting Iberia, or the countries of Spain and Portugal. Mesoamerican - a native or inhabitant of the region of Meso-America. Civilization - the stage of human social and cultural development and organization that is considered most advanced. Pre-Columbian - relating to the history and cultures of the Americas before the arrival of Columbus in 1492.
Prerequisite Skills	• identify and explain the geographic factors responsible for the location of economic activities in places and regions; (6.5A) • identify geographic factors such as location, physical features, transportation corridors and barriers, and distribution of natural resources that influence a society's ability to control territory (6.5B) • analyze the effects of physical and human geographic patterns and processes on the past and describe their impact on the present, including significant physical features and environmental conditions that influenced migration patterns and shaped the distribution of culture groups today (9.1.A) • trace the historical development of the civil rights movement in the 19th, 20th, and 21st centuries, including the 13th, 14th, 15th, and 19th amendments (US.9A) • describe the roles of political organizations that promoted civil rights, including ones from African American, Chicano, American Indian, women's, and other civil rights movements (US.9B)
Misconceptions	Latinos are a modern people and do not have ancient origins There is no delineation between the Latin American experience and the Iberian experience.

Instructional Strategies	Best Practices for All, Essential for English Learners (ELs) Adaptations for All, Essential for Specially Designed Instruction (SDI) Social Studies Instructional Framework and Best Practices Engaged Literacy Strategy Engaged Literacy Strategy chart 4 R's of Culturally Responsive Instruction Social Emotional Learning Sample Activities FWISD Learning Model Cultural Relevant Instruction and Coaching

High Leverage Standards in the Unit

TEKS	Example – Unit Level Taught Directly	Unit Level Specificity
SPTSS.1D	examine the role of diverse communities in the context of the selected topic;	Students will examine the relationship between Latin American Countries and the United States in various contexts.
SPTSS.1E	analyze ethical issues raised by the selected topic in historic, cultural, and social contexts;	Throughout each unit, students will examine the social, economic, geographic, and historical factors that informs the question "Who are Latinos?"

SPTSS.2C	read narrative texts critically and identify points of view from the historical context surrounding an event and the frame of reference that influenced the participants.	Students will use primary and secondary sources to examine narratives and counter narratives to understand that Latino/a history is American history.
Process Standards	SPTSS.3ABCDEF	
NOTE		

Resources

DOL resources as indicated:
DOL 1: Pre-Colonial Indigenous American Civilizations (1.5 Days)
DOL 2: Spain Pre-1492 (1 Day)
DOL 3: Summative – Latino Origins (.5 / 1 Day)

Harvest of Empire – Juan Gonzalez

ConnectEd Online Resources – MY.FWISD.ORG
African and African-American History and Culture Infusion Curriculum

Latino(a) History and Culture Infusion Curriculum
SB30 Resources

Harvest of Empire. Juan Gonzalez trailer
Pew Research Center: Hispanic Trends, data sets
PBS Latino Americans Digital Resources

Digital Monitoring

N/A

Critical Components

19 TAC Chapter 113. Texas Essential Knowledge and Skills for Social Studies

Texas College and Career Readiness Standards

National Council for the Social Studies

Wineburg, Sam. Thinking Like a Historian: Historical Thinking: Memorizing Facts and Stuff?

Wineburg, S.S., Martin, D. & Monte-Sano, C. (2011) Reading like a historian: Teaching literacy in middle and high school history classrooms.

Adams, Caralee. (July 1, 2013). Reviving History Instruction: What's Old is New Again, Education Week.

Lesh, Bruce A., (2011) "Why Won't You Just Tell Us the Answer?

"Teaching Historical Thinking Grades 7-12." Steinhouse Publishers

Sample Assessment Items

Formative Assessment Examples

Written responses
Four Corners
Stop and Jot
3-2-1
Get the Gist
Socratic discussion
Collect information using a graphic organizer
Conduct research using primary and secondary sources.
Use maps to understand the spatial organization of the world
Employ Think-Pair-Share strategies to facilitate class discussions

Summative Examples

Unit 2 Summative Activity

Instructional Standards

Process TEKS	TEKS	TECH	CCR
SPTSS.3ABCDEF	SPTSS.1ABCDEFG, SPTSS.2ABCDEFGH	1D, 4ACE	1.C.1a, II.B4a. I.A.6b

English Language Proficiency Standards

In order for ELLS to be successful, they must acquire both social and academic language proficiency in English. Effective instruction in second language acquisition involves giving ELLs opportunities to listen, speak, read, and write at their current English development while gradually increasing the linguistic complexity of the English they read and hear, and are expected to speak and write.

Learning Strategies - 1.A, 1.E, 1.G, 1.H

Listening - 2.C, 2.E, 2.H

Speaking - 3.B, 3.E, 3.H

Reading - 4.D, 4.G, 4.J, 4.K

Proficiency Level Descriptors

SPTSS Latino/a Studies
Unit 2 : Pre-Colonial Indigenous American Civilization and Iberian History

DOL 1 –Early Indigenous Civilization

Research and create an annotated map demonstrating the development of Indigenous Civilizations to develop a "welcome to our civilization" introduction guide for indigenous civilizations.

Resources:
- *Harvest of Empire Book*
- *Linked Resources*
- *Blank Latin America Map*

TEKS: SPTSS.1ABCDEFG, SPTSS.2ABCDEFGH
ELPS: 1C, 2E, 3EH
Process skills: SPTSS.3ABCDEF

Social Studies DOL Criteria Rubric	
Advanced Understanding - 4 • The idea is perceptive and reflects an awareness of the complexities of the text. • The text evidence used to support the idea is specific and well chosen. • The combination of the idea/text evidence demonstrates a deep understanding of the text.	**Emerging Understanding - 2** • The idea is reasonable, but does not contain text evidence. • The idea is reasonable, but the text evidence is flawed. • The idea needs more explanation or specificity. • The idea represents only a literal reading of the text, with or without text evidence.
Proficient Understanding - 3 • The idea is reasonable and goes beyond a literal reading of the text. • The text evidence used to support the idea is accurate and relevant. • The idea/text evidence used to support it are clearly linked. • The combination of the idea/text evidence demonstrates a good understanding of the text.	**Beginner Understanding - 1** • The idea is not an answer to the question asked. • The idea is incorrect because it is not based on the text. • The idea is too general vague or unclear to determine whether it is reasonable. • No idea is present …because it merely repeats verbatim, or "echoes" the text evidence.

Preview

Facilitate a think pair share.

Think- What do you know about Mesoamerican / Indigenous Cultures?

Inform students they will watch a brief video summary of Mesoamerican culture, and have them jot down familiar ideas they recognize from the video.

Latinx Lesson Lunes #1 - Aztecs, Olmecs, Mayans, and Incan Empire

Pair students to discuss their recordings

Share out at a whole group

Engage

Present the following information to students and discuss how it might change or enhance the typical Latin American narrative.

☐ Agriculture has existed in present-day Latin America for at least 10,000 years;
☐ Over 50 million indigenous people inhabited the Americas in 1492;
☐ The earliest known civilization in present day Latin America is as old as Ancient Egypt;
☐ Ancient Peru is considered one of the world's six "pristine civilizations"
☐ The Olmec civilization is one of the three civilizations of the world where writing first emerged and developed independently;

Students will create an annotated map by researching the location of the listed civilizations and labeling the blank map. Students should also annotate their map with date ranges as well as any other pertinent information.

Norte Chico
Chavín
Olmec
Aztec
Maya
Carib
Taíno

Research Resources

Infinity of Nations
The Ancient Americas – The Field Guide - Educator
The Americas Timeline

Top 10 Latin America
5 amazing archaeological discoveries in Latin America
Early Latin American Civilizations
10 Ancient Americans

Timelines

http://www.famsi.org/research/pohl/chronology.html
https://www.ancient.eu/timeline/Mesoamerica/

Process

Select at least one indigenous civilization and develop a "welcome to our civilization" introduction guide for each civilization. The guide could look like a welcome packet for someone moving in. This could include "need to knows," history, and explanation of systems such as government. The guide should not only explain the significance of the civilization, but also prove that it was indeed a civilization.

Traits of a Civilization.

SPTSS Latino/a Studies
Unit 2: Pre-Colonial Indigenous American Civilizations and Iberian History

DOL 2 – Spain Pre-1492

Cite modern examples of the remnants of cultural diffusion stemming from Spain prior to 1492 and create a reflection of diverse origins of Latinos.

Resources:
- *Harvest of Empire Book*
- *Linked Videos*

TEKS: SPTSS.1ABCDEFG, SPTSS.2ABCDEFGH
ELPS: 1C, 2E, 3EH
Process skills: SPTSS.3ABCDEF

Social Studies DOL Criteria Rubric	
Advanced Understanding - 4 • The idea is perceptive and reflects an awareness of the complexities of the text. • The text evidence used to support the idea is specific and well chosen. • The combination of the idea/text evidence demonstrates a deep understanding of the text.	**Emerging Understanding - 2** • The idea is reasonable, but does not contain text evidence. • The idea is reasonable, but the text evidence is flawed. • The idea needs more explanation or specificity. • The idea represents only a literal reading of the text, with or without text evidence.
Proficient Understanding - 3 • The idea is reasonable and goes beyond a literal reading of the text. • The text evidence used to support the idea is accurate and relevant. • The idea/text evidence used to support it are clearly linked. • The combination of the idea/text evidence demonstrates a good understanding of the text.	**Beginner Understanding - 1** • The idea is not an answer to the question asked. • The idea is incorrect because it is not based on the text. • The idea is too general vague or unclear to determine whether it is reasonable. • No idea is present …because it merely repeats verbatim, or "echoes" the text evidence.

Preview

Watch the video clip below and debrief by discussing the similarities between Spanish and Arabic. Ask students to make connections to other examples of cultural similarities that stem from an intertwined past.

Similarities Between Spanish And Arabic

Engage

Use Google Maps to demonstrate the physical relationship between Latin America, Spain, and North Africa. Explain that they are connected, especially in the conversation of Latino origins. Discuss the listed ideas below that will be further explained in the linked videos.

☐ Before 1492, Spain itself was repeatedly colonized by numerous tribes and empires;
☐ The Moorish Empire of Arabia and Northern Africa, which was Islamic, ruled Spain for over 700 years;
☐ The Islamic influence of the Moors in Spain is still evident in the architecture, language, arts, politics, and religions of Spain and Latin America to this day.

Have students review the resources below with the purpose of citing the following.
1. Examples of Culture
2. Effects of Cultural Diffusion
3. Effects Conflict has on Cultural Diffusion

Who were the Moors? - National Geographic
Sevilla, Spain: The Moors and Alcazar
Moorish Spain 1933 – Optional
Spain's Islamic Legacy source of Controversy – Focus on Europe

Facilitate a round robin using the prompt below.

How does the continued survival of culture integration reflect the current Latino American experience? How can that be demonstrated by current culture and society?

Process

Create a written reflection, how does information regarding a Moorish influence on Spain better inform your understanding of Latino Culture? Share out if time is available.

SPTSS Latino/a Studies
Unit 2: Pre-Colonial Indigenous American Civilization and Iberian History

DOL 3 – Summative: Latino

Summative: Create a semantic map to organize findings and respond to an "I used to think, but now I know" prompt regarding the origins of Latino Peoples.

Resources:
- *Harvest of Empire Book*
- *Linked Articles*

TEKS: SPTSS.1ABCDEFG, SPTSS.2ABCDEFGH
ELPS: 1C, 2E, 3EH
Process skills: SPTSS.3ABCDEF

Social Studies DOL Criteria Rubric	
Advanced Understanding - 4	**Emerging Understanding - 2**
• The idea is perceptive and reflects an awareness of the complexities of the text. • The text evidence used to support the idea is specific and well chosen. • The combination of the idea/text evidence demonstrates a deep understanding of the text.	• The idea is reasonable, but does not contain text evidence. • The idea is reasonable, but the text evidence is flawed. • The idea needs more explanation or specificity. • The idea represents only a literal reading of the text, with or without text evidence.
Proficient Understanding - 3	**Beginner Understanding - 1**
• The idea is reasonable and goes beyond a literal reading of the text. • The text evidence used to support the idea is accurate and relevant. • The idea/text evidence used to support it are clearly linked. • The combination of the idea/text evidence demonstrates a good understanding of the text.	• The idea is not an answer to the question asked. • The idea is incorrect because it is not based on the text. • The idea is too general vague or unclear to determine whether it is reasonable. • No idea is present …because it merely repeats verbatim, or "echoes" the text evidence.

Preview

Have student pairs collaborate to predict their genetic makeup. Have them consider their family tree, ethnicity, and history of migration. Each student should consider the breakdown in terms of 100%.

Engage

Watch the video clip found in the blog below from 0:00 – 3:51, and 4:28 -4:58.

https://blog.23andme.com/ancestry-reports/latino-ancestry/

Present the quote below to students. Facilitate a round robin to discuss how this information challenges or confirms their belief about Latino Origins.

"You see all of those different ancestries in each of these groups, Bryc explains. The average African-American genome, for example, is 73.2% African, 24% European, and 0.8% Native American, the team reports online today in *The American Journal of Human Genetics*. Latinos, meanwhile, carry an average of 18% Native American ancestry, 65.1% European ancestry (mostly from the Iberian Peninsula), and 6.2% African ancestry." – Sciencemag.org

Supplemental Data - https://www.cell.com/ajhg/fulltext/S0002-9297(14)00476-5

Create a diagram that represents this data and annotate the diagram with information learned during this unit, which may provide background to the allotments of Latino genetic makeup. Consider facilitating an online portfolio folder, where students use studies, maps, and primary sources to explain these origins. Remind students of ideas examined in this unit as well as the information below.

☐ Latinos/as have diverse origins and ancestries.
 Individuals have history, and this history combines ancestry, context, and experience;
☐ Many modern customs, languages, foods, and religious practices have roots in ancient traditions;
☐ Social Studies curricula can tend to pay an undue amount of attention to Anglo/European societies and their relationships with indigenous peoples.

Introduce the idea of a semantic map to students, which like a web allows students to collect and organize their thoughts, however, does give an opportunity to creatively make connections across various concepts. Have students create a semantic map with "Latino Origins" at the center.

Semantic Map Background

http://mavoigt.weebly.com/semantic-maps.html

https://iris.peabody.vanderbilt.edu/module/ss2/cresource/q1/p02/link-semantic-map/

Process

Have students respond to the following prompt followed by a brief explanation.

When considering Latino Origins, I used to think _____, but now I know _____.

6. Social Studies Core Course Infusion

Elementary

LHC themes are infused into learning experiences where students develop an understanding of themselves and the world around them. Geography, customs, symbols, traditions, and contributions of individuals are emphasized. At grades four and five, LHC themes are infused to an introductory survey of Texas history (Grade 4) and United States history (Grade 5).

Middle & High School

LHC themes are infused into an exploration of geography, history, and culture within the context of the contemporary world in Grade 6; and, deeper studies of Texas history in Grade 7 and United States history in Grade 8. Students will learn with increasing depth and complexity how historical narratives form and why multiple perspectives and counter-narratives are necessary to uncover an accurate story about the past.

All LHC themes are addressed through the disciplinary lens of geography, world history, United States history from 1877 to present, economics, and government. In addition, students further develop their understanding about the origins of and motivations behind dominant narratives. A focus of learning experiences at high school prepares students to transfer their understanding in ways that connect the history and culture of Latino communities with the contemporary Latinx experience and, more broadly, the human experience. Latinx Studies may be taken for core social studies graduation credit.

Content Maps by Grade Level

The tables on following pages list sample learning activities by course/grade level.

Table 7.1 - Sample Learning Activities: Elementary School

LS Theme	Grade	Course Name	Unit	Lesson Example
1	K	Self, Home, Family, and Classroom (thematic)	8: Christopher Columbus	Students will investigate the meaning of Indigenous Peoples' Day, which takes place on the second Monday in October (the same date given to Columbus Day). Avoid reading children's literature or teaching about Columbus as a hero who discovered America. Colonization and the tremendous harm to Native peoples brought on by Columbus's explorations are not appropriate to teach students in Kindergarten. Recommended children's literature: *We Are Grateful: Otsaliheliga* by Traci Sorell. This book was written by a citizen of the Cherokee Nation, and the topic is gratitude. Background reading for teacher: https://www.splcenter.org/news/2019/10/12/weekend-read-monday-observe-indigenous-peoples-day

Courtesy of TCU CRES Consultants (the authors).

(Continues)

LS Theme	Grade	Course Name	Unit	Lesson Example
-	K	Self, Home, Family, and Classroom (thematic)	12: Veterans Day	Students will investigate photographs of veterans to define what it means to be a veteran in honor of Veterans Day. Tell students that they will be looking at some photos of special people today called veterans. One at a time, show 4-6 historical and contemporary photos of veterans including women and people of color. Ask students to look closely at each photo and help the teacher find "clues" about what it means to be a veteran in each photo, such as helmets, uniforms, marching, medals, planes, etc. Record students' clues as they are identified on a chart and circle the clues on a smart board if possible. Summarize the lesson by restating the clues and explaining that a veteran is someone who is serving in the military or who has ever served in the military (e.g., army, navy, air force). Assessment-ask students to draw or write an answer to the following: "I think a veteran is someone who _____ because _____." See links for suggested photos from the Library of Congress, the National Archives, and The University of Texas at Austin's Voices Oral History Project. Other photos can be found online.
-	K	Self, Home, Family, and Classroom (thematic)	24: Presidents' Day	Students will explore leadership and qualifications for president. Extend Presidents' Day lessons so students are exposed to more than biographies of George Washington and Abraham Lincoln. Include discussion of the first and only black president to date, and the possibility of women being elected president. Recommended children's literature: *Of Thee I Sing: A Letter to My Daughters* by Barack Obama. The book includes references to Washington, Lincoln, César Chávez, Jackie Robinson, and other male and female individuals who pursued their dreams and made an impact on society.
-	K	Self, Home, Family, and Classroom (thematic)	27-29: Jobs	Students will discuss various jobs people have. Instructional materials such as children's literature should include people of color and women/women of color. Recommended children's literature: *Mighty Mommies and Their Amazing Jobs: A STEM Career Book for Kids* by Donald Jacobsen.

(Continues)

LS Theme	Grade	Course Name	Unit	Lesson Example
3,4	1	Classroom, School, and Community (Thematic)	4: Looking at our world	Students will conduct an oral history with family members to learn about their cultural heritage. Display children's countries of origin on a map of the world. Recommended children's literature: *Dreamers* by Yuyi Morales, the story of a migrant family from Mexico.
3	1	Classroom, School, and Community (Thematic)	5: Traditions We Share	Students will read about and discuss the origin and purpose of the holiday Día de los Muertos (Day of the Dead). Use children's literature to introduce Day of the Dead and compare to Memorial Day when people remember loved ones who are no longer living. Recommended children's literature: *Calavera Abecedario: A Day of the Dead Alphabet Book* by Jeannette Winter; *Dia de Los Muertos* by Roseanne Greenfield Thong.
7	1	Classroom, School, and Community (Thematic)	5: Traditions we share	Students will discuss and illustrate family traditions. Have students talk to family members about traditions they share and share their findings with the class and represent a favorite tradition through artwork/illustrations. Recommended children's literature: *Family Pictures, 15th Anniversary Edition/Cuadros de familia, Edición Quinceañara* by C. L. Garza or *The Keeping Quilt* by P. Polacco.
-	1	Classroom, School, and Community (Thematic)	6: Our past, our present	Students will be exposed to Latinx and women inventors. Recommended children's literature: selections from the book *Girls Think of Everything: Stories of Ingenious Inventions by Women* by C. Thimmesh; and *Marvelous Mattie: How Margaret E. Knight Became an Inventor* by E. A. McCully. Introduce Guillermo González Camarena, an electrical engineer from Mexico whose inventions led to the first color TV broadcast in Mexico (1963). His inventions were adapted by NASA for a 1979 Voyager mission.

(Continues)

LS Theme	Grade	Course Name	Unit	Lesson Example
7	2	Local Community (thematic)	1: My community, my country	Students will expand their understanding of what it means to be a citizen. Complicate the textbook's notion of citizenship by recognizing some students and their family members may not have US citizenship or they may be undocumented. Help children understand that citizenship can also mean belonging to and caring for a group such as your school/neighborhood/community. Work with the class to establish 3-5 classroom citizenship norms (class/playground rules) based on student input. Hold daily or weekly morning meetings with the class in which students, as classroom citizens, can discuss local community events and other issues affecting their lives/families.
-	2	Local Community (thematic)	2: Working to meet our needs	Students will explore various jobs/careers that have a range of financial benefits. Complicate or decenter the textbook's emphasis on capitalism by discussing the dignity of work, regardless of financial rewards. Expose students to jobs and careers that make people happy but do not necessarily have high salaries. Invite guest speakers to talk about the work that they enjoy (e.g., artists, librarians).
-	2	Local Community (thematic)	3: Elementary history fair	Students will select History Fair topics related to Latinx studies. Potential biographies for the History Fair: Ellen Ochoa, first Latina astronaut; Octaviano Larrazolo, first Latino US Senator; Roberto Clemente, Major League Baseball player from Puerto Rico who became the first Latin American to be inducted to the National Baseball Hall of Fame; Dolores Huerta and César Chávez, civil rights activists and labor leaders; Sylvia Mendez, a child involved in a landmark California desegregation case who won the Presidential Medal of Freedom in 2011; Irma Lerma Rangel, the first Mexican American woman elected to the Texas House of Representatives.

(Continues)

LS Theme	Grade	Course Name	Unit	Lesson Example
6	2	Local Community (thematic)	6: Our nation past and present	Students will write about Latinx activists during the Civil Rights Movement. First, lead students through primary source analysis with a photo of migrant farm workers from the Library of Congress. Ask students to observe and discuss what they see, what they think, and what they wonder about the photo. Sample questions: Where might the men be going? What do you think the temperature is like outside, and what makes you think so? Talk about the photo's title, "Off to the melon fields." Who has eaten watermelon before? Where does watermelon come from? How does watermelon get to the grocery store or market? (See link to Library of Congress handout for leading photograph analysis.) Use the photo (or similar photo) to introduce the notion of people working hard without getting paid fairly. Two people who worked with others to make life better for hard working people like these were César Chávez and Dolores Huerta. Recommended children's literature: *Harvesting Hope: The Story of César Chávez* by K. Krull; *Dolores Huerta: A Hero to Migrant Workers* by S. Warren; *Side by Side/Lado a Lado: The Story of Dolores Huerta and César Chávez* by M. Brown. After reading about these two individuals, work with students to write a simple Bio Poem about each using a simple template: I am…I see…I hear…I think…I wonder… I am… Sample: I am César Chávez. I see laborers holding up signs while they are on strike. I hear hundreds of people shouting "Huelga!" (strike). I wonder if we can convince grape growers to pay laborers better. I am a leader.
1	2	Local Community (thematic)	6: Our nation and present	Students will discuss the presence of Indigenous peoples prior to and after colonization (e.g., 13 colonies). Correct the textbook's comment that Native Americans "lost land" (p. 192) by explaining that the lands were stolen. (Note that the children's book *Encounter* by J. Yolen is not recommended.)

(Continues)

LS Theme	Grade	Course Name	Unit	Lesson Example
-	3	Communities and the World (thematic)	4: Elementary History Fair	Students will select History Fair topics related to Latinx studies. Potential biographies for the History Fair: Ellen Ochoa, first Latina astronaut; Octaviano Larrazolo, first Latino US Senator; Roberto Clemente, Major League Baseball player from Puerto Rico who became the first Latin American to be inducted to the National Baseball Hall of Fame; Dolores Huerta and César Chávez, civil rights activists and labor leaders; Sylvia Mendez, a child involved in a landmark California desegregation case who won the Presidential Medal of Freedom in 2011; Irma Lerma Rangel, the first Mexican American woman elected to the Texas House of Representatives
6	3	Communities and the World (thematic)	6: Citizenship	Students will understand that not all women won the right to vote when the Nineteenth Amendment was ratified. Show students 2-3 historical photos of women participating in women's suffrage marches and meetings. Ask them to look closely at the photos and identify what they see, what they think is happening and why, and what they wonder about the images. Draw students' attention to the fact that people of color are missing from the photos or are found in very limited numbers. Discuss implications of this historical time period, and connect the conversation to present day voting rights. In the present day, who is still excluded from the right to vote, and what do students think about this? Links to suggested photos are provided from the Library of Congress and the National Archives: https://www.docsteach.org/documents/document/-flag-bearer-womens-rights https://www.docsteach.org/documents/document/-marching-suffrage-parade-dc https://www.loc.gov/resource/hec.07355/ http://www.loc.gov/teachers/usingprimarysources/r-sources/Analyzing_Photographs_and_Prints.pdf http://www.loc.gov/teachers/usingprimarysources/resources/Primary_Source_Analysis_Tool.pdf

(Continues)

LS Theme	Grade	Course Name	Unit	Lesson Example
6	3	Communities and the World (thematic)	7: A Growing Nation	Students will learn about school segregation among Mexican American children. Teach about the landmark desegregation case in California that took place several years before *Brown v. Board of Education*. Recommended children's literature: *Separate Is Never Equal: Sylvia Mendez and Her Family's Fight for Desegregation* by Duncan Tonatiuh. Show students a video of President Obama awarding Mendez the Presidential Medal of Freedom: https://www.youtube.com/watch?v=aXKBSm3sQ2w
2	4	Texas History (chronological)	3: Early History of Texas	Students will identify contributions of indigenous people who inhabited the land now known as Texas. Use a K-W-L chart (what we Know, what we Want to know, what we Learned) to discuss what students know about Native Americans who inhabited Texas long ago. Who were they? What skills did they have? How did they live? What happened to them? Have students work in small groups to research various tribes (Caddo, Jumano, Tonkawa, Karankawa), identify where they lived on a map of present-day Texas, and write a short report. Teachers should look closely for bias in student resources. Highlight agricultural ingenuity and other contributions of indigenous peoples. Suggested student resource: American Indians Timeline through the Bullock Texas State History Museum: https://www.thestoryoftexas.com/discover/campfire-stories/native-americans. Additional background for teachers: Handbook of Texas Online https://tshaonline.org/handbook-search-results and Handbook of Tejano History https://tshaonline.org/handbook/tejano

(Continues)

LS Theme	Grade	Course Name	Unit	Lesson Example
3	4	Texas History (chronological)	6: Revolution and the Republic of Texas	Students will expand their understanding about the Battle of the Alamo by comparing information in the textbook to other sources and multiple perspectives. Recommended children's literature: *Voices of the Alamo* by Sherry Garland; *Enrique Esparza and the Battle of the Alamo* by Susan Taylor Brown. The book about Enrique Esparza includes a readers theater script that students can read aloud and discuss. After examining multiple texts about what happened at the Alamo, have students revisit the textbook's description and discuss what additional information they have learned. Resource Link: https://www.amazon.com/Voices-Alamo-History-Sherry-Garland/dp/1589802225/ref=sr_1_1?key-words=voices+of+the+alamo&qid=1579479919&s=books&sr=1-1
5	4	Texas History (chronological)	9: Growing State	Students will identify contributions of Mexican American Emma Tenayuca, an activist in the 1930s in Texas. Suggested literature: *That's Not Fair! / ¡No Es Justo!: Emma Tenayuca's Struggle for Justice/La lucha de Emma Tenayuca por la justicia* by Carmen Tafolla. This is a biography about Emma Tenayuca, a Mexican American activist from San Antonio who led a successful strike for pecan shellers working in Texas factories. After reading the book aloud, have students create a character map in which they draw Emma and add illustrations/words to summarize who she advocated for, what she did, when she led the strike, where the strike took place, and why she led the strike.
7	4	Texas History (chronological)	Texas Government	Students will identify contributions of elected Latinx officials who have served and are serving in local and state offices. Examples are Carlos Flores, Fort Worth City Council, District 2, and former San Antonio mayors Henry Cisneros (1981–1989) and Julián Castro (2009–2014).

(Continues)

LS Theme	Grade	Course Name	Unit	Lesson Example
1	5	U.S. History: 1565 to present (chronological)	1: Age of Exploration	Students will explore the question, "How should Columbus be remembered?" by re-examining the heroic myth surrounding the Columbus narrative. Study the number of cities and states who have recently replaced Columbus Day with Indigenous Peoples Day. Questions for students to investigate are: What reasons are given for changing to Indigenous Peoples Day? How have people responded to this change? How might thinking about Indigenous Peoples Day change the way we think about European explorers and colonizers of the 1500s to the present day? Recommended children's literature: *A Coyote Columbus Story* by Thomas King. Recommended teacher resource: *Rethinking Columbus: The Next 500 Years* by Bill Bigelow and Bob Peterson, and Debbie Reese's website https://americanindiansin-childrensliterature.blogspot.com Link: https://www.amazon.com/Coyote-Columbus-Story-Thomas-King/dp/0888998309/ref=sr_1_1?crid=CF5PLU1JSJLE&keywords=coyote+columbus+story&qid=1581180649&sprefix=coyote+Columbus%2Caps%2C174&sr=8-1 Link: https://www.amazon.com/Rethinking-Columbus-Next-500-Years/dp/094296120X/ref=sr_1_1?crid=2K4RT04ZGWSB5&keywords=rethinking+columbus+the+next+500+years&qid=1581177951&sprefix=rethinking+Columbus+the%2Caps%2C182&sr=8-1

(Continues)

LS Theme	Grade	Course Name	Unit	Lesson Example
4	5	U.S. History: 1565 to present (chronological)	11: Industry and Immigration	Students will investigate present-day migration from Mexico into the US through children's literature. Expand the unit to include perspectives beyond European immigrants of the East Coast. Recommended children's literature: *My Diary from Here to There/Mi diario de aqui hasta alla* by Amada Irma Perez; *Pancho Rabbit and the Coyote: A Migrants Tale* by Duncan Tonatiuh; *La Frontera: El Viaje Con Papa / My Journey with Papa* by Deborah Mills. Links: https://www.amazon.com/Diary-Here-There-diario-hasta/dp/0892392304/ref=sr_1_1?crid=3L7DEPAHOEJ1A&keywords=my+diary+from+here+to+there&qid=1581199130&sprefix=my+diary+-fro%2Caps%2C179&sr=8-1 https://www.amazon.com/Pancho-Rabbit-Coyote-Mexican-American-Childrens-ebook/dp/B00C8A3IFO/ref=sr_1_1?keywords=Pancho+Rabbit+and+the+Coyote%3A+A+Migrants+Tale.&qid=1581199779&s=books&sr=1-1 https://www.amazon.com/Frontera-Border-Journey-Spanish-English/dp/178285388X/ref=pd_cp_14_2/130-8304226-3114203?_encoding=UTF8&pd_rd_i=178285388X&pd_rd_r=6407b7d3-c7b0-413d-99b9-e0b9652c68ea&pd_rd_w=MrB7C&pd_rd_wg=EL2hO&pf_rd_p=592dc715-8438-4207-b7fa-4c7afdeb6112&pf_rd_r=CQY8MBKBFRM6YCY4Z49H&psc=1&refRID=CQY8MBKBFRM6YCY4Z49H

(Continues)

LS Theme	Grade	Course Name	Unit	Lesson Example
5	5	U.S. History: 1565 to present (chronological)	14: World War II	Students will identify Mexican Americans who made contributions at home and abroad during World War II. Have students compare and contrast images of J. Howard Miller's (1943) Rosie the Riveter and Robert Valadez's (2009) Rosita (see https://robertvaladez.com/artwork/1137759-Rosita.html for background information). Compare the colors, the details, and the slogans in both images. Show students photos of Latina women in the military such as WWII airplane mechanic Josephine Kelly Ledesma Walker, whose story is archived in the University of Texas VOCES Oral History Project https://voces.lib.utexas.edu/collections/world-war-ii?field_military_branch_tid=All&field_story_tags_tid=86&field_place_of_interview_state_tid=All Additional background information for teachers: 1. Army infantry unit made up entirely of Mexican Americans: 36th Division, 141st Regiment, 2nd Battalion, Company E. They fought in the Italian Campaign (see the book *Patriots from the Barrio* by Dave Gutierrez). 2. Puerto Rican 65th Infantry unit fought during WWII and the Korean War (see https://history.army.mil/html/forcestruc/lineages/branches/inf/0065in.htm) Links: https://voces.lib.utexas.edu/collections/world-wa https://voces.lib.utexas.edu/collections/stories/jo https://voces.lib.utexas.edu/collections/world-wa

(Continues)

LS Theme	Grade	Course Name	Unit	Lesson Example
7	5	U.S. History: 1565 to present (chronological)	15: The Cold War	Students will use primary and secondary sources to identify Latino contributions to the Vietnam War. Students will be introduced to:
				1. Naval Commander Everett Alvarez (1937–) Alvarez was a Californian and a Vietnam POW for 8 years who was later awarded two Purple Heart Medals and numerous other honors.
				2. Master Sergeant Roy Benavidez (1935-1998). Benavidez was a Green Beret from Texas who was a 1981 Congressional Medal of Honor recipeint for bravery during the Vietnam War.
				Primary sources: 1. Show a 2-minute US Navy video of Commander Everett Alvarez speaking on YouTube: https://www.youtube.com/watch?v=QiTgAs2m8-c. Show a photo from the Ronald Reagan Presidential Library & Museum website—President Ronald Reagan awarding Benavidez the Congressional Medal of Honor https://www.reaganlibrary.gov/sites/default/files/archives/photographs/large/c822-13.jpg
				Secondary sources: 1. Show a 4-minute biography of Everett Alvarez on YouTube https://www.youtube.com/watch?v=mgpH-Jq2L4u4
				2. Have students read a summary of Benavidez's heroic acts on the US Army website: https://www.army.mil/article/148297/army_intelligence_showcases_medal_of_honor_recipients
				Background information for teachers: Everett Alvarez https://www.history.navy.mil/content/history/nhhc/research/library/research-guides/modern-biographical-files-ndl/modern-bios-a/alvarez-everrett-jr.html; Roy Benevides: https://tshaonline.org/handbook/online/artic

Table 7.2 - Sample Learning Activities: Middle and High School

LS Theme	Grade	Course Name	Unit	Lesson Example
3	6	People, Places, and Societies of the Contemporary World (regional)	3 / North America: The Growth of the United States	2.5 "Expansion & Industrialization" (96–97): Students will understand the importance of The Treaty of Guadalupe Hidalgo (1848) and the Gadsden Purchase (1853) in the US in acquiring Southwestern territories and how this directly impacted Texas. 2.6 "Civil War & Reconstruction" (98–99): Students will discuss other Civil War generals alongside Robert E. Lee and Ulysses S. Grant, including Gen. Diego Archuleta (Union) who was New Mexican and the first Latino to ever reach the rank of brigadier general, and Col. Ambrosio Jose Gonzales (Confederacy), artillery commander for South Carolina, Georgia, and Florida.
5	6	People, Places, and Societies of the Contemporary World (regional)	8 / South America: Building Economies	Students will discuss the role of activism and protest in the shaping and formation of Brazil. Students will examine the arts' ability (e.g. Caetano Veloso) to express this through its various forms, from visual art to musical lyrics. Students will discuss the impact these forms of protest had on the shaping of economies via policy reform induced under social pressures.
7	6	People, Places, and Societies of the Contemporary World (regional)	11 / Africa: Physical Geography and How Big is Africa?	Students will expand the question of "How big is Africa?" to include the following points: 1) The misrepresentation of the size/shapes/longitudinal positioning of the source continents of the peoples of the Latino diaspora (Africa and S. America); and 2) The labeling of Europe and America as "Up" while South America and Africa as "Down"(i.e. why is North up and South down? etc.). Teachers could use this video as a conversation starter: https://youtu.be/v-VX-PrBRtTY

Courtesy of TCU CRES Consultants (the authors).

(Continues)

LS Theme	Grade	Course Name	Unit	Lesson Example
6	7	Texas History	14 / Growth and Change 1950s-1969	Students will discuss the 1968 student walkouts in San Antonio in answering the question: "What economic, social, and political events affected Texans in the 1950s and 1960s?" Students will understand the reforms demanded by Mexican American students during this period and the specific ways those demands were answered or not by the Texas government. Source: https://stmuhistorymedia.org/edgewood-isd-chicano-walkouts-learning-about-the-growing-history-of-discrimination-in-san-antonio-schools/
2	7	Texas History	1 / Regions and Native Americans of Texas	Students will expand the discussion of Native Americans beyond tribes and explore the mestizaje nature of the population as the Spanish colonists appeared and settled. Students will simultaneously define and draw distinct lines between tribes while also understanding how Native American culture and identity also became interwoven with the Spanish to some degree.
3	7	Texas History	5 / From Revolution to Republic	Students will discuss how many native Texans, that is, Tejanos, also supported the overthrow of Mexican rule. Students will examine specific examples of this including the only two native Texans to sign the Texas Declaration of Independence, José Francisco Ruiz, a school teacher, and José Antionio Navarro, Ruiz's nephew. Students will also discuss the physician and diplomat Lorenzo de Zavala, though born in the Yucatan, as the other Spanish-surnamed signatory. He also designed the Texas flag, and is credited with having a major role in the drafting of the document. Students will note the importance of Tejano defenders of the Alamo, and to acknowledge the conflicting stories about their role.

(Continues)

LS Theme	Grade	Course Name	Unit	Lesson Example
1, 2	8	Early U.S. pre-1877	1 / The Development of the 13 Original Colonies	Students will examine pre-colonial Native American populations and an indigenous-centered narrative of the Spanish colonies in the future US. The first learning experience could introduce students to the great corn societies of Central Mexico that migrated north into what is now the US Southwest (such as the Hohokam of the Salt River Valley) and later spread across all of North America (including to the Iroquois / Haudenosaunee confederation of the Great Lakes). The next learning experience could add the Spanish colonies of St. Augustine and Santa Fe, the two earliest permanent settlements in the territory that becomes the US. It's important to emphasize that Spanish was the first European language spoken, and Catholicism was a dominant religion. A third learning experience could include discussion of the "Indian Slave Trade" that connected the English, French, and Spanish empires, the hacienda economic system established by the Spanish, and indigenous resistance to enslavement, missionization, and economic exploitation. A prominent example should be the Pueblo Revolt of 1680.
2	8	Early U.S. pre-1877	2 / The Revolutionary Era	Students will explore the history and contributions of Bernardo de Gálvez (1746–1786), the governor of Spanish Louisiana and a key player in the American Revolution. Gálvez provided critical supplies for the Continental Army as early as 1777 before helping finance and coordinate a successful American siege of a British fort in Illinois in 1779. Then, after Spain had declared war on Britain, Gálvez raised a multiracial/-multiethnic battalion that ended the British occupation of Florida and drove them out of the Gulf South. One of Gálvez's officers, Don Francisco Saavedra de Sangronis, raised tens of millions of dollars (in 2020 dollars) to resupply the beleaguered Continental Army, which he delivered along with thousands of reinforcement troops. In short, Gálvez and his men played a key role in helping the newly independent US win the revolution and its independence.

(Continues)

LS Theme	Grade	Course Name	Unit	Lesson Example
3	8	Early U.S. pre-1877	6 / Industry, Expansion, and Reform	Students will reassess the US government's expansion west by centering the experiences of Mexicans in Texas and California. The Texas revolt of 1835–36 should include critical analysis of Juan Seguín, Lorenzo de Zavala, and other Mexican leaders in Tejas. Looking at both Texas and California through the 1840s, students will explore the myths embedded in the Spanish Fantasy Past celebrated in the public history of missions and instead read primary sources about the indigenous and mestizo presence, including their forced labor and dispossession in the countryside and their exclusion from the mines during the Gold Rush. Students will read the "All-Mexico" movement and the racist thinking that drove both its proponents and detractors. Students can then analyze the Treaty of Guadalupe-Hidalgo as well as the debates in which the US Senate elected not to ratify Article X, thereby leaving Mexican land grants subject to confiscation by Anglos. Perhaps most important, students will learn about the waves of Mexican immigrants who came to the US during the Porfiriato (1876–1910) and during and after the Revolution (1910–1930), helping them to supplement existing narratives of European and Chinese immigration during the Gilded Age and Progressive Era. Pages 15-20 of the introductory essay provide additional guidance and content for this unit.

(Continues)

LS Theme	Grade	Course Name	Unit	Lesson Example
4, 7	9	World Geography	2 / Concepts in Context: United States and Canada (20 instructional days)	Students will gain an understanding of US immigration debates and policies, including the critical Johnson-Reed Immigration and Nationality Act (1924), which imposed quotas on migrants from Europe and created the category of "illegal alien" but did not impose quotas on Latin Americans. Students then turn to the failed Box Bills (1928–29), which attempted to impose restrictions on Mexican migration but were not passed due to opposition from growers and industrialists in the US Southwest and South—white businessmen who depended on Mexican labor. Students will explore the Hart-Celler act of 1965 and its prioritization of family reunification and the unexpected demographic transitions in the US since its passage. Last, students will understand the Immigration Reform and Control Act (1986), signed by Ronald Reagan, that gave amnesty to unauthorized migrants while imposing sanctions on employers who hired undocumented workers, and the Clinton-era Illegal Immigration Reform and Immigrant Responsibility Act of 1996, which dramatically expanded the border wall and authorized immigration enforcement by local governments (section 287g).

(Continues)

LS Theme	Grade	Course Name	Unit	Lesson Example
6, 7, 3	9	World Geography	3 / Concepts in Context - Latin America	Students will explore the radical political and social movement of Latin America and connect them to diasporic Latinx communities in the US and to US imperialism in the region. Specific examples include: the resistance to the United Fruit Company and the expropriation of foreign plantations in Guatemala, which resulted in the US CIA coup that deposed democratically elected President Jacobo Arbenz; the Mexican PRI government's crackdown on student protestors in Mexico City beginning with the 1968 Olympics; US complicity in the Argentine "dirty war" of the 1970s; US support for the contras that overthrew democratically elected socialist governments in El Salvador and Nicaragua, including massacres of indigenous peoples in these countries; and the new Zapatista uprising of 1994 in Chiapas, Mexico. Students will also explore how US Latinos and other radicals supported the ordinary people and leftist revolutionaries of Latin America in each of these moments and places, including ties between Chicano Movement activists and Fidel Castro's Cuba and Sandinista Nicaragua and, later, the Committee in Solidarity with the People of El Salvador (CISPES), the sanctuary movement in the US in the 1980s, and the anti-globalization "Battle in Seattle" in 1999 that included Zapatista calls for the liberation of Chiapas.
4, 5	9 10	World Geography	10 / Concepts in Context: United States and the World	Students will understand the creation of "Juan Crow" segregation in the US Southwest. The latter includes the creation of segregated neighborhoods and public accommodations (e.g., movie theaters and restaurants); separate and unequal schools; targeted policing, police brutality, and state-sanctioned violence; political disenfranchisement; and a racial division of labor that confined Mexican Americans to the dirtiest, low-paid, and most dangerous jobs, often including migratory agricultural labor. Students will also explore the ways Mexican Americans built communities and resisted their poor treatment.

(Continues)

LS Theme	Grade	Course Name	Unit	Lesson Example
5	10	World History	11 / The World at War	Students will understand and discuss the role of Mexican Americans in WWII both in the US and abroad. Specific details could include a discussion of the all-Mexican American Army battalion in WWII (Company E, 2nd Battalion, 141st Regiment, 36th Division; see "Patriots From the Barrio" by David Gutierrez) and/or the Sleepy Lagoon Incident and Zoot Suit Riots in Los Angeles.
2, 1	10	World History	8 / European Expansion and Colonization	Students will be exposed to more detailed information on the Latinx experience of European expansion in the Americas, especially related to the Spanish colonization of Mexico and indigenous responses and resistance. Specific topics include the effects of Spanish influence on social order, including the spread of Spanish language and Catholicism, as well as the impositions of slavery, large-scale war, and infectious diseases that were crucial to Spain's success in establishing sustainable colonies in the New World. Students should also address the survivance and sovereignty of non-European communities, such as indigenous nations and African-descended Maroon societies founded by rebellion. Other key details include the spread of Catholicism through missionaries and the creation of the "Castas" system of categorizing race and status.

(Continues)

LS Theme	Grade	Course Name	Unit	Lesson Example
3	11	World History	10 / The Industrial Revolution and Imperialism	Students should focus in this unit on the emergence and growth of Latin American national identities, from Mexican Independence to Puerto Rican annexation, and on the effects of US expansionism in Latin America and the present-day US Southwest. Specific examples include the US-Mexico War and the subsequent Treaty of Guadalupe Hidalgo (1848), in which the US acquired most of Mexico's land mass, and the War of 1898 and subsequent Treaty of Paris, in which the US conquered Guam and the Philippines in the Western Pacific and Puerto Rico in the Caribbean. Students will also understand the history of filibusters in greater Latin America and the motivations, means, and outcomes of borderland rebellions such as the Cortina Wars. Students should also explore the distinctly opposed positions on slavery of the US vs. Mexico (and much of Latin America) that resulted in the US withholding support for independence/revolutions in Latin America. On the other hand, students should learn that US Latinos and African Americans supported their counterparts in Latin America as they resisted European and US imperialism (see, for example, Paul Ortiz, *An African American and Latinx History of the United States*).
1, 3	11	US History 1877 to present	1 / The US during reconstruction	Students will review the status of Native Americans and Mexican Americans in the US prior to the Civil War and trace their treatment and living conditions in the period immediately after the war. Students will understand how the US military continued fighting in the West to complete the conquest of the region, often at the expense of indigenous and Mexicano people. Students will compare/contrast policies towards these groups related to other elements of postwar policy, all of which sought to incorporate the US West and South to the more populated East.

(Continues)

LS Theme	Grade	Course Name	Unit	Lesson Example
4	11	US History 1877 to present	3 / The Progressive Era	Students will discuss how this period is critical in the formation of US Latino communities. Mass migration began in the 1880s and picked up in the early 20th century, accelerating after the Mexican Revolution began in 1910. For example, Mexicanos migrated through El Paso (the Ellis Island of the Southwest) and formed major enclaves in Los Angeles, San Antonio, and beyond. They organized *mutualistas* as the key forms of community self-help. And they created enclaves of Mexican culture and defended themselves against racism by creating vibrant barrios across the Southwest. Most worked as laborers on railroads, in mines and fields, and beyond. They formed all-Mexicano and interethnic unions like the Japanese-Mexican Labor Association. Students will examine modern-day examples of these formations. Sources: George J. Sanchez, *Becoming Mexican American*; Emilio Zamora, *The World of the Mexican Worker in Texas*, among others.
5	11	US History 1877 to present	8 / Post War America	Students will consider the question: "What were the causes of prosperity in the 1950s?" in relation to information about the Bracero Program (1942–64) and "Operation Wetback" (1954). In doing so, students will discuss the role of "cheap labor" in fueling prosperity for wider US society. Students will also understand the difficulties many Mexican Americans and other Latinos had in accessing their rights under the "GI Bill," including late payments (a problem for those seeing the tuition benefit) and redlining, which made it difficult for many to buy a home in a neighborhood where they might obtain a loan. Students will also discuss how many Mexican Americans were nonetheless able to use the GI Bill to attend college in significant numbers for the first time even as "discrimination limited social mobility." Last, students will explore how the "Baby Boom" dovetails with the explosive growth of the Latino population post-WWII and especially after 1965. See Zaragosa Vargas, *Crucible of Struggle*.

(Continues)

LS Theme	Grade	Course Name	Unit	Lesson Example
2	12	Government	N/A	Students will expand the discussion of "American" government by including the Latino/a Studies perspective and including background on the alternative forms of government and law that existed in what is now the US. For example, Spanish colonial rule, operative in New Mexico and other places, offered women greater freedoms and legal rights than English Common law, which is the system that ultimately won out. For instance, Spanish colonial women were able to file lawsuits, own and operate ranches, bequeath inheritance to children or others, etc. Students will discuss how these seemingly small differences impact what is codified in law and then translated into social norms. For example, how Anglo-American colonial women's existence and support was entirely dependent on men because of legal restrictions in English common law. Students will debate how alternative foundations could play out in gender dynamics, among other social norms. Sources include Deena Gonzalez, *Refusing the Favor* and Sarah Deutsch, *No Separate Refuge*.
	12	Economics	N/A	Throughout the course, students should learn about the "outsize role" of immigrants in creating small businesses, revitalizing main streets, and boosting employment. In some states, immigrants accounted for 40 percent of all new businesses founded in the early 21st century, according to a working paper published by the National Bureau of Economic Research. Latino immigrants in particular rebuilt America's small towns, including across the South, and its major cities. Most US metropolises would have experienced population *loss* had it not been for immigration; Latinos especially have solved the nation's urban crisis, as argued by Andrew Sandoval-Strausz in *Barrio America*. Additionally, Latinx small business growth, whether immigrant or US born, outstrips that among all other demographic groups. Latinx communities are profoundly entrepreneurial, in sharp contrast to the stereotypes of Latino laziness.

Annotated Bibliography: Latinx Literature and Social Studies

Kindergarten – 1st Grade

1. Brown, M. *Waiting for the Biblioburro*. Tricycle Press, 2011. [Grade level: K-3]

(From the publisher:)
Ana loves stories. She often makes them up to help her little brother fall asleep. But in her small village there are only a few books, and she has read them all. One morning, Ana wakes up to the clip-clop of hooves, and there before her is the most wonderful sight: a traveling library resting on the backs of two burros: all the books a little girl could dream of, with enough stories to encourage her to create one of her own. Inspired by the heroic efforts of real-life librarian Luis Soriano, award-winning picture book creators Monica Brown and John Parra introduce readers to the mobile library that journeys over mountains and through valleys to bring literacy and culture to rural Colombia, and to the children who wait for the BiblioBurro.

2. Garza, C. L. *Family Pictures, 15th Anniversary Edition / Cuadros de familia, Edición Quinceañara*. Children's Book Press, 2005. [Grade level: 1-2]

(From the publisher:)
Family Pictures is the story of Carmen Lomas Garza's girlhood: celebrating birthdays, making tamales, finding a hammerhead shark on the beach, picking cactus, going to a fair in Mexico, and confiding to her sister her dreams of becoming an artist. These day-to-day experiences are told through fourteen vignettes of art and a descriptive narrative, each focusing on a different aspect of traditional Mexican American culture. The English-Spanish text and vivid illustrations reflect the author's strong sense of family and community. For Mexican Americans, Carmen Lomas Garza offers a book that reflects their lives and traditions. For others, this work offers insights into a beautifully rich community.

(Review by Ina Rimpau – Parents' Choice®)
This is the illustrator and storyteller's bilingual memoir of growing up in Texas, fully immersed in her family's Mexican traditions. The illustrations are painted in a flat, naïve style, bringing out the details of celebrations and everyday activities from cakewalk scholarship fundraisers to visits from the curandera to eating watermelon on the porch on a hot summer evening. There is always a mix of ages and generations, emphasizing activities all members of a family enjoy in their own ways. Lomas Garza explains the paintings, supplying additional information, making this book an introduction to the artistic process as well as a family history.

3. Jacobsen, D., Evans, G., Hoffman, D. J., & Silea, M. *Mighty Mommies and Their Amazing Jobs!: A STEM Career Book for Kids*. Memphis, TN: Donald Jacobsen, 2019.

(From the publisher:)
Mighty Mommies and Their Amazing Jobs is an engaging and easy-to-read rhyming picture book that teaches children about STEM careers (doctor, dentist, scientist, paleontologist) and service careers (firefighter, police officer, teacher). This book is packed with colorful illustrations and a simple discussion of what each job entails.

4. Johnston, T. *P is for Piñata: A Mexico Alphabet*. Sleeping Bear Press, 2008. [Grade level: K-2]

(From the publisher:)
The country of Mexico has long been a popular travel destination. But there's much more to enjoy and appreciate than just sunshine and warm temperatures when exploring this region with its ancient

history and proud traditions. Enjoy an A-Z tour of our neighbor to the south in *P is for Piñata: A Mexico Alphabet*. Young readers can visit the tomb of a Mayan king, experience the life of the vaquero (Mexican cowboy), attend the world-famous Ballet Folklórico de Mèxico, and sample the everyday treat that was once known as the "food of the gods." From folk art to famous people to the original "hot dog," the treasures of Mexico are revealed in *P is for Piñata*. Vibrant artwork perfectly captures the flavor, texture, and spirit of its landscape and culture.

5. Lainez, R. C. *Rene Has Two Last Names / Rene Tiene Dos Apellidos*. Arte Público Press, 2009. [Grade level: K-2]

(From the publisher:)
Young Rene is from El Salvador, and he doesn't understand why his name has to be different in the United States. When he writes Colato, he sees his paternal grandparents, Rene and Amelia. When he writes Lainez, he sees his maternal grandparents, Angela and Julio. Without his second last name, Rene feels incomplete, like a hamburger without the meat or a pizza without cheese or a hot dog without a wiener. His new classmates giggle when Rene tells them his name. "That's a long dinosaur name," one says. "Your name is longer than an anaconda," laughs another. But Rene doesn't want to lose the part of him that comes from his mother's family. So when the students are given a project to create a family tree, Rene is determined to explain the importance of using both of his last names. On the day of his presentation, Rene explains that he is as hard-working as Abuelo Rene, who is a farmer, and as creative as his Abuela Amelia, who is a potter. He can tell stories like his Abuelo Julio and enjoys music like his Abuela Angela.

6. McCully, E. A. *Marvelous Mattie: How Margaret E. Knight Became an Inventor*. New York, NY: Farrar, Straus, Giroux, 2006.

(From the publisher:)
With her sketchbook labeled My Inventions and her father's toolbox, Mattie could make almost anything: toys, sleds, and a foot warmer. When she was just twelve years old, Mattie designed a metal guard to prevent shuttles from shooting off textile looms and injuring workers. As an adult, Mattie invented the machine that makes the square-bottom paper bags we still use today. However, in court, a man claimed the invention was his, stating that she "could not possibly understand the mechanical complexities." Marvelous Mattie proved him wrong, and over the course of her life earned the title of "the Lady Edison."

7. Mora, P. *Doña Flor: A Tall Tale about a Giant Woman with a Great Big Heart*. Dragonfly Books, 2010. [Grade level: Pre K-2]

(From the publisher:)
Doña Flor is a giant lady who lives in a tiny village in the American Southwest. Popular with her neighbors, she lets the children use her flowers as trumpets and her leftover tortillas as rafts. Flor loves to read, too, and she can often be found reading aloud to the children. One day, all the villagers hear a terrifying noise: it sounds like a huge animal bellowing just outside their village. Everyone is afraid, but not Flor. She wants to protect her beloved neighbors, so with the help of her animal friends, she sets off for the highest mesa to find the creature. Soon enough, though, the joke is on Flor and her friends, who come to rescue her, as she discovers the small secret behind that great big noise. The creators of Tomás and the Library Lady, Pat Mora and Raul Colón, have once again joined together. This time they present a heartwarming and humorous original tall tale—peppered with Spanish words and phrases—about a giant lady with a great big heart.

8. Morales, Y. *Just a Minute: A Trickster Tale and Counting Book*. Chronicle Books, 2016. [Grade level: K-3]

(From the publisher:)
This original trickster tale, with its vivacious illustrations and dynamic read-aloud text, is at once a spirited tribute to the rich traditions of Mexican culture and a perfect introduction to counting in both English and Spanish.

(Review from Goodreads:)
In this original trickster tale, Señor Calavera arrives unexpectedly at Grandma Beetle's door. He requests that she leave with him right away. "Just a minute," Grandma Beetle tells him. She still has one house to sweep, two pots of tea to boil, three pounds of corn to make into tortillas—and that's just the start! Using both Spanish and English words to tally the party preparations, Grandma Beetle cleverly delays her trip and spends her birthday with a table full of grandchildren and her surprise guest. This spirited tribute to the rich traditions of Mexican culture is the perfect introduction to counting in both English and Spanish. The vivacious illustrations and universal depiction of a family celebration are sure to be adored by young readers everywhere.

9. Morales, Y. *Dreamers*. Neal Porter Books, 2018. [Grade level: K-2]

(From the publisher:)
Dreamers is a celebration of what migrants bring with them when they leave their homes. It's a story about family. And it's a story to remind us that we are all dreamers, bringing our own gifts wherever we roam. Beautiful and powerful at any time but given particular urgency as the status of our own Dreamers becomes uncertain, this is a story that is both topical and timeless. The lyrical text is complemented by sumptuously detailed illustrations, rich in symbolism. Also included are a brief autobiographical essay about Yuyi's own experience, a list of books that inspired her (and still do), and a description of the beautiful images, textures, and mementos she used to create this book. A parallel Spanish-language edition, *Soñadores*, is also available.

10. Mora, P. *The Rainbow Tulip*. Puffin Books, 2003. [Grade level: K-1]

(From the publisher:)
Stella loves her family and her Mexican heritage, but she doesn't always like being different from the other kids at school. Now her class is going to dance around the Maypole at the school's May parade, and Stella wants her tulip costume to be special, even if she won't look like the other girls at school. Sometimes being different can be exciting. This touching story that celebrates diversity is based on author Pat Mora's mother's childhood and is brought to life by Elizabeth Sayles's evocative paintings.

11. Neal, J. M. *Alma and How She Got Her Name/ Alma y come obtuvo su nombre*. Candlewick, 2018. [Grade level: Preschool-3]

(From the publisher:)
If you ask her, Alma Sofia Esperanza José Pura Candela has way too many names: six! How did such a small person wind up with such a large name? Alma turns to Daddy for an answer and learns of Sofia, the grandmother who loved books and flowers; Esperanza, the great-grandmother who longed to travel; José, the grandfather who was an artist; and other namesakes, too. As she hears the story of her name, Alma starts to think it might be a perfect fit after all — and realizes that she will one day have her own story to tell. In her author-illustrator debut, Juana Martinez-Neal opens a treasure box of discovery for children who may be curious about their own origin stories or names.

(From *School Library Journal:*)
It's said there's a story behind every name, and Alma Sofia Esperanza José Pura Candela is surely a moniker worthy of six tales. After complaining that her name is so long that it "never fits," Alma's father shares stories with the girl about the people she's been named after, including a book lover, an artist, and a deeply spiritual woman, among others. Martinez-Neal, the recipient of the 2018 Pura Belpré Illustrator Award for *La Princesa and the Pea*, works in print transfers with graphite and colored pencils for these images, limiting her palette to black, charcoal gray, and blushes of color. The round, stylized figure of the girl, dressed in pink striped pants and a white shirt, pops against the sepia pages (reminiscent of old family photo albums). As Alma's namesakes emerge from the shadows when they are introduced, they and their distinguishing items (books, plants, paintbrushes, etc.) are highlighted in a pale gray-blue. The softly colored images and curvilinear shapes that embrace the figures evoke a sense of warmth and affection. At the story's end, the only tale readers have not heard is Alma's. "You will make your own story," states her father. VERDICT: A beautifully illustrated, tender story to be shared with all children, sure to evoke conversations about their names.—Daryl Grabarek, *School Library Journal.*

12. Obama, B. *Of Thee I Sing: A Letter to My Daughters*. London: Puffin, 2018.

(From the publisher:)
In this poignant message to his daughters, Barack Obama has written a moving tribute to thirteen groundbreaking Americans and the ideals that have shaped our nation. From the artistry of Georgia O'Keeffe, to the courage of Jackie Robinson, to the patriotism of George Washington, Obama sees the traits of these heroes within his own children, and within all of America's children. Breathtaking, evocative illustrations by award-winning artist Loren Long at once capture the personalities and achievements of these great Americans and the innocence and promise of childhood. This beautiful book celebrates the characteristics that unite all Americans, from our nation's founders to generations to come. It is about the potential within each of us to pursue our dreams and forge our own paths. It is a treasure to cherish with your family forever.

13. Polacco, P. *The Keeping Quilt*. New York: Simon & Schuster Books for Young Readers, 1998.

(From the publisher:)
"We will make a quilt to help us always remember home," Anna's mother said. "It will be like having the family in back home Russia dance around us at night." And so it was. From a basket of old clothes, Anna's babushka, Uncle Vladimir's shirt, Aunt Havalah's nightdress, and an apron of Aunt Natasha's become The Keeping Quilt, passed along from mother to daughter for almost a century. For four generations the quilt is a Sabbath tablecloth, a wedding canopy, and a blanket that welcomes babies warmly into the world. In strongly moving pictures that are as heartwarming as they are real, Patricia Polacco tells the story of her own family and the quilt's further story that remains a symbol of their enduring love and faith. This anniversary edition includes fifteen pages of original material describing the quilt's journey and its home at the Mazza Museum in Findley, Ohio.

14. Pinkney, M. *I Am Latino: The Beauty in Me*. Hachette Book Group, 2007. [Grade Level: PreK-3]

(From the publisher:)
I Am Latino: The Beauty in Me is a celebration of Latino children in all of their various shades, cultures, and customs. Poetic, affirmative text accompanies the bright and striking photographs of children and uses the five senses to lead the reader on an exploration of Latino foods, music, language, and more. "Use your senses and you will see, / there is beauty in everything." In this celebration of Latino children, Myles Pinkney's joyous photographs and Sandra Pinkney's buoyant text showcase traditional food, music, and more through each of the five senses. From dancing the salsa and the tango to smelling delicious empanadas and mouthwatering tamales, to treasuring time with family members

and even learning Spanish words and phrases along the way, this is the perfect way to celebrate Latino culture. The beloved husband-and-wife team celebrates Latino children in all of their various shades, cultures, and customs. Full color.

15. Sorell, T. *We Are Grateful: Otsaliheliga*. Watertown, MA: Charlesbridge, 2018.

(From the publisher:)
The word otsaliheliga (oh-jah-LEE-hay-le-gah) is used by members of the Cherokee Nation to express gratitude. Beginning in the fall with the new year and ending in summer, follow a full Cherokee year of celebrations and experiences. Appended with a glossary and the complete Cherokee syllabary, originally created by Sequoyah.

16. Thimmesh, C., & Sweet, M. *Girls Think of Everything: Stories of Ingenious Inventions by Women*. Boston, MA: Houghton Mifflin, 2018.

(From the publisher:)
This updated edition of the bestselling *Girls Think of Everything*, by Sibert-winner Catherine Thimmesh and Caldecott Honor winner Melissa Sweet, retains all the integrity of the original but includes expanded coverage of inventions (and inventors) to better reflect our diverse and technological world. Ages: 10 to 12. Author: Catherine Thimmesh is the award-winning author of many books for children, including *Team Moon*, winner of the Sibert Medal. Her books have received numerous starred reviews, appeared on best books lists, and won many awards, including the IRA Children's Book Award and Minnesota Book Award.

17. Thong, R., & Ballesteros, C. *Día de Los Muertos*. Chicago, IL: Albert Whitman & Company, 2015.

(From the publisher:)
It's Dia de Los Muertos (Day of the Dead), and children throughout the pueblo, or town, are getting ready to celebrate! They decorate with colored streamers, calaveras, or sugar skulls, and pan de muertos, or bread of the dead. There are altars draped in cloth and covered in marigolds and twinkling candles. Music fills the streets. Join the fun and festivities, learn about a different cultural tradition, and brush up on your Spanish vocabulary, as the town honors their dearly departed in a traditional, time-honored style.

18. Tonatiuh, D., & Vega, E. de la., *Dear Primo: A Letter to My Cousin*. New York: Scholastic, Inc., 2017.

(From the publisher:)
Dear Primo covers the sights, sounds, smells, and tastes of two very different childhoods, while also emphasizing how alike Charlie and Carlitos are at heart. Spanish words are scattered among the English text, providing a wonderful way to introduce the language and culture of Mexico to young children. Inspired by the ancient art of the Mixtecs and other cultures of Mexico, Tonatiuh incorporates their stylized forms into his own artwork.

19. Well, C. *Opuestos: Mexican Folk Art Opposites in English and Spanish*. Cico Puntos Press, 2009. [Grade level: PreK-2]

(From the publisher:)
(First Concepts in Mexican Folk Art/Board book) Brothers Martín and Quirino, along with other family members, carved these figures from the wood of the flowering jacaranda tree. All are farmers but supplement their income carving these beautiful creatures in the little mountain town of La Union Tejalapam, Oaxaca. Bilingual and whimsical authentic hand-painted animals from Oaxaca teach kids about opposites in Spanish and English.

(From *School Library Journal*:)
Oaxacan folk art in the form of hand-carved wood sculptures abounds in this bilingual concept book about opposites. Contrasting concepts include inside and outside, high and low, and left and right, to name a few. At the turn of each page, readers see brightly painted wood characters set against equally vibrantly colored background pages that effortlessly convey the concept the author sets out to teach. On each spread, the English and Spanish words for a single concept face the opposing concept. This attractive volume conveys the concept in a unique and inviting fashion and provides youngsters with an introduction to some Mexican art in the process.–Rhonda L. Jeffers, Coweta Public Library System, Newnan, GA.

20. Weill, C. *ABeCedarios: Mexican Folk Art ABCs in English and Spanish*. Cinco Puntos Press, 2007. [Grade Level: Preschool-4]

(From the publisher:)
Review from: https://www.cincopuntos.com:
Every ABC book worth its cover price is bound to have bright colors and big letters. But not every ABC book has magical hand-carved animals to illustrate every letter. And very few alphabet books present those letters in more varieties than English! Very few alphabet books except the *ABeCedarios*, that is! In this brightly colored book, the alphabet is presented in both Spanish and English, and includes the four additional letters—and whimsical animals—that make the Spanish alphabet so much fun. The famous folk artists, brothers Moisés and Armando Jiménez, carved the wonderful animal figures that illustrate each letter in *ABeCedarios*. Working with their wives and children in the beautiful village of Arrazola in Oaxaca, Mexico, they carved and painted each enchanting animal by hand. For many centuries, people in Oaxaca have carved wood to make toys and household objects. However, it was Moisés's and Armando's grandfather Manuel who started making animal figures. Now more than sixty families in Arrazola make their living from wood carving.

21. Winter, J. *Calavera abecedario: A Day of the Dead Alphabet*. Houghton Mifflin/Harcourt, 2006. [Grade level: Preschool-3]

(From the publisher:)
Every year Don Pedro and his family make papier-mâché skeletons, or calaveras, for Mexico's Day of the Dead fiesta. From the Angel and Doctor to the Mariachi and Unicornio, there's a special calavera for each letter of the alphabet. Come dance with them! Includes a glossary of Spanish words and an author's note.

(Review from: https://www.kirkusreviews.com:)
This visually exciting alphabet book makes a fine companion to Winter's *Day of the Dead* (1997). Boldly colored borders frame the brilliant-hued folk-like images and vivid white text superimposed on a black background. First she tells of a Mexico City family preparing the papier-mâché skeletons (calaveras) for annual *Day of the Dead* celebrations as they have for several generations. The alphabet portion includes an array of charming skeletons in various poses, including an angel, a witch (bruja), bride and bridegroom (novia and novio), mariachi, and zapatero (shoemaker). The letter K is represented by Frida Kahlo, Y by a yucca, and W, which doesn't exist in Spanish, is pushed off the page. An alphabet glossary notes differences between the Spanish and English alphabets and provides English translations of the Spanish words. An author's note discusses Mexican fiestas and Don Pedro Linares, whose life inspired the story.

2nd Grade – 3rd Grade

22. Alarcon, F. X. *Angels Ride Bikes and Other Fall Poems: Los Angeles Andan En Bicicleta y Otros Poemas del Otono*. Madison, WI: Cooperative Children's book Center, 2000. [Grade level: 2-4]

(From the publisher:)
In this bilingual poetry book, Francisco X. Alarcon invites young readers to experience fall in Los Angeles—the City of the Angels—where dreams can come true. In the poet's whimsical imagination, mariachis play like angels, angels ride bikes, and the earth dances the "cha-cha-cha." Alarcon celebrates the simple joys and trials of everyday life: a visit to the outdoor market, the arrival of the ice cream vendor, the first day of school. He honors his family and pays tribute to his mother, who taught him that with hard work and education, he could realize his dreams. Maya Christina Gonzalez's spirited images perfectly complement each poem, bringing to life the people and places in Alarcon's childhood.

23. Brown, M. *Tito Puente, Mambo King/Rey Del Mambo*. HarperCollins, 2013. [Grade level: Preschool-3]

(From the publisher:)
In this vibrant bilingual picture book biography of musician Tito Puente, readers will dance along to the beat of this mambo king's life. Tito Puente loved banging pots and pans as a child, but what he really dreamed of was having his own band one day. From Spanish Harlem to the Grammy Awards—and all the beats in between—this is the true-life story of a boy whose passion for music turned him into the "King of Mambo." Award-winning author-illustrator duo Monica Brown and Rafael López bring the remarkable story of this talented legend to life in this Pura Belpré Honor Book. Supports the Common Core State Standards.

24. Brown, M. *Side by Side/Lado a lado: The Story of Dolores Huerta and César Chávez/La Historia de Dolores Huerta y César Chávez*. HarperCollins, 2010. [Grade level: Preschool-3; Lexile measure: 870L]

(From the publisher:)
Colorful, bilingual portrayal of the lives of Delores Huerta and César Chávez, who grew up as migrant workers and teamed to change conditions for generations to follow. Every day, thousands of farmworkers harvested the food that ended up on kitchen tables all over the country. But at the end of the day, when the workers sat down to eat, there were only beans on their own tables. Then Dolores Huerta and César Chávez teamed up. Together they motivated the workers to fight for their rights and, in the process, changed history. Award-winning author Monica Brown and acclaimed illustrator Joe Cepeda join together to create this stunning tribute to two of the most influential people of the twentieth century.

(Review from *Booklist*:)
This picture book pairs the dual stories of powerful activists César Chávez and Dolores Huerta. When Chávez was a child, his family lost their home and became migrant farmworkers, and Chávez had to drop out of school to work. As an adult, he continued to work in the fields. When Huerta was young, she moved to California, where her mother let poor farmworkers stay at her hotel for free, and when she grew up, she taught farmworkers' children. Each double-page spread features text in both Spanish and English, with Huerta's story on the left, and Chávez's on the right-hand side. Cepeda's bright mixed-media images convey the dramatic stories. One scene shows Chávez fleeing poisonous pesticides sprayed from an overhead plane, and in another, particularly striking spread, Chávez and Huerta come together to lead a 340-mile march to demand better living and working conditions for farmworkers. A long final note aimed at parents and teachers will also draw young readers, who can move from this introduction to longer biographies of the inspiring leaders.

25. Campoy, F. I. & Ada, F. A. *Tales Our Abuelitas Told: A Hispanic Folktale Collection*. Simon & Schuster, 2007. [Grade level: K-4]

(From the publisher:)
Once upon a time, in a land far away . . . These stories have journeyed far—over mountains, deserts, and oceans—carried by wind, passed on to us by our ancestors. Now they have found their way to you. A sly fox, a bird of a thousand colors, a magical set of bagpipes, and an audacious young girl . . . A mixture of popular tales and literary lore, this anthology celebrates Hispanic culture and its many roots—Indigenous, African, Arab, Hebrew, and Spanish. F. Isabel Campoy and Alma Flor Ada have retold twelve beloved stories that embody the lively spirit and the rich heritage of Latino people.

26. Garza, X. *Maximilian & the Mystery of the Guardian Angel: A Bilingual Lucha Libre Thriller*. Cinco Puntos Press, 2011. [Grade level: 2-5; Lexile measure: 820L]

(From the publisher:)
Margarito acts like any other eleven-year-old aficionado of lucha libre. He worships all the players. But in the summer just before sixth grade, he tumbles over the railing at a match in San Antonio and makes a connection to the world of Mexican wrestling that will ultimately connect him—maybe by blood!—to the greatest hero of all time: the Guardian Angel.

27. Krull, K., & Morales, Y. *Harvesting Hope: The Story of César Chávez*. San Diego, CA: Harcourt, 2003.

(From the publisher:)
César Chávez dedicated his life to helping American farmworkers. As a child growing up in California during the Great Depression, he picked produce with his family. César saw firsthand how unfairly workers were treated. As an adult, he organized farm workers into unions and argued for better pay and fair working conditions. He was jailed for his efforts, but he never stopped urging people to stand up for their rights. Young readers will be inspired by the fascinating life story of this champion of social justice.

28. Medina, J. *Juana and Lucas*. Candlewick, 2016. [Grade level: K-3]

(From the publisher:)
Juana loves many things — drawing, eating Brussels sprouts, living in Bogotá, Colombia, and especially her dog, Lucas, the best amigo ever. She does not love wearing her itchy school uniform, solving math problems, or going to dance class. And she especially does not love learning the English. Why is it so important to learn a language that makes so little sense? But when Juana's abuelos tell her about a special trip they are planning—one that Juana will need to speak English to go on—Juana begins to wonder whether learning the English might be a good use of her time after all. Hilarious, energetic, and utterly relatable, Juana will win over los corazones — the hearts — of readers everywhere in her first adventure, presented by namesake Juana Medina.

(From *School Library Journal*:)
Juana lives in Bogotá, Colombia, with her dog Lucas. She loves Brussels sprouts, drawing, and especially the comic book superhero Astroman. She most definitely does not like learning "the English." When her teacher says learning English is going to be a "ton of fun," Juana knows that it will really be "nada de fun." Her abuelo, or Abue for short, is a brain surgeon and tries to explain to Juana how learning English can be very useful. He also has a bribe—if Juana learns English, he will take her to the Spaceland amusement park in Florida, where only English is spoken, even by her hero Astroman. Medina has written a first-person narrative filled with expressive description. Spanish words are used throughout, and their meaning is made clear through context. As both author and illustrator, Medina is able to integrate the text and illustrations in unique ways, including spreads in which Juana tells us

why, for example, she strongly dislikes her school uniform or why Mami is the most important person in her life. Font design is also used creatively, such as when Medina traces the arc of a soccer ball hit hard enough to be sent "across the field." VERDICT: An essential selection that creates multicultural awareness, has distinguished and appealing design elements, and has a text that is the stuff of true literature.—Tim Wadham, formerly at Puyallup Public Library, WA.

29. Morales, Y. *Viva Frida*. Roaring Brook Press, 2014. [Grade level: K-4]

(From the publisher:)
Viva Frida is Yuyi Morales's love letter to Frida Kahlo. The depth of Morales's admiration for the groundbreaking Mexican surrealist painter comes through in every expertly prepared page spread. Morales incorporates acrylic painting, stop-motion puppetry, and other three-dimensional elements into a series of dioramas, photographed by her collaborator, Tim O'Meara. The result is eye-popping. Each spread bursts with jewel-like colors and captivating details, including Mexican textiles, bits of jewelry, and animal fur. Clay figures representing Frida, her husband, Diego, and their animal friends are central to each diorama. Readers familiar with Kahlo's work will recognize iconic elements in the injured fawn, the monkey, Frida's famous eyebrows, her hand-shaped earrings, and much more. A simple and brief poetic text in Spanish and English complements each page's visual design. *Viva Frida* is a stunner that understandably caught the attention of important list-makers.

30. Nye, N. S. *The Tree Is Older Than You Are: A Bilingual Gathering of Poems & Stories from Mexico*. Aladdin, 1998. [Grade level: 2-4]

(From the publisher:)
This gathering of poems and stories, told in both the original Spanish and translated English, transcends borders as it invites readers into a shared world of ideas, visions, and dreams. Sixty-four great Mexican writers and painters are collected here, including Rosario Castellanos, Alberta Blanco, Octavio Paz, and Julio Galan.

31. Otheguy, E. *Martí's Song for Freedom / Martí y sus versos por la Libertad*. Lee & Low Books, 2017. [Grade level: 3-7]

(From the publisher:)
A bilingual biography of José Martí, who dedicated his life to the promotion of liberty, the abolishment of slavery, political independence for Cuba, and intellectual freedom. Written in verse with excerpts from Martí's seminal work, *Versos Sencillos*.

(Review from *Kirkus Reviews*)
Weaving in work from poet and Cuban freedom fighter José Martí, Otheguy presents a sensitive portrayal of the revolutionary. Told in stanzas paired alongside Domínguez's Spanish translation, Martí's life story faces detailed, evocative full-page paintings, some painful (Martí witnessed the horrors of slavery), others celebratory. If the text sometimes feels workmanlike, it's only because the included bits of Martí's poetry are so strong and searing. In bringing an important life back into the conversation during divided political times, this book spotlights a steadfast hero and brilliant writer still worth admiring today.

(Review from *Booklist*:)
Cuban poet and political activist José Martí witnessed an injustice at a young age and gave his life trying to right that wrong. He opposed slavery in Cuba and knew that the only way to end it would be to free Cuba from Spain's rule. Cuban American author Otheguy illuminates the life of a young man endeavoring to make a difference through affecting bilingual verses, which make Cuba's complicated

history with slavery and colonialism accessible to young readers. By incorporating excerpts of Martí's writing into the narration, Otheguy introduces a new generation of readers to an important champion of human rights. Vidal's gouache artwork captures the beauty and the injustice of which Martí wrote, showcasing his country's vibrant colors, as in the pinks and oranges of the sunset, and illustrating the harsh treatment of enslaved Africans, who are shown performing backbreaking labor in sugarcane fields. Dominguez's excellent Spanish translation makes Martí's story available to a wide audience, and the text offers significant additional information via an afterword on Cuba's history, a selected bibliography, and excerpts from Martí's *Versos Sencillos*. Otheguy and Vidal tell a timely story that will inspire many to fight for equality and sings songs for freedom.—*Booklist,* starred review.

32. Schimel, L. *Let's Go See Papa!* Groundwood Books, 2011. [Grade level: 2-4]

(From the publisher:)
The little girl in this story likes Sundays best of all—it's the day her father calls. She hasn't seen him for over a year because he works far away across the ocean in the United States. She writes in her notebook every day, keeping a record of everything that happens to share with him when she finally sees him again. And she thinks about the fun they used to have when he was home—taking their dog Kika to the park and buying freshly baked bread together. Then one Sunday her father asks if she and her mother would like to join him, and she's surprised by her mixed feelings. It means leaving her grandmother, her friend . . . and Kika behind. This is a powerful story from a young child's perspective about what it's like to have an absent parent and to have to leave your home, country, and those you love for a new life.

(Review from *Publishers Weekly*:)
Rivera fills the pages with poignant, angular portraits and telling details. For some children (and even adults) it may be too somber, but there will be readers who will admire the heroine's stoicism and faith in the importance of having her family whole again. Reading level 2nd and 3rd grade; appropriate for read aloud Ages 4-7. *Publishers Weekly* Copyright PWxyz, LLC. All rights reserved.

33. Taylor, S. T. *Enrique Esparza and the Battle of the Alamo.* Lerner Publishing Group, 2011. [Grade level: 2-4]

(From the publisher:)
In early 1836, trouble broke out in Texas. Texas was part of Mexico, yet many of its settlers wanted to fight for independence. Mexican General Santa Anna and his army came to battle the Texans in San Antonio at the Alamo. Eight-year-old Enrique Esparza witnessed the battle. His father was a soldier with the Texas army. The whole Esparza family had taken shelter at the Alamo, but they knew it might be dangerous. Would they survive? In the back of this book, you'll find a script and instructions for putting on a reader's theater performance of this adventure. At our companion website—www.historyspeaksbooks.com—you can download additional copies of the script plus sound effects, background images, and more ideas that will help make your reader's theater performance a success.

34. Tonatiuh, D. *Pancho Rabbit and the Coyote: A Migrants Tale.* Abrams Books, 2013. [Grade level: 1-4]

(From the publisher:)
In this allegorical picture book, a young rabbit named Pancho eagerly awaits his papa's return. Papa Rabbit traveled north two years ago to find work in the great carrot and lettuce fields to earn money for his family. When Papa does not return, Pancho sets out to find him. He packs Papa's favorite meal—mole, rice and beans, a heap of warm tortillas, and a jug of aguamiel—and heads north. He meets a coyote, who offers to help Pancho in exchange for some of Papa's food. They travel together until the food is gone and the coyote decides he is still hungry . . . for Pancho! Duncan Tonatiuh brings to light the hardship and struggles faced by thousands of families who seek to make better lives for themselves and their children by illegally crossing the border.

35. Tonatiuh, D. *Separate is Never Equal: Sylvia Mendez and Her Family's Fight for Desegregation*. Harry N. Abrams, 2014. [Grade level: 1-4]

(From the publisher:)
Almost ten years before *Brown vs. Board of Education*, Sylvia Mendez and her parents helped end school segregation in California. An American citizen of Mexican and Puerto Rican heritage who spoke and wrote perfect English, Mendez was denied enrollment to a "Whites only" school. Her parents took action by organizing the Hispanic community and filing a lawsuit in federal district court. Their success eventually brought an end to the era of segregated education in California.

36. Torres, J. *Finding the Music/En Pos de la Música*. Lee & Low Books, 2015. [Grade level: 1-5]

(From the publisher:)
When Reyna accidentally breaks Abuelito's vihuela, a small guitar-like instrument, she ventures out into the neighborhood determined to find someone who can help her repair it. No one can fix the vihuela, but along the way Reyna gathers stories and mementos of Abuelito and his music. Still determined, Reyna visits the music store, where the owner gives her a recording of Abuelito's music and promises that they can fix the vihuela together. Reyna realizes how much she's learned about Abuelito, his influence in the community, and the power of his music. She returns to her family's restaurant to share Abuelito's gifts with Mama and is happier still finally to hear the sweet sounds of Abuelito's music for herself. With lively illustrations by Renato Alarcão, the tradition of mariachi music comes to life in this bilingual story. Winner of Lee & Low's New Voices Award, *Finding the Music* is a heartwarming tale of family, community, and the music that brings them all together.

(From *School Library Journal*:)
Torres, winner of the 2011 Lee & Low Books New Voices Award, here offers readers a charming bilingual story that showcases the power of music as an intergenerational unifier. . . A rich addition for those who enjoy music and its influence in community and family unity.—Sujei Lugo, Boston Public Library, MA.

37. Warren, S. E., & Casilla, R. *Dolores Huerta: A Hero to Migrant Workers*. Las Vegas, NV: Two Lions, 2012.

(From the publisher:)
Dolores is a teacher, a mother, and a friend. She wants to know why her students are too hungry to listen, why they don't have shoes to wear to school. Dolores is a warrior, an organizer, and a peacemaker. When she finds out that the farm workers in her community are poorly paid and working under dangerous conditions, she stands up for their rights. This is the story of Dolores Huerta and the extraordinary battle she waged to ensure fair and safe workplaces for migrant workers. The powerful text, paired with Robert Casilla's vibrant watercolor-and-pastel illustrations, brings Dolores's amazing journey to life A timeline, additional reading, articles, websites, and resources for teachers are included.

4th Grade – 5th Grade
38. Argueta, J. *Somos Como Las Nubes We Are Like the Clouds*. Groundwood Books, 2016. [Grade level: 4-6]

(From the publisher:)
Why are young people leaving their country to walk to the United States to seek a new, safe home? Over 100,000 such children have left Central America. This book of poetry helps us to understand why and what it is like to be them. This powerful book by award-winning Salvadoran poet Jorge Argueta describes the terrible process that leads young people to undertake the extreme hardships and risks involved in the journey to what they hope will be a new life of safety and opportunity. A refugee from El Salvador's war in the eighties, Argueta was born to explain the tragic choice confronting

young Central Americans today who are saying goodbye to everything they know because they fear for their lives. This book brings home their situation and will help young people who are living in safety to understand those who are not.

(From *Publishers Weekly*:)
"Compelling, timely and eloquent, this book is beautifully illustrated by master artist Alfonso Ruano ... Poems written in Spanish and English poignantly address the struggles of child refugees fleeing Central America for the US. Ages 7–12. (Oct.)" *Publishers Weekly* Copyright PWxyz, LLC. All rights reserved.

39. Alvarez, J. *Return to Sender*. Alfred A. Knopf, 2009. [Grade level: 4-6; Lexile Measure: 890L]

(From Scholastic:)
"After Tyler's father is injured in a tractor accident, his family is forced to hire migrant Mexican workers to help save their Vermont farm from foreclosure."

40. Bigelow, B., & Peterson, B. *Rethinking Columbus: The Next 500 Years*, 2nd ed. Milwaukee, WI: Rethinking Schools, 1998.

(From the publisher:)
Why rethink Christopher Columbus? Because the Columbus myth is a foundation of children's beliefs about society. Columbus is often a child's first lesson about encounters between different cultures and races. The murky legend of a brave adventurer tells children whose version of history to accept, and whose to ignore. It says nothing about the brutality of the European invasion of North America. We need to listen to a wider range of voices. We need to hear from those whose lands and rights were taken away by those who "discovered" them. Their stories, too often suppressed, tell of 500 years of courageous struggle, and the lasting wisdom of native peoples. Understanding what really happened to them in 1492 is key to understanding why people suffer the same injustices today. More than eighty essays, poems, interviews, historical vignettes, and lesson plans reevaluate the myth of Columbus and issues of indigenous rights. *Rethinking Columbus* is packed with useful teaching ideas for kindergarten through college.

41. Carlson L. M., ed. *Cool Salsa: Bilingual Poems on Growing Up Latino in the United States*. Square Fish, 2013. [Grade level: 4-5]

(From the publisher:)
Growing up Latino in America means speaking two languages, living two lives, learning the rules of two cultures. *Cool Salsa* celebrates the tones, rhythms, sounds, and experiences of that double life. Here are poems about families and parties, insults and sad memories, hot dogs and mangos, the sweet syllables of Spanish and the snag-toothed traps of English. Here is the glory—and pain—of being Latino American. Latino Americans hail from Cuba and California, Mexico and Michigan, Nicaragua and New York, and editor Lori M. Carlson has made sure to capture all of those accents. With poets such as Sandra Cisneros, Martín Espada, Gary Soto, and Ed Vega, and a very personal introduction by Oscar Hijuelos, this collection encompasses the voices of Latino America. By selecting poems about the experiences of teenagers, Carlson has given a focus to that rich diversity; by presenting the poems both in their original language and in translation, she has made them available to us all. As you move from memories of red wagons to dreams of orange trees to fights with street gangs, you feel *Cool Salsa*'s musical and emotional cross rhythms. Here is a world of exciting poetry for you, y tú también.

(Review from *School Library Journal*:)
"The Spanish translations capture the sense of the English so well that without the translator's byline one would be hard pressed to discern the original language. The same is true for those few poems translated from Spanish to English. This is . . . excellent enrichment material for literature courses."

42. King, T., & Monkman, K. *A Coyote Columbus Story*. Toronto ON: Groundwood Books, 2018.

(From the publisher:)
A retelling of the Christopher Columbus story from a Native point of view turns this tale on its ear! Coyote, the trickster, creates the world and all the creatures in it. She is able to control all events to her advantage until a funny-looking red-haired man named Columbus changes her plans. He is unimpressed by the wealth of moose, turtles, and beavers in Coyote's land. Instead he is interested in the human beings he can take to sell in Spain. Thomas King uses a bag of literary tricks to shatter the stereotypes surrounding Columbus's voyages. In doing so, he invites children to laugh with him at the crazy antics of Coyote, who unwittingly allows Columbus to bring about the downfall of her human friends. And he makes the point that history is influenced by the culture of the reporter.

43. McCall, G. G. *Summer of the Mariposas*. Tu Books, 2012. [Grade level: 4-5; Lexile 840]

(From the publisher:)
When Odilia and her four sisters find a dead body in the swimming hole, they embark on a hero's journey to return the dead man to his family in Mexico. But returning home to Texas turns into an odyssey that would rival Homer's original tale. With the supernatural aid of ghostly La Llorona via a magical earring, Odilia and her little sisters travel a road of tribulation to their long-lost grandmother's house. Along the way, they must outsmart a witch and her Evil Trinity: a wily warlock, a coven of vicious half-human barn owls, and a bloodthirsty livestock-hunting chupacabra. Can these fantastic trials prepare Odilia and her sisters for what happens when they face their final test, returning home to the real world, where goddesses and ghosts can no longer help them?

44. Mills, D. *La Frontera: El Viaje con Papa / My Journey with Papa*. Chicago: American Library Association, 2018.

(From the publisher:)
Join a young boy and his father on a daring journey from Mexico to Texas to find a new life. They'll need all the resilience and courage they can muster to safely cross the border—la frontera—and to make a home for themselves in a new land.

45. Petrillo, V. *A kid's Guide to Latino History: More than 50 Activities*. Chicago Review Press, 2009. [Grade level: 2-4]

(From *School Library Journal*:)
History and hands-on activities introduce children to the Latino cultures that are shaping our society. The book addresses a broad historical scope, from pre-Columbian culture in the Americas to present-day debates about undocumented immigration to the United States. . . . An excellent resource for enriching children's understanding of these cultures.—Mary Landrum, Lexington Public Library, KY.

46. Perez, A. I. *My Diary from Here to There: Mi diario de aquí hasta allá*. Children's Book Press, 2002. [Grade level: 3-5]

(From the publisher:)
This English/Spanish story begins as young Amada overhears her parents whisper of moving from Mexico to Los Angeles, where greater opportunity awaits. As she and her family journey north, Amada

records in her diary her fears, hopes, and dreams for their lives in the United States. Full-color illustrations.

47. Roback, D., J. M. Brown, and J. Britton. *My Diary from Here to There / Mi Diario de aqui hasta alla*. San Francisco, CA: Children's Book Press, 2002.

(From the publisher:)
A young girl describes her feelings when her father decides to leave their home in Mexico to work in the United States.

48. Ryan, M. P. *The Dreamer / El Soñador*. Scholastic, 2010. [Grade level: 3-6]

(From the publisher:)
Neftalí is a dreamer. He loves words, birds, forests, and the sky. But his father expects him to be practical, concentrate on his studies, and prepare for a career in business. Slowly Neftalí learns to believe in himself, defy his father, and trust his own vision . . . a vision that makes him grow up to become one of the foremost poets of the twentieth century. This imaginative exploration of the boyhood of Pablo Neruda takes readers on a rare journey of the heart and imagination, and brings hope and confidence to every child who has struggled against the odds and dreamed of a larger world.

49. Soto, G. *The Skirt*. Demco Media, 1994. [Grade level: 4-6]

(From the publisher:)
Miata has left the beautiful folklórico skirt her mother wore in Mexico on the bus. She was going to wear the skirt on Sunday when her dance group performed folklórico. Can Miata and her friend Ana rescue the precious skirt in time? A warm-hearted story about a contemporary Mexican American family. "Light, easy reading . . . offering readers a cast and situations with which to identify, whatever their own ethnic origins." — *The Bulletin*.

50. Stavans, I. *Wachale!: Poetry and Prose about Growing Up Latino in America*. Cricket Books/Marcaot, 2001. [Grade level: 3-6]

(From the publisher:)
This groundbreaking bilingual anthology, carefully designed for middle readers, is a mosaic of voices demonstrating the energy, creativity, and diversity of the fastest-growing minority group in America. Wachale! (Spanglish for "watch out!") includes folk tales, stories, and poems in both English and Spanish, and brief autobiographical essays by both well-established and emerging writers representing all shades of Latinos, such as Chicanos in the Southwest, Puerto Ricans in New York, and Cubans in Florida, as well as Dominicans, Guatemalans, and other subgroups. Geared toward ten- to thirteen-year-olds, this is a window to Latino experiences north of the Rio Grande.

51. Tafolla, C., Teneyuca, S., & Ybáñez, T. *That's Not Fair: Emma Tenayuca's Struggle for Justice = No Es Justo! : La lucha de Emma Tenayuca por la Justicia*. San Antonio, TX: Wings Press, 2008.

(From the publisher:)
A vivid depiction of the early injustices encountered by a young Mexican-American girl in San Antonio in the 1920s, this book tells the true story of Emma Tenayuca. Emma learns to care deeply about poverty and hunger during a time when many Mexican Americans were starving to death and working unreasonably long hours at slave wages in the city's pecan-shelling factories. Through astute perception, caring, and personal action, Emma begins to get involved, and eventually, at the age of twenty-one, leads 12,000 workers in the first significant historical action in the Mexican American

struggle for justice. Emma Tenayuca's story serves as a model for young and old alike about courage, compassion, and the role everyone can play in making the world more fair.

52. Tonatiuh, D. *Funny Bones: Posada and His Day of the Dead Calaveras*. Harry N. Abrams, 2015. [Grade level: 2-5]

(From the publisher:)
Funny Bones tells the story of how the amusing calaveras—skeletons performing various every day or festive activities—came to be. They are the creation of Mexican artist José Guadalupe (Lupe) Posada (1852–1913). In a country that was not known for freedom of speech, he first drew political cartoons, much to the amusement of the local population but not the politicians. He continued to draw cartoons throughout much of his life, but he is best known today for his calavera drawings. They have become synonymous with Mexico's Día de los Muertos (Day of the Dead) festival. Juxtaposing his own art with that of Lupe's, author Duncan Tonatiuh brings to light the remarkable life and work of a man whose art is beloved by many but whose name has remained in obscurity. The book includes an author's note, bibliography, glossary, and index.

(From *School Library Journal*:)
"The beautifully expressive Day of the Dead-inspired illustrations on heavy paper pages sport borders of bones, grinning skeletons, and Tonatiuh's signature figures shown in profile, influenced by the ancient Mexican art of his ancestors. . . . A stunning work, with great possibilities for lesson plans or tie-ins with Day of the Dead.—Toby Rajput, National Louis University, Skokie, IL

53. Tonatiah, D. *Danza!: Amalia Hernández and El Ballet Folklórico de México*. Harry N. Abrams, 2017. [Grade level: 1-6]

(From the publisher:)
Danza! is a celebration of Hernández's life and of the rich history of dance in Mexico. As a child, Amalia always thought she would grow up to be a teacher until she saw a performance of dancers in her town square. She was fascinated by the way the dancers twirled and swayed, and she knew that someday she would be a dancer, too. She began to study many different types of dance, including ballet and modern, under some of the best teachers in the world. Hernández traveled throughout Mexico studying and learning regional dances. Soon she founded her own dance company, El Ballet Folklórico de México, where she integrated her knowledge of ballet and modern dance with folkloric dances. The group began to perform all over the country and soon all over the world, becoming an international sensation that still tours today.

(From *School Library Journal*:)
"Part biography and part homage to the history of Mexican dance, this essential, first-ever children's biography of Amalia Hernández is a vivid celebration of Mexican culture, art, and life, and a timely release in anticipation of the 100th anniversary of Hernández's birth."—Natalie Romano, Denver Public Library

6th Grade – 8th Grade, Middle School TEKS

■ *Grade 6: People, Places, and Societies of the Contemporary World*
■ *Grade 7: Texas*
■ *Grade 8: History of the US, Colonial through Reconstruction*

1. Ada, A. F. *Under the Royal Palms: A Childhood in Cuba.* New York: Antheneum Books for Young Readers, 1998. [Grade level: 4-7]

   (From the publisher:)
   In this companion volume to Alma Flor Ada's *Where the Flame Trees Bloom,* the author offers young readers another inspiring collection of stories and reminiscences drawn from her childhood on the island of Cuba. Through those stories we see how the many events and relationships she enjoyed helped shape who she is today. Heartwarming, poignant, and often humorous, this collection encourages children to discover the stories in their own lives—stories that can help inform their own values and celebrate the joys and struggles we all share no matter where or when we grew up.

2. Ada, F. A. *Yes! We Are Latinos* Wattertown, MA: Charlesbridge, 2016. [Grade level: 8-12]

   (From the publisher:)
   Thirteen young Latinos and Latinas living in America are introduced in this book celebrating the rich diversity of the Latino and Latina experience in the United States. Free-verse fictional narratives from the perspective of each youth provide specific stories and circumstances for the reader to better understand the Latino people's quest for identity. Each profile is followed by nonfiction prose that further clarifies the character's background and history, touching upon important events in the history of the Latino American people, such as the Spanish Civil War, immigration to the US, and the internment of Latinos with Japanese ancestry during World War II.

3. Agosin, M. and L. White. *I Lived on Butterfly Hill.* New York: Atheneum Books for Young Readers, 2015. [Grade level: 5-9 / Age 10-14]

   (From the publisher:)
   Celeste Marconi is a dreamer. She lives peacefully among friends and neighbors and family in the idyllic town of Valparaiso, Chile—until the time comes when even Celeste, with her head in the clouds, can't deny the political unrest that is sweeping through the country. Warships are spotted in the harbor, and schoolmates disappear from class without a word. Celeste doesn't quite know what is happening, but one thing is clear: no one is safe, not anymore. The country has been taken over by a government that declares artists, protestors, and anyone who helps the needy to be considered "subversive" and dangerous to Chile's future. So Celeste's parents—her educated, generous, kind parents—must go into hiding before they, too, "disappear." To protect their daughter, they send her to America. As Celeste adapts to her new life in Maine, she never stops dreaming of Chile. But even after democracy is restored to her home country, questions remain: Will her parents reemerge from hiding? Will she ever be truly safe again? Accented with interior artwork, steeped in the history of Pinochet's catastrophic takeover of Chile, and based on many true events, this multicultural ode to the power of revolution, words, and love is both indelibly brave and heartwrenchingly graceful.

4. Alvarez, Julia. *Return to Sender.* New York: Yearling, 2010. [Grade level: 3-7 / Age 8-12]

   (From the publisher:)
   After Tyler's father is injured in a tractor accident, his family is forced to hire migrant Mexican workers to help save their Vermont farm from foreclosure. Tyler isn't sure what to make of these workers. Are they undocumented? And what about the three daughters, particularly Mari, the oldest, who is proud of her Mexican heritage but also increasingly connected to her American life. Her family lives

in constant fear of being discovered by the authorities and sent back to the poverty they left behind in Mexico. Can Tyler and Mari find a way to be friends despite their differences? In a novel full of hope, but with no easy answers, Julia Alvarez weaves a beautiful and timely story that will stay with readers long after they finish it.

5. Brown, S. *Caminar*. Sommerville, MA: Candlewick, 2016. [Grade level: 6-8]

(From the publisher:)
Carlos knows that when the soldiers arrive with warnings about the Communist rebels, it is time to be a man and defend the village, keep everyone safe. But Mama tells him not yet—he's still her quiet moonfaced boy. The soldiers laugh at the villagers, and before they move on, a neighbor is found dangling from a tree, a sign on his neck: Communist. Mama tells Carlos to run and hide, then try to find her . . . Numb and alone, he must join a band of guerillas as they trek to the top of the mountain where Carlos's abuela lives. Will he be in time, and brave enough, to warn them about the soldiers? What will he do then? A novel in verse inspired by actual events during Guatemala's civil war, *Caminar* is the moving story of a boy who loses nearly everything before discovering who he really is.

6. Delacre, L. *US in Progress: Short Stories about Young Latinos*. New York: HarperCollins, 2017. [Grade level: 3-7]

(From the publisher:)
Acclaimed author and Pura Belpré Award honoree Lulu Delacre's beautifully illustrated collection of twelve short stories is a groundbreaking look at the diverse Latinxs who live in the United States. In this book, you will meet many young Latinxs living in the United States, from a young girl whose day at her father's burrito truck surprises her to two sisters working together to change the older sister's immigration status, and more. Turn the pages to experience life through the eyes of these boys and girls whose families originally hail from many different countries; see their hardships, celebrate their victories, and come away with a better understanding of what it means to be Latino in the US today.

7. Diaz, A. *The Only Road*. New York. Simon & Schuster, 2016. [Grade level: 3-7]

(From the publisher:)
Jaime is sitting on his bed drawing when he hears a scream. Instantly he knows: Miguel, his cousin and best friend, is dead. Everyone in Jaime's small town in Guatemala knows someone who has been killed by the Alphas, a powerful gang that's known for violence and drug trafficking. Anyone who refuses to work for them is hurt or killed—like Miguel. With Miguel gone, Jaime fears that he is next. There's only one choice: Accompanied by his cousin Ángela, Jaime must flee his home to live with his older brother in the United States. Inspired by true incidents, *The Only Road* tells an individual story of a boy who feels that leaving his home and risking everything is his only chance for a better life. It is a story of fear and bravery, love and loss, strangers becoming family, and one boy's treacherous and life-changing journey. Jamie and Ángela's experiences may be unapologetically realistic, but they also demonstrate the resiliency of the human spirit.

8. Engle, M. *Bravo! Poems about Amazing Hispanics*. New York: Henry Holt and Co., 2017. [Grade level: 3-7]

(From the publisher:)
Musician, botanist, baseball player, pilot—the Hispanics featured in this collection come from many different backgrounds and from many different countries. Celebrate their accomplishments and their contributions to collective history and a community that continues to evolve and thrive today! Poems spotlight Aida de Acosta, Arnold Rojas, Baruj Benacerraf, César Chávez, Fabiola Cabeza de Vaca, Félix Varela, George Meléndez Wright, José Martí, Juan de Miralles, Juana Briones, Julia de Burgos, Louis

Agassiz Fuertes, Paulina Pedroso, Pura Belpré, Roberto Clemente, Tito Puente, Tomás Rivera, and Ynés Mexia.

9. Engle, M. *Silver people: Voices from the Panama Canal.* New York: HMH Books for Young Readers, 2016. [Grade level: 7-9]

(From the publisher:)
One hundred years ago, the world celebrated the opening of the Panama Canal, which connected the world's two largest oceans and signaled America's emergence as a global superpower. It was a miracle, this path of water where a mountain had stood—and creating a miracle is no easy thing. Thousands lost their lives, and those who survived worked under the harshest conditions for only a few silver coins a day. From the young "silver people" whose back-breaking labor built the Canal to the denizens of the endangered rainforest itself, this is the story of one of the largest and most difficult engineering projects ever undertaken, as only Newbery Honor-winning author Margarita Engle could tell it.

10. Grande, R. *The Distance Between Us: A Memoir.* New York: Washington Square Press, 2013. [Grade level: 3-7 / Age 8-12]

(From the publisher:)
The original version of this memoir was written for general audiences. This review is based on an advance reader's copy of the young readers' edition.

(Description and review by Lila Quintero Weaver:)
Echoes of Cinderella reverberate throughout Reyna Grande's forceful and captivating memoir of a family torn apart by internal and external stressors, centered in a years-long separation across the US-Mexico border. Due to the physical and cultural distances that develop between members of the family, Reyna spends much of her childhood feeling like an orphan. The memoir begins as her mother, Juana, leaves Reyna and her two siblings under the care of Evila, the children's paternal grandmother. Motivated by the promise of steady work and higher wages, Reyna's father has already left Mexico for El Otro Lado, and this happened so long ago that four-year-old Reyna must rely on a framed photo to remember what he looks like. Later, Juana decides she must migrate, too, and although she vows to return within a year, the separation stretches out much longer, stranding her children—Reyna, Mago, and Carlos—in a bleak, loveless existence. Even as the three siblings tend to chores and subsist on meager rations, Abuelita Evila lavishes treats and special privileges on Élida, another grandchild living under her roof. Although some of Élida's spoils come from the money that Juana and her husband send for their children's necessities, the couple remains unaware of these abuses. Each time they call to speak with their kids, Evila hovers nearby to make sure they don't disclose anything negative. When Juana returns from her two-and-a-half year absence, she is almost unrecognizable to Reyna. Her hair is dyed bright red, her clothes are much fancier than anything she used to wear, and there is a new baby in her arms. Worse yet, she demonstrates a chilling degree of detachment toward her children. Before long, Juana acquires a boyfriend and foists all four kids off on their other abuelita—a far poorer, but kinder woman whose house is a one-room shack constructed of bamboo sticks. A river nearby subjects the house to serious flooding.

11. Joseph, L. *The Color of My Words.* New York: HarperCollins, 2019. [Grade level: 3-7]

(From the publisher:)
Twelve-year-old Ana Rosa is a blossoming writer growing up in the Dominican Republic, a country where words are feared. Yet there is so much inspiration all around her—watching her brother search for a future, learning to dance and to love, and finding out what it means to be part of a community—that Ana Rosa must write it all down. As she struggles to find her own voice and a way to make it

heard, Ana Rosa realizes the power of her words to transform the world around her—and to transcend the most unthinkable of tragedies.

12. Soto, G. *Jessie de La Cruz: Profile of a United Farm Worker.* New York: Persea Books, 2001. [Grade level: 6-9]

(From the publisher:)
This inspiring story of Jessie De La Cruz, the United Farmer Workers, and la Causa is told as only Gary Soto—novelist, essayist, poet, and himself a field laborer during his teens—can tell it, with respect, empathy, and deep compassion for the working poor. A field worker from the age of five, Jessie knew poverty, harsh working conditions, and the exploitation of Mexicans and all poor people. Her response was to take a stand. She joined the fledgling United Farm Workers union and, at Cesar Chavez's request, became its first woman recruiter. She also participated in strikes, helped ban the crippling short-handle hoe, became a delegate to the Democratic National Convention, testified before the Senate, and met with the Pope. Jessie's life story personalizes an historical movement and shows teens how an ordinary woman became extraordinary through her will to make change happen, not just for herself but for others.

13. Weaver, L. Q. *My Year in the Middle.* Somerville, MA: Candlewick, 2018. [Grade level: 3-7]

(From the publisher:)
In a racially polarized classroom in 1970 Alabama, Lu's talent for running track makes her a new best friend—and tests her mettle as she navigates the school's social cliques. *Miss Garrett's classroom is like every other at our school. White kids sit on one side and black kids on the other. I'm one of the few middle-rowers who split the difference.* Sixth-grader Lu Olivera just wants to keep her head down and get along with everyone in her class. Trouble is, Lu's old friends have been changing lately—acting boy crazy and making snide remarks about Lu's newfound talent for running track. Lu's secret hope for a new friend is fellow runner Belinda Gresham, but in 1970 Red Grove, Alabama, blacks and whites don't mix. As segregationist ex-governor George Wallace ramps up his campaign against the current governor, Albert Brewer, growing tensions in the state—and in the classroom—mean that Lu can't stay neutral about the racial divide at school. Will she find the gumption to stand up for what's right and to choose friends who do the same?

9th Grade – 12th Grade, High School TEKS
- *Grade 9: World Geography*
- *Grade 10: World History*
- *Grade 11: US History Since 1877*
- *Grade 12: US Government*

14. Alsaid, A. *North of Happy.* New York: Harlequin Teen, 2017. [Grade level: YA]

(From the publisher:)
Carlos Portillo has always led a privileged and sheltered life. A dual citizen of Mexico and the US, he lives in Mexico City with his wealthy family, where he attends an elite international school. Always a rule follower and a parent pleaser, Carlos is more than happy to tread the well-worn path in front of him. He has always loved food and cooking, but his parents see it as just a hobby. When his older brother, Felix—who has dropped out of college to live a life of travel—is tragically killed, Carlos begins hearing his brother's voice, giving him advice and pushing him to rebel against his father's plan for him. Worrying about his mental health, but knowing the voice is right, Carlos runs away to the United States and manages to secure a job with his favorite celebrity chef. As he works to improve his skills in the kitchen and pursue his dream, he begins to fall for his boss's daughter—a fact that could end his career before it begins. Finally living for himself, Carlos must decide what's most important to him and where his true path really lies.

15. Andreu, M. E. *The Secret Side of Empty*. New York: Running Press Kids, 2015. [Grade level: YA]

(From the publisher:)
M.T. is undocumented. But she keeps that a secret. As a straight-A student with a budding romance and loyal best friend, M.T.'s life seems as apple-pie American as her blondish hair and pale skin. But she hides two facts to the contrary: her full name of Monserrat Thalia and her status as an undocumented immigrant. But it's getting harder to hide now that M.T.'s a senior. Her school's National Honor Society wants her to plan their trip abroad, her best friend won't stop bugging her to get her driver's license, and all everyone talks about is where they want to go to college. M.T. is pretty sure she can't go to college, and with high school ending and her family life unraveling, she's staring down a future that just seems hopeless. In the end, M.T. will need to trust herself and others to stake a claim in the life that she wants. Told in M.T.'s darkly funny voice and full of nuanced characters, *The Secret Side of Empty* is a poignant but unsentimental look at what it's like to live as an "illegal" immigrant, how we're shaped by the secrets we keep, and how the human spirit ultimately always triumphs.

16. Canales, V. *The Tequila Worm*. New York: Wendy Lamb Books, 2017. [Grade level: YA]

(From the publisher:)
Sofia comes from a family of storytellers. Here are her tales of growing up in the barrio, full of the magic and mystery of family traditions: making Easter *cascarones*, celebrating el Día de los Muertos, preparing for quinceañera, rejoicing in the Christmas *nacimiento*, and curing homesickness by eating the tequila worm. When Sofia is singled out to receive a scholarship to an elite boarding school, she longs to explore life beyond the barrio, even though it means leaving her family to navigate a strange world of rich, privileged kids. It's a different *mundo*, but one where Sofia's traditions take on new meaning and illuminate her path.

17. Chambers, V. *The Go Between*. New York: Delacorte Press, 2017. [Grade level: 7-12]

(From the publisher:)
She is the envy of every teenage girl in Mexico City. Her mother is a glamorous telenovela actress. Her father is the go-to voiceover talent for blockbuster films. Hers is a world of private planes, chauffeurs, paparazzi, and gossip columnists. Meet Camilla del Valle, or Cammi to those who know her best. When Cammi's mom gets cast in an American television show and the family moves to LA, things change, and quickly. Her mom's first role is playing a not-so-glamorous maid in a sitcom. Her dad tries to find work, but dreams about returning to Mexico. And at the posh, private Polestar Academy, Cammi's new friends assume she is a scholarship kid, the daughter of a domestic. At first Cammi thinks that playing along with the stereotypes will teach her new friends a lesson. But the more she lies, the more she wonders: Is she only fooling herself?

18. Cofer, Judith Ortiz. *The Line of the Sun*. Athens, GA: University of Georgia Press, 1989. [Grade level: YA]

(From the publisher:)
María is a girl caught between two worlds: Puerto Rico, where she was born, and New York, where she now lives in a basement apartment in the barrio. While her mother remains on the island, María lives with her father, the super of their building. As she struggles to lose her island accent, María does her best to find her place within the unfamiliar culture of the barrio. Finally, with the Spanglish of the barrio people ringing in her ears, she finds the poet within herself. In lush prose and spare, evocative poetry, Pura Belpré Award-winner Judith Ortiz Cofer weaves a powerful and emotionally satisfying novel, bursting with life and hope.

19. Engle, M. *The Surrender Tree: Poems of Cuba's Struggle for Freedom.* New York: Square Fish, 2010. [Grade level: YA]

(From the publisher:)
It is 1896. Cuba has fought three wars for independence and still is not free. People have been rounded up in reconcentration camps with too little food and too much illness. Rosa is a nurse, but she dares not go to the camps. So she turns hidden caves into hospitals for those who know how to find her. Black, white, Cuban, Spanish—Rosa does her best for everyone. Yet who can heal a country so torn apart by war? Acclaimed poet Margarita Engle has created another breathtaking portrait of Cuba. *The Surrender Tree* is a 2009 Newbery Honor Book, the winner of the 2009 Pura Belpré Medal for Narrative and the 2009 Bank Street—Claudia Lewis Award, and a 2009 Bank Street—Best Children's Book of the Year.

20. Engle, M. *The Poet Slave of Cuba: A Biography of Juan Francisco Manzano.* New York: Square Fish, 2011. [Grade Level: YA]

(From the publisher:)
A lyrical biography of a Cuban slave who escaped to become a celebrated poet. Born into the household of a wealthy slave owner in Cuba in 1797, Juan Francisco Manzano spent his early years by the side of a woman who made him call her Mama, even though he had a mama of his own. Denied an education, young Juan still showed an exceptional talent for poetry. His verses reflect the beauty of his world, but they also expose its hideous cruelty. Powerful, haunting poems and breathtaking illustrations create a portrait of a life in which even the pain of slavery could not extinguish the capacity for hope. *The Poet Slave of Cuba* is the winner of the 2008 Pura Belpre Medal for Narrative and a 2007 Bank Street—Best Children's Book of the Year.

21. Grande, R. *Across A Hundred Mountains.* New York: Washington Square Post, 2007. [Grade level: YA]

(From the publisher:)
Across a Hundred Mountains is a stunning and poignant story of migration, loss, and discovery as two women—one born in Mexico, one in the United States—find their lives joined in the most unlikely way. After a tragedy separates her from her mother, Juana Garcia leaves her small town in Mexico to find her father, who left his home and family two years before to find work in America, el otro lado, and rise above the oppressive poverty so many of his countrymen endure. Out of money and in need of someone to help her across the border, Juana meets Adelina Vasquez, a young woman who left her family in California to follow her lover to Mexico. Finding each other—in a Tijuana jail—in desperate circumstances, they offer each other much needed material and spiritual support and ultimately become linked forever in the most unexpected way. The phenomenon of Mexican immigration to the United States is one of the most controversial issues of our time. While it is often discussed in terms of the political and economic implications, Grande, with this brilliant debut novel and her own profound insider's perspective, puts a human face on the subject. Who are the men, women, and children whose lives are affected by the forces that propel so many to risk life and limb, crossing the border in pursuit of a better life?

22. Jaramillo, A. *La Linea: A Novel.* New York: Square Fish, 2006. [Grade level: YA]

(From the publisher:)
Miguel has dreamed of joining his parents in California since the day they left him behind in Mexico six years, eleven months, and twelve days ago. On the morning of his fifteenth birthday, Miguel's wait is over. Or so he thinks. The trip north to the border—*la línea*—is fraught with dangers. Thieves. Border guards. And a grueling, two-day trek across the desert. It would be hard enough to survive alone.

But it's almost impossible with his tagalong sister in tow. Their money gone and their hopes nearly dashed, Miguel and his sister have no choice but to hop the infamous *mata gente* as it races toward the border. As they cling to the roof of the speeding train, they hold onto each other, and to their dreams. But they quickly learn that you can't always count on dreams—even the ones that come true.

Note: Readers will encounter frequent terms and phrases in Spanish, not always translated, but whose meanings are usually discernible through context.

23. Jensen, K. *Here we are: Feminism for the Real World.* Chapel Hill: Algonquin Young Readers, 2017. [Grade level: YA]

(From the publisher:)
Let's get the feminist party started! *Here We Are* is a scrapbook-style teen guide to understanding what it really means to be a feminist. It's packed with essays, lists, poems, comics, and illustrations from a diverse range of voices, including TV, film, and pop-culture celebrities and public figures such as ballet dancer Michaela DePrince and her sister Mia, politician Wendy Davis, as well as popular YA authors like Nova Ren Suma, Malinda Lo, Brandy Colbert, Courtney Summers, and many more. Altogether, the book features more than forty-four pieces, with an eight-page insert of full-color illustrations. *Here We Are* is a response to lively discussions about the true meaning of feminism on social media and across popular culture and is an invitation to one of the most important, life-changing, and exciting parties around.

Note: Three essays in particular are from a Latino perspective: "Pretty Enough" by Alida Nugent, "The 'Nice Girl' Feminist" by Ashley Hope Pérez, and "Many Stories, Many Roads" by Daniel José Older.

24. Jimenez, J. *Bloodline.* Houston: Pinata Books Arte Publico Press, 2016. [Grade level: YA]

(From the publisher:)
In his junior year, seventeen-year-old Abraham learns how to drive a stick shift. He falls in love for the first time. And he has been in three fights and suspended twice, all before Thanksgiving. His grandmother and her girlfriend, the ones who have raised him, fear for his life and the hard future that awaits him. "He needs a father," his grandmother says. "He needs a man. I can't do this, Becky. We can't. Not on our own." Soon, his Uncle Claudio, the son with a fat police file who has hurt his mother so many times, is back in the house. Determined to make a man of his nephew, he takes the boy to the gym and shows him how to use free weights and become bigger and stronger. Meanwhile, Abraham's feelings for his friend Ophelia grow, and she tries to understand why he fights. "This will end badly," she warns. "Nothing good can come from this." At school, Abraham learns about genetics, and he wonders if people are born bad. Is it in their DNA? Was he born to punch and kick and scream and fight and destroy things because of the genes in his body? Is that what happened to his father? All he knows is that his father is dead and his mother is gone. In Joe Jimenez's striking debut novel for teens, a young man struggles with his family's refusal to talk about the violence that has plagued it and what it means to become a man. Does a boy need a father to become a good man?

25. Manzano, S. *The Revolution of Evelyn Serrana.* New York: Scholastic Press. 2014. [Grade level: YA]

(From the publisher:)
There are two secrets Evelyn Serrano is keeping from her Mami and Papo: her true feelings about growing up in her Spanish Harlem neighborhood, and her attitude about Abuela, her sassy grandmother who's come from Puerto Rico to live with them. Then, like an urgent ticking clock, events erupt that change everything. The Young Lords, a Puerto Rican activist group, dump garbage in the street and set it on fire, igniting a powerful protest. When Abuela steps in to take charge, Evelyn is thrust into the action. Tempers flare, loyalties are tested. Through it all, Evelyn learns important

truths about her Latino heritage and the history makers who shaped a nation. Infused with actual news accounts from the time period, Sonia Manzano has crafted a gripping work of fiction based on her own life growing up during a fiery, unforgettable time in America, when young Latinos took control of their destinies.

26. Martinez, E. *500 Years of Chicana Women's History.* New Brunswick: Rutgers University Press, 2008. [Grade level: YA]

(From the publisher:)
Named the 2009 AAUP Best of the Best—Outstanding Book Distinction. The history of Mexican Americans spans more than five centuries and varies from region to region across the United States. Yet most of our history books devote at most a chapter to Chicano history, with even less attention to the story of Chicanas. *500 Years of Chicana Women's History* offers a powerful antidote to this omission with a vivid, pictorial account of struggle and survival, resilience and achievement, discrimination and identity. The bilingual text, along with hundreds of photos and other images, ranges from female-centered stories of pre-Columbian Mexico to profiles of contemporary social justice activists, labor leaders, youth organizers, artists, and environmentalists, among others. With a distinguished, seventeen-member advisory board, the book presents a remarkable combination of scholarship and youthful appeal. In the section on jobs held by Mexicanas under US rule in the 1800s, for example, readers learn about flamboyant Doña Tules, who owned a popular gambling saloon in Santa Fe, and Eulalia Arrilla de Pérez, a respected curandera (healer) in the San Diego area. Also covered are the "repatriation campaigns" of the Midwest during the Depression that deported both adults and children, 75 percent of whom were US-born and knew nothing of Mexico. Other stories include those of garment, laundry, and cannery worker strikes, told from the perspective of Chicanas on the ground. From the women who fought and died in the Mexican Revolution to those marching with their young children today for immigrant rights, every story draws inspiration. Like the editor's previous book, *500 Years of Chicano History* (still in print after thirty years), this thoroughly enriching view of Chicana women's history promises to become a classic.

27. McCall, G. G. *All the Stars Denied.* New York. Lee & Low Books, 2018. [Grade level: YA]

(From the publisher:)
In the heart of the Great Depression, Rancho Las Moras, like everywhere else in Texas, is gripped by the drought of the Dust Bowl, and resentment is building among white farmers against Mexican Americans. All around town, signs go up proclaiming "No Dogs or Mexicans" and "No Mexicans Allowed." When Estrella organizes a protest against the treatment of *tejanos* in their town of Monteseco, Texas, her whole family becomes a target of "repatriation" efforts to send Mexicans "back to Mexico"—whether they were ever Mexican citizens or not. Dumped across the border and separated from half her family, Estrella must figure out a way to survive and care for her mother and baby brother. How can she reunite with her father and grandparents and convince her country of birth that she deserves to return home? There are no easy answers in the first YA book to tackle this hidden history.

28. Nazario, S. *Enrique's Journey: The Story of a Boy's Dangerous Odyssey to Reunite with His Mother.* New York: Random House Trade Paperbacks, 2007. [Grade level: YA]

(From the publisher:)
Based on the *Los Angeles Times* newspaper series that won two Pulitzer Prizes, this astonishing story puts a human face on the ongoing debate about immigration reform in the United States. Now a beloved classic, this page-turner about the power of family is a popular text in classrooms and a touchstone for communities across the country to engage in meaningful discussions about this essential American subject. *Enrique's Journey* recounts the unforgettable quest of a Honduran boy looking for his mother, eleven years after she is forced to leave her starving family to find work in the United

States. Braving unimaginable peril, often clinging to the sides and tops of freight trains, Enrique travels through hostile worlds full of thugs, bandits, and corrupt cops. But he pushes forward, relying on his wit, courage, hope, and the kindness of strangers.

29. Roman, M. J., ed. *Afro-Latin@ Reader: History & Culture in the United States.* Durham: Duke University Press Books, 2010. [Grade level: YA]

(From the publisher:)
The Afro-Latin@ Reader focuses attention on a large, vibrant, yet oddly invisible community in the United States: people of African descent from Latin America and the Caribbean. The presence of Afro-Latins in the United States (and throughout the Americas) belies the notion that Blacks and Latins are two distinct categories or cultures. Afro-Latins are uniquely situated to bridge the widening social divide between Latins and African Americans; at the same time, their experiences reveal pervasive racism among Latins and ethnocentrism among African Americans. Offering insight into Afro-Latin life and new ways to understand culture, ethnicity, nation, identity, and antiracist politics, *The Afro-Latin@ Reader* presents a kaleidoscopic view of Black Latins in the United States. It addresses history, music, gender, class, and media representations in more than sixty selections, including scholarly essays, memoirs, newspaper and magazine articles, poetry, short stories, and interviews. While the selections cover centuries of Afro-Latin history, since the arrival of Spanish-speaking Africans in North America in the mid-sixteenth century, most of them focus on the past fifty years. The central question of how Afro-Latins relate to and experience US and Latin American racial ideologies is engaged throughout, in first-person accounts of growing up Afro-Latin, a classic essay by a leader of the Young Lords, and analyses of US census data on race and ethnicity, as well as in pieces on gender and sexuality, major-league baseball, and religion. The contributions that Afro-Latins have made to US culture are highlighted in essays on the illustrious Afro-Puerto Rican bibliophile Arturo Alfonso Schomburg and music and dance genres from salsa to mambo, and from boogaloo to hip hop. Taken together, these and many more selections help to bring Afro-Latins in the United States into critical view.

30. Weaver, L. Q. *Darkroom: A Memoir in Black and White.* Tuscaloosa: University of Alabama Press, 2012. [Grade level: YA]

(From the publisher:)
Darkroom: A Memoir in Black and White is an arresting and moving personal story about childhood, race, and identity in the American South, rendered in stunning illustrations by the author, Lila Quintero Weaver. In 1961, when Lila was five, she and her family emigrated from Buenos Aires, Argentina, to Marion, Alabama, in the heart of Alabama's Black Belt. As educated, middle-class Latino immigrants in a region that was defined by segregation, the Quinteros occupied a privileged vantage from which to view the racially charged culture they inhabited. Weaver and her family were firsthand witnesses to key moments in the civil rights movement. But *Darkroom* is her personal story as well: chronicling what it was like being a Latina girl in the Jim Crow South, struggling to understand both a foreign country and the horrors of our nation's race relations. Weaver, who was neither black nor white, observed very early on the inequalities in the American culture, with its blonde and blue-eyed feminine ideal. Throughout her life, Lila has struggled to find her place in this society and fought against the discrimination around her.

7. K-12 Latinx Studies Resources

Latinx History Timeline
From PBS, *Latino Americans*, https://www.pbs.org/latino-americans/en/timeline/

1565	Saint Augustine brings the first European settlement to the United States, introducing Catholicism and the Spanish language in Florida.
1598	New Mexico is settled by the Spanish—making it the largest and oldest Spanish settlement in the Southwest.
1607	The colony of Jamestown is founded in Virginia.
1691	Texas is made a separate Spanish province with Don Domingo de Terán as its governor.
1692	Explorer Diego de Vargas leads an expedition in search of salt deposits in and around the Guadalupe Mountains, becoming the first non-Indian visitor to this area.
1718	The mission at San Antonio is founded—it becomes one of the most prosperous and most important missions.
1776	While the American colonies in the East declare their independence from Great Britain, the Spanish celebrate the founding of San Francisco in the West.
1789	The Bill of Rights is adopted.
1810	Separatist movements begin in Latin America.
1821	The first Anglo settlers arrive in the Mexican state of Texas after being invited by the government of Mexico, which had recently declared its independence.
1829	Slavery in Mexico is abolished by the new republican government that emerged after independence from Spain (1821).
1833	The government of the Republic of Mexico challenges the power of the Catholic Church—ordering its missions secularized and land holdings broken up. Antonio López Santa Anna is named president of Mexico.
1834	Mexico's president, Antonio López Santa Anna, dissolves the Congress to rule all Mexico with an iron hand. Texans and "Tejanos" unite in opposition.
1835	In the autumn of 1835, Texans and Tejanos rise in rebellion against the oppressive Mexican government.
1836	On the February 23, Mexico's Antonio López Santa Anna takes possession of San Antonio.
	On March 6, day 13 of the siege, Santa Anna's forces breach the Alamo defenses. All the defenders of the Alamo, 189 men, are killed.
	On April 21, after joining forces with Sam Houston's army, Juan Seguín defeats the Mexican army in the Battle of San Jacinto—a battle that lasted all of eighteen minutes.
1837	Seguin is named Military Commander of West Texas, Senator, and later Mayor.
1842	Seguin flees to Mexico, escaping Anglo threats.
1845	Texas is officially annexed to the United States—which angers the Mexican government. Conflict over the official border line arises.

1846	In April, Mexico and the United States go to war over disputed territory.
	On June 14, Military Commander of California Mariano Guadalupe Vallejo is awakened by an angry mob of Anglo settlers—forcing him to sign the Articles of Capitulation to make California an independent republic.
1848	Mexico surrenders.
1853	Antonio López Santa Anna returns to power as president of Mexico, and during his time in office sells the land between Yuma, Arizona, and the Mesilla Valley, New Mexico, to the United States.
1859	Cigar factories are built in Florida, Louisiana, and New York, bringing an influx of working-class Cubans to the growing industry in the United States.
1862	The Homestead Act is passed in Congress, allowing squatters in the West to settle and claim vacant lands—many of which were owned by Mexicans.
1868	Angered by three hundred years of Spanish rule, Cubans rise up in revolt. Many leave for Europe and the United States, and the Fourteenth Amendment to the US Constitution is adopted, declaring all people of Hispanic origin born in the United States as US citizens.
1870	The Spanish government frees the slaves it owns in Cuba and Puerto Rico.
1872	Puerto Rican representatives in Spain win equal civil rights for the colony.
1873	Slavery is abolished in Puerto Rico.
1890	Juan Seguín, the lone survivor of the Alamo, dies. Eighty years later, his body would be returned to Texas and buried with honors.
1892	The *Partido Revolucionario Cubano* is created to organize the independence movements in Cuba and Puerto Rico.
1895	Cuban rebels stage an insurrection, led by the poet Jose Martí.
1897	Spain grants Cuba and Puerto Rico autonomy and home rule.
1898	On February 15, in Havana Harbor, Cuba, an explosion destroys a US battleship—killing 266 men aboard. The United States subsequently declares war on Spain. The war lasts thirteen weeks.
	The Cuban Revolutionary Party (Partido Revolucionario Cubano) strikes a deal with the US Congress: in exchange for the rebels' cooperation with US military intervention, the United States promises to leave Cuba at the end of the war.
	The United States acquires Puerto Rico through war and claims it as a territory.
1901	Under the Platt Amendment, the United States limits Cuban independence as written into the Cuban Constitution. The United States reserves the right to build a naval base on Cuba and enforces that Cuba cannot sign treaties with other countries or borrow money unless it is deemed agreeable to the United States. With these parameters in place, the US government hands the government of Cuba over to the Cuban people.
	The Federación Libre de los Trabajadores (Free Federation of Workers) becomes affiliated with the American Federation of Labor, which in turn breaks from its prior policy of excluding non-whites.

1902	The Reclamation Act is passed, dispossessing many Hispanic Americans of their lands.
	Cuba declares its independence from the United States.
1910	The Mexican Revolution begins as a revolt against President Porfirio Díaz. The railroads that had once served as a means for trade and development now serve as the main escape from the violence of the revolution.
1917	Puerto Ricans are granted US citizenship.
	In February, Congress passes the Immigration Act of 1917, which enforces a literacy requirement on all immigrants.
	On April 6, the United States declares war against Germany, joining WWI.
	With many able-bodied American men off to war, "temporary" Mexican workers are encouraged and permitted to enter the United States to work.
	In May, the Selective Service Act becomes law, obligating Mexican immigrants in the United States to register for the draft even though they are not eligible.
1921	Limits on the number of immigrants allowed in the United States are imposed for the first time in the country's history.
1925	The "Border Patrol" is created by Congress.
1932	The United States government begins to deport Mexicans. Between 300,000 and 500,000 Mexican Americans would be forced out of the United States in the 1930s.
1933	The Roosevelt administration reverses the policy of English as the official language in Puerto Rico.
	Cuban dictator Gerardo Machado is overthrown.
1934	The Platt Amendment, which restricted the Cuban government, is annulled.
1940s	As WWII sets in, many Latinos enlist in the US military—as a proportion, the largest ethnic group serving in the war.
	The Fair Employment Practices Act is passed, eliminating discrimination in employment.
1943	On August 23, Macario Garcia becomes the first Mexican national to receive a US Congressional Medal of Honor, yet is refused service at the Oasis Café near his home in Texas.
	Prompted by the WWII labor shortage, the US government launches an agreement with Mexico to import temporary workers (braceros), to fill the void in agricultural work.
1944	D-day invasion of Europe on June 6.
	The Servicemen's Readjustment Act of 1944 is passed, providing settlements for veterans. Mexican American veterans, however, have trouble receiving these benefits.
	Operation Bootstrap, a program initiated by Puerto Rico to encourage industrialization and to meet US labor demands, fuels a large wave of migrant workers to the United States.
1947	Puerto Rico gains political autonomy when it becomes a commonwealth.
1948	Dr. Hector Garcia, a witness to racial injustice, begins holding meetings for Mexican Americans to voice their concerns, and in March they establish a new Mexican American movement: the American GI Forum.

This group gets national attention after a Latino soldier killed in action, Pvt. Felix Z. Longoria, is refused burial in Texas. Senator Lyndon B. Johnson, appalled by this blatant bigotry, makes arrangements for Longoria to be buried at the prestigious Arlington National Cemetery.

1950   The US Congress advances Puerto Rico's political status from protectorate to commonwealth.

1951   The Bracero Program is formalized as the Mexican Farm Labor Supply Program and the Mexican Labor Agreement, and will bring an annual average of 350,000 Mexican workers into the United States until its end in 1964.

1954   In the case *Hernández v. The State of Texas*, the Supreme Court recognizes that Latinos are suffering inequality and profound discrimination, paving the way for Hispanic Americans to use legal means to fight for their equality. This is the first Supreme Court case briefed and argued by Mexican American attorneys.

1954–58 Operation Wetback is put into place by the US government. The initiative is a government effort to locate and deport undocumented workers—over the four-year period, 3.8 million people of Mexican descent are deported.

1956   Nearly a dozen bills are introduced into the Senate to preserve segregation. Henry B. González, determined to stop them, stages an effective filibuster, speaking for twenty-two straight hours. He would later represent San Antonio in Congress.

1958   The landmark production of *West Side Story* premieres on Broadway, chronicling the racial tensions of the '40s and '50s.

1959   Fidel Castro and his band of revolutionaries march into Havana, following an armed revolt that ends in the overthrow of military dictator Fulgencio Batista.

1960   John F. Kennedy runs for President, with Lyndon B. Johnson as his running mate. Johnson enlists in the help of Dr. Hector Garcia to help carry the Latino vote. Garcia forms "Viva Kennedy" clubs, greatly aiding Kennedy's narrow victory.

        On October 24, a ship called the City of Havana ferries Cubans fleeing Fidel Castro's reign. Over the next three years, more than 200,000 Cubans flee to Miami.

1961   On April 17, 1,400 US-trained Cuban exiles invade Cuba—within 72 hours, Fidel Castro's forces easily defeat the Bay of Pigs Invasion.

        Aspira (Aspire) is founded to promote the education of Hispanic youth and acquires a national following, serving Puerto Ricans wherever they live in large numbers.

        West Side Story is made into a film; the role of Anita goes to a Puerto Rican, Rita Moreno, who takes home an Academy Award for her performance.

        Rafael Leonidas Trujillo, dictator of the Dominican Republic, is assassinated in a CIA-backed plot.

1962   US reconnaissance planes discover Soviet missiles in Cuba. Travel to and from Cuba is prohibited. The United States blocks a Soviet plan to establish missile bases in Cuba. The Soviet Premier withdraws the missiles on the condition that the United States publicly declares it will not invade Cuba.

        After the Community Service Organization turns down César Chávez's request, as their president, to organize farm workers, César and Dolores Huerta resign from the CSO. They form the National Farm Workers Association.

1963	On November 22, President John F. Kennedy is assassinated, leaving Lyndon B. Johnson as his successor. President Johnson appoints more Mexican Americans to positions in government than any president before; he passes landmark legislation advocating desegregation.
1964	Congress passes the Civil Rights Act of 1964. The act establishes affirmative action programs, prohibiting discrimination on the basis of gender, creed, race, or ethnic background: "to achieve equality of employment opportunities and remove barriers that have operated in the past" (Title VII). The Equal Employment Opportunity Commission (EEOC) is also established through Title VII to prevent job discrimination.
	The Bracero Program, the government program initially put in place during WWII, ends. It brought Mexican laborers into the country to replace the American men who were fighting overseas. When the war ended the program continued.
1966	Striking workers are subjected to physical and verbal attacks throughout their peaceful demonstrations, and on March 16, the Senate Subcommittee on Migratory Labor held hearings in Delano.
	March 17, the morning following the hearings, César Chávez sets out with 100 farmworkers to begin his pilgrimage to the San Joaquin Valley. After twenty-five days, their numbers swell from hundreds to an army of thousands.
	On Easter Sunday, the state capital is finally in sight. With public sympathy mounting and the spring growing season upon them, growers finally agree to meet with union representatives.
1967	With Martin Luther King Jr. organizing in the South and César Chávez organizing in California, East LA high school teacher Sal Castro begins looking for ways to organize students.
1968	On March 6, a walkout is planned and coordinated among East LA high schools. Approximately 10,000 students peacefully walk out of four schools and are joined by parents and supporters. Police are sent to maintain order—and things get out of hand.
	Following the police riot, on March 7 the students walk out again. The walkouts continue for two weeks until the demands are met.
	Just days after the opening of the HemisFair in San Antonio, Chicano high school students stage walkouts—first in San Antonio, then in thirty-nine towns across Texas, eventually spreading to nearly 100 high schools in ten states.
	José Ángel Gutiérrez is the mastermind behind much of this activism.
1970	Herman Badillo is elected into the US House of Representatives, making him the first Puerto Rican to serve in Congress.
	In Crystal City, Texas, José Ángel Gutiérrez forms a political party, La Raza Unida ("The United Race").
	Elections in April see an unprecedented victory for Chicanos. Gutiérrez is elected county judge, and La Raza Unida controls not only the school board, but city and county government as well.
1973	Miami officially becomes bilingual, following a referendum sponsored by its growing Cuban community.
	Maurice Ferre becomes mayor of Miami, making him the first Puerto Rican to lead a major city in the mainland United States.

1974	Willie Velasquez of San Antonio organizes thousands of voter registration drives across the Southwest, encouraging the Latino population to vote. He notices, however, that the problem is not the number of Latino voters, but the electoral system. He later would file voting rights lawsuits—never losing a case.
	Congress passes the Equal Educational Opportunity Act to create equality in public schools by offering bilingual education to Hispanic students.
1978	Russian-born immigrant Emmy Shafer spearheads a campaign to put an end to bilingualism and make English the official language of Miami. Her push for an English-only Miami is a harbinger of broader anti-immigrant sentiment that would spread across the country in the late twentieth and early twenty-first century.
1980	In the spring, Fidel Castro announces that any Cuban who wishes to leave may do so. Shortly after this declaration, a ramshackle armada sails from South Florida to the port of Mariel.
	Over a period of five months, more than 125,000 Cubans arrive in South Florida. The newly arrived Cubans are quickly branded as mentally ill or criminal, following a CBS News story. Although only 4 percent are from mental hospitals, more than 25,000 have criminal records. The media perpetuates the stereotype of mentally ill or criminal in shows and movies such as *Miami Vice* and *Scarface*.
	The English-only campaign comes roaring back, with Emmy Shafer again at the helm. In the 1980 election, voters approve the ordinance to end official bilingualism.
1986	Seeking to bring illegal immigration under control while maintaining a stable agricultural labor force, President Ronald Reagan signs the Immigration Reform and Control Act (IRCA). It is intended to toughen US immigration law; border security is to be enforced and employers are now required to monitor the immigration status of their employees. It also, however, grants amnesty to nearly three million immigrants—mostly Mexicans—who had quietly slipped across the border during the 1970s and '80s.
1987	The National Hispanic Leadership Institute addresses the underrepresentation of Latinas in the corporate, nonprofit, and political arenas.
1988	Voter rights advocate Willie Velasquez dies in May, and is posthumously honored with the Presidential Medal of Freedom—the highest civilian peacetime award.
1990	President George Bush appoints the first woman and first Hispanic surgeon general of the United States: Antonia C. Novello.
1991	The proposed North American Free Trade Agreement (NAFTA) between Canada, the United States, and Mexico expands and exploits the maquiladora concept, which offers potential tax reductions to US businesses.
1992	A series of peace agreements finally ends the bloodshed in El Salvador.
1993	Ellen Ochoa becomes the first Hispanic woman to go to space aboard the Space Shuttle Discovery.
	President Bill Clinton names Federico Peña as secretary of Transportation and Henry Cisneros as secretary of Housing and Urban Development, making the two the first Hispanics to hold those positions. He also appoints Norma Cantú, former director of the Mexican American Legal Defense and Education Fund, to the position of assistant secretary for Civil Rights within the Department of Education. Twenty-five other Hispanics are appointed to positions needing Senate confirmation under this presidency.

1994   NAFTA takes effect, eliminating all tariffs between Canada, Mexico, and the United States within fifteen years. Imports from the *maquiladoras* become duty-free.

On November 8, Californians pass Proposition 187 with 59 percent of the vote. This bans undocumented immigrants from receiving public education and benefits such as welfare and subsidized health care (with the exception of emergency services); makes it a felony to manufacture, distribute, sell, or use false citizenship or residence documents; and requires any city, county, or state officials to report any suspected or apparent illegal aliens.

1996   Proposition 187 is ruled unconstitutional, on the grounds that only the federal government has the authority to regulate immigration. Eliseo Medina spearheads the movement to file lawsuits against Proposition 187.

Medina becomes the first Mexican American vice president of the Service Employees International Union.

2003   Hispanics are pronounced the nation's largest minority group—surpassing African Americans.

CHLI is the premier organization founded by members of Congress to advance the Hispanic Community's Economic Progress with a focus on social responsibility and global competitiveness.

2004   Anti-immigrant sentiment reaches a tipping point when Arizonans organize a group of volunteers known as "The Minutemen" to patrol the border.

2005   In April, the Minutemen began patrolling the border. They report unauthorized border crossings or other illegal activity to the US Border Patrol.

Antonio Villaraigosa becomes the first Mexican American mayor of Los Angeles in more than a century.

2008   The Freedom Tower is designated a National Historic Landmark, considered the "Ellis Island of the South" for its role as the Cuban Assistance Center in Miami during 1962–1974, offering nationally sanctioned relief to Cuban refugees.

2009   Puerto Rican Sonia Sotomayor is sworn in as the first Latina Supreme Court Justice.

2010   With no new comprehensive federal immigration policy in place, states began to enact their own.

In April, Arizona Governor Jan Brewer signs the broadest and toughest anti–illegal immigrant law in US history. The legislation, SB-1070, cracks down on anyone harboring or hiring undocumented immigrants and gives local police unprecedented powers.

Marco Rubio, a second-generation Cuban American, is elected US Senator from Florida.

2011   Georgia enacts its own version of Arizona's SB-1070—anyone stopped without a driver's license or proof of residency can be handed over to the immigration authorities.

2013   Hispanics make up about one-sixth of the US population—nearly 51 million people. By the middle of the century, the Latino population is expected to reach 127 million—nearly 30 percent of the projected population of the country.

Titles in FWISD Campus Libraries

Elementary School

Lower Grades
1. *Lola Levine, Drama Queen*, Monica Brown
2. *Arrorró, Mi Niño: Latino Lullabies and Gentle Games*, Lulu Delacre
3. *Little Chanclas*, José Lozano
4. *Rudas: Niño's Horrendous Hermanitas*, Yuyi Morales
5. *Turning Pages: My Life Story*, Sonia Sotomayor
6. *An Illustrated Treasury of Latino Read-Aloud Stories*, Maite Suarez-Rivas

Upper Grades
7. *Lucky Broken Girl*, Ruth Behar
8. *Charlie Hernández and the League of Shadows*, Ryan Calejo
9. *Latino Americans and Religion*, Frank DePietro
10. *Freddie Ramos Rules New York*, Jacqueline Jules
11. *Merci Suárez Changes Gears*, Meg Medina
12. *Latino Folklore and Culture*, Bill Palmer

Middle School

13. *Marcus Vega Doesn't Speak Spanish*, Pablo Cartaya
14. *Voices in First Person: Reflections on Latino Identity*, Lori Marie Carlson
15. *Latino Rainbow: Poems about Latino Americans*, Carlos Cumpián
16. *Bravo!*, Margarita Engle
17. *Looking Out, Looking In: Anthology of Latino Poetry*, William Luis
18. *Pig Park*, Claudia Guadalupe Martínez
19. *Sammy Sosa: An Authorized Biography*, Carrie Muskat
20. *Amazing Hispanic American History: A Book of Answers for Kids*, George Ochoa

High School

21. *Voices of the US Latino Experience*, Rodolfo F. Acuna and Guadalupe Compean
22. *Roberto Clemente: The Pride of Puerto Rico*, Gerry Boehme
23. *Home is Everything: The Latino Baseball Story*, Marcos Bretón
24. *Icons of Latino America: Latino Contributions to American Culture*, Roger Bruns
25. *Red Hot Salsa: Bilingual Poems on Being Young and Latino in the United States*, Lori Marie Carlson
26. *Voices in First Person: Reflections on Latino Identity*, Lori Marie Carlson
27. *Latino Visions: Contemporary Chicano, Puerto Rican, and Cuban American Artists*, James D. Cockcroft
28. *Windows into My World: Latino Youth Write Their Lives*, Sarah Cortez
29. *You Don't Have a Clue: Latino Mystery Stories for Teens*, Sarah Cortez
30. *César Chávez: Civil Rights Activist*, Bárbara Cruz
31. *Paper Dance: 55 Latino Poets*, Victor Hernández Cruz, Leroy V. Quintana, and Virgil Suárez
32. *Spare Parts: Four Undocumented Teenagers, One Ugly Robot, and the Battle for the American Dream*, Joshua Davis
33. *Latino Cuisine and its Influence on American Foods: The Taste of Celebration*, Jean Ford
34. *Latino Baseball Legends*, Lew Freedman
35. *Latino Athletes*, Ian C. Friedman
36. *Yo, Alejandro: My (Our) Story / Mi (nuestra) historia*, Alejandro Gac-Artigas
37. *Latino American Folktales*, Thomas A. Green
38. *The US Latino Community*, Margaret Haerens

39. *Latino Migrant Workers: America's Harvesters*, Christopher Hovius
40. *Latino Americans and Immigration Laws: Crossing the Border*, Miranda Hunter
41. *The Story of Latino Civil Rights: Fighting for Justice*, Miranda Hunter
42. *Latino Food Culture*, Zilkia Janer
43. *Becoming María: Love and Chaos in the South Bronx*, Sonia Manzano
44. *Latino Arts and their Influence on the United States: Songs, Dreams, and Dances*, Rory Makosz
45. *Dream Things True: A Novel*, Marie Marquardt
46. *Latino Writers and Journalists*, Jamie Martínez Wood
47. *The Latino Religious Experience: People of Faith and Vision*, Kenneth McIntosh
48. *Diego Rivera: Mexican Muralist*, Mariana Medina
49. *Frida Kahlo: Self-Portrait Artist*, Mariana Medina
50. *Notable Latino Americans*, Matt Meier
51. *The Latino Holiday Book: From Cinco de Mayo to Día de los Muertos—The Celebrations and Traditions of Hispanic-Americans*, Valerie Menard
52. *Latino Americans in Sports, Film, Music, and Government: Trailblazers*, Richard Mintzer
53. *Isabel Allende: Award-Winning Author*, Jeanne Nagle
54. *Pablo Neruda: Nobel Prize-Winning Poet*, Jeanne Nagle
55. *It's All in the Frijoles: 100 Famous Latinos Share Real-Life Stories, Time-Tested dichos, Favorite Folktales, and Inspiring Words of Wisdom*, Yolanda Nava
56. *Latinos in Science, Math, and Professions*, David E. Newton
57. *Riding Low on the Streets of Gold*, Judith Ortiz Cofer
58. *Latinos in the Arts*, Steven Otfinoski
59. *Latino America: A State-by-State Encyclopedia*, Mark Overmyer-Velázquez
60. *Latino and African American Athletes Today: A Biographical Dictionary*, David L. Porter
61. *Latino Folklore and Culture: Stories of Family, Traditions of Pride*, Ellyn Sanna
62. *Las mamis: Favorite Latino Authors Remember Their Mothers*, Esmeralda Santiago and Joie Davidow
63. *Latino Economics in the United States*, Eric Schwartz
64. *César Chávez*, Ilan Stavans
65. *Latina Writers*, Ilan Stavans
66. *Quinceañera*, Ilan Stavans
67. *Great Lives from History: Latinos*, Carmen Tafolla and Martha P. Cotera
68. *Sonia Sotomayor: First Latina Supreme Court Justice*, John Torres
69. *The Latino Student's Guide to College Success*, Leonard A. Valverde

Webliography of National and Local Resources

Latino Americans: 500 Years of History (https://apply.ala.org/latinoamericans)

> This website has been developed to support prospective applicants and grant recipients of Latino Americans: 500 Years of History, produced by the National Endowment for the Humanities and the American Library Association. Latino Americans: 500 Years of History is part of an NEH initiative, The Common Good: Humanities in the Public Square, and features the PBS documentary series *Latino Americans*, a production of WETA Washington, DC; Bosch and Co., Inc.; and Latino Public Broadcasting (LPB). We invite you to learn more about the national advisory group involved in this effort and the resources developed to support organizations that received a grant. Inquiries about Latino Americans: 500 Years of History may be directed to the ALA Public Programs Office. Most of the following resources are linked from the Latino Americans "Resources" page.

1. *Viva Mi Historia!* - The Story of Fort Worth Latino Families (https://holatarrantcounty.org/vivamihistoria/)

On September 26 and October 17, 2015, a team of researchers with the Civil Rights in Black and Brown Oral History Project (https://crbb.tcu.edu/) at TCU interviewed dozens of Fort Worth residents at a pair of events sponsored by the City of Fort Worth Human Relations Unit. The result is *Viva Mi Historia!*: The Story of Fort Worth Latino Families. The purpose of the project was to collect and curate an inclusive history of Latino Fort Worth told from the perspective of the residents who lived it. Under the direction of Dr. Max Krochmal of TCU, the interviewers—graduate students from surrounding institutions—captured memoirs and testimonies from forty-three veterans of foreign wars, activists, retired professionals, social workers, laborers, school administrators, business owners, and educators. Each of the interviewees shared personal stories that spanned from recollections of the Great Depression and World War II to the Civil Rights movement and Reagan revolution. They told family tales of immigration from the first massive wave sparked by the Mexican Revolution in 1910 to the most recent stimulated by the North American Free Trade Agreement (NAFTA) in the 1990s.

The original Latino Fort Worth site was created by CRBB research assistant and former TCU PhD student Moisés Acuña-Gurrola, now an assistant professor of history at California State University, Bakersfield. Gurrola also curated and wrote the six multimedia essays listed on the "Interview Themes" pages: Migration, the Barrios, Schools & Churches, Activism & Public Service, Work & Entrepreneurship, and Arts & Culture (hover over "Theme," then click the theme title using the drop-down menu). The site is now hosted by HOLA Tarrant County.

2. *Mujeres Poderosas* (https://mkrochmal1.wixsite.com/latino-fort-worth/mujeres-poderosas)

The purpose of the study is to investigate the role of religion in helping Latinas in Fort Worth and surrounding communities overcome a variety of obstacles to achieve success as professional women. The Latinx community has often been marginalized by a wider community dominated by Anglo males. Women have often been the most vulnerable. Yet Latinas have struggled to overcome great obstacles and have risen to become strong role models for younger generations of Latinas, other younger ladies, and the community as a whole. In their attempt to overcome such difficulties many have turned to religion as a source of inspiration and strength. To be sure, not all have found religion to be as supportive as they needed it to be. This project seeks to highlight the role of religion in the lives of successful Latinas. *Mujeres Poderosas* is directed by Dr. Santiago Piñón, Jr., Texas Christian University.

3. Historians of Latino Americans (HOLA) Tarrant County (https://holatarrantcounty.org/)

Formed out of a desire to create a history of Latinas and Latinos in Tarrant County, the Historians of Latino Americans (HOLA), a non-profit organization, aims to research, document, and archive our work and to share it with the community. Our hope is that this information will lead to a better understanding and appreciation of the role that Latinas and Latinos have played in the civil, educational, and cultural history of our county. The website hosts a series of oral history projects, public history exhibitions, and published and unpublished writings. Former FWISD teacher and CRES team member Cecilia Hill is one of the HOLA leaders.

Oral History Resources

1. The American Folklife Center at the Library of Congress (http://www.loc.gov/folklife/index.html)

   The online version of "Folklife and Fieldwork: An Introduction to Field Techniques" (http://www.loc.gov/folklife/fieldwork/index.html) is an important resource for those interested in planning local history programs that will document and preserve the unique personal stories of Latino Americans in our diverse communities. Applicants may also wish to consult the list of additional online resources for local and oral history programming (http://www.loc.gov/folklife/fieldwork/internetlinks.html) compiled by the American Folklife Center.

2. Latina/o Diaspora in the Americas Project (LDAP) (https://oral.history.ufl.edu/projects/latinao-diaspora-in-the-americas-project/)

   The Latina/o Diaspora in the Americas Project, newly founded in 2014, is a growing archive of one hundred-plus oral histories dedicated to creating space for Latina/os to share their historical experiences related to identity, immigration reform, labor conditions, education, and civil rights. The site includes tutorials for beginning a new project, deeds of gift examples, and other tools for implementing oral history projects.

3. Veterans History Project (http://www.loc.gov/vets/)

   The Veterans History Project of the American Folklife Center collects, preserves, and makes accessible the personal accounts of American war veterans so that future generations may hear directly from veterans and better understand the realities of war. Stories can be told through personal narratives, correspondence, and visual materials. More information about the collection and how to participate (http://www.loc.gov/vets/kit.html) is available on the project website.

3. Voces Oral History Center, University of Texas (https://voces.lib.utexas.edu/)

   Voces Oral History Center is dedicated to recording and disseminating the stories of US Latinas and Latinos and weaving the many perspectives into our historical narrative at the national, state, and local levels.

5. Civil Rights in Black and Brown Oral History Project (https://crbb.tcu.edu/)

   Not one but two civil rights movements flourished in mid-twentieth century Texas, and they did so in intimate conversation with one another. While most research on American race relations has utilized a binary analytical lens—examining either "black" vs. "white" or "Anglo" vs. "Mexican"—the *Civil Rights in Black and Brown Oral History Project* collects, interprets, and disseminates new oral history interviews with members of all three groups. Its website includes a publicly accessible, free, and user-friendly multimedia digital humanities database that provides video clips from the interviews to researchers as well as teachers, students, journalists, activists, and the public. The site includes interviews related to Fort Worth.

Historical and Cultural Resources

1. Bridging *Historias* through Latino History and Culture: An NEH Bridging Cultures at Community Colleges Project (http://bridginghistorias.gc.cuny.edu/)

> Funded by the NEH, Bridging *Historias* addresses the increasingly influential body of scholarship on the importance of Latinx culture in American history that remains under-represented in most college history textbooks and teaching collections. The website contains the research and teaching materials used by forty-two community college faculty and administrators in the greater New York City region, including scholarly talks and teaching presentations by visiting lecturers. The website is designed to provide scholarly resources for incorporating Latino history and culture into the humanities classroom, and for the general public.

2. Humanities Texas Traveling Exhibitions (http://www.humanitiestexas.org/)

> The Humanities Texas exhibitions program circulates traveling exhibitions on a variety of topics including:

> ■ In His Own Words: The Life and Work of César Chávez
> http://www.humanitiestexas.org/exhibitions/list/by-title/his-own-words-life-and-work-cesar-chavez

> ■ *Vaquero*: Genesis of the Texas Cowboy
> http://www.humanitiestexas.org/exhibitions/list/by-title/vaquero-genesis-texas-cowboy

> ■ *Voces Americanas*: Latino Literature in the United States
> http://www.humanitiestexas.org/exhibitions/list/by-title/voces-americanas-latino-literature-united-states

> Information including rental prices are included for each exhibit.

3. *Latino Americans* documentary http://www.pbs.org/latino-americans/en/

> *Latino Americans* is a landmark six-hour documentary featuring interviews with nearly one hundred Latinos and more than five hundred years of history. It is a production of WETA Washington, DC; Bosch and Co., Inc.; and Latino Public Broadcasting (LPB); in association with Independent Television Service (ITVS). The *Latino Americans* website offers:

> ■ Complete episode descriptions
> http://www.pbs.org/latino-americans/en/episode-guide/

> ■ Videos of the full series as well as clips that highlight areas of interest
> http://www.pbs.org/latino-americans/en/watch-videos/

> ■ Access to supporting lesson plans and activities
> http://www.pbs.org/latino-americans/en/education/

4. The Latino Intersections Resource Center (https://journals.dartmouth.edu/latinox/resource_center/)

> The Latino Intersections Resource Center, a part of the Latino Journal Intersections website, is affiliated with the Department of Spanish and Portuguese and the Latin American, Latino & Caribbean Studies Program at Dartmouth College, Hanover, New Hampshire. It receives funding and support from the Dartmouth College Library System. The Resource Center's mission is to create a gateway to resources that facilitate access to internet-based information to, from, or about the Latino community in the United States.

5. National Park Services: American Latino Heritage Projects (http://www.nps.gov/history/heritageinitiatives/latino/)

> The National Park Service American Latino Heritage projects explore how the legacy of American Latinos can be recognized, preserved, and interpreted for future generations. This website highlights projects undertaken by National Park Service parks and programs as part of the Service's commitment to telling the American Latino story. Projects vary from increased interpretation, collaboration with community organizations, and the production of scholarly documentation.

Latinxs in the US and Their Contributions
Research by Danyelle Greene, Adrian College student and Idali Feliciano, Director of Multicultural Programs, September 2011. Permission is granted to use this resource.

1. US Latino Patriots: From the American Revolution to Afghanistan http://pewhispanic.org/files/reports/17.3.pdf

2. Hispanic Americans History http://history-world.org/hispanics.htm

3. Contributions in different areas http://www.neta.com/~1stbooks/dod2.html

4. Hispanic Threads in America http://www.ma.iup.edu/Pueblo/latino_cultures/contrib.html

5. Famous Firsts by Hispanic Americans http://www.infoplease.com/ipa/A0933896.html

6. Hispanic Heritage Month—Activities/Facts http://www.factmonster.com/spot/hhm1.html

7. Hispanic American History (Encyclopedia) http://www.encyclopedia.com/topic/Hispanic_Americans.aspx

8. Hispanic American Heritage http://www.madisonvoices.com/hispanicheritage/timeline.htm

9. Some Famous Hispanic/Latino Americans http://www.personal.psu.edu/faculty/c/s/csr4/PSU3/Hispanic-Latino-Americans/Hispanic-Latino-Americans.html

10. Hispanic Americans http://usa.usembassy.de/society-hispanics.htm

11. Hispanic Contributions to the United States http://hispaniccontributions.org/pManager_E.asp?pid=home_E

12. US-Mexican War http://www.pbs.org/kera/usmexicanwar/index_flash.html

13. Some Contributions by Some Hispanic Americans http://mije.org/features/hispanic-heritage-month?gclid=CN29rNXyn6sCFe4AQAodQ12dhw

14. Era of Hispanic American Hero http://www.youtube.com/watch?v=gu-2-_g-Fjs

15. Hispanics in Military Service http://www.houstonculture.org/hispanic/memorial.html

16. Hispanic American History http://www.ouramericanhistory.com/

17. African American and Hispanic Progressive http://www.youtube.com/watch?v=r7tn71w58RI

18. Hispanic Influences in Pop Culture http://www.msnbc.msn.com/id/21134540/vp/31405202#31405202

Cultural Aspects

19. Vista Magazine www.vistamagazine.com

20. Pew Hispanic Research www.pewhispanic.org

21. Timeline in Hispanic American History www.galegroup.com/free_resources/chh/timeline

22. English Borrows Spanish words www.infoplease.com/spot/spanishwords1.html

Puerto Rican Contributions

23. Famous Puerto Ricans http://daytranslations.com/famous_puerto_rican_people.aspx

24. Famous Puerto Ricans http://www.buzzle.com/articles/famous-puerto-ricans.html

25. Famous Puerto Ricans http://www.topuertorico.org/culture/famousprA-C.shtml

26. Puerto Rican Americans http://www.everyculture.com/multi/Pa-Sp/Puerto-Rican-Americans.html

27. Puerto Rican Americans http://www.wfu.edu/aes/Puerto%20Rican.php

28. Puerto Rican Facts http://www.topuertorico.org/people.shtml

29. Puerto Rican Facts http://www.britannica.com/EBchecked/topic/482879/Puerto-Rico/54528/Language-and-religion

30. Cultural Diversity: Eating in America http://ohioline.osu.edu/hyg-fact/5000/pdf/5257.pdf

31. Puerto Rican Cuisine http://www.lifeintheusa.com/food/puertorico.htm

32. Economic Status of Puerto Ricans http://www.irp.wisc.edu/publications/focus/pdfs/foc102d.pdf

33. Puerto Rican Immigrants and Migrants http://www.americansall.com/PDFs/02-americans-all/9.9.pdf

34. Puerto Ricans living in the US http://www2.scholastic.com/browse/subarticle.jsp?id=1933

35. Puerto Rican Community http://www.bateylink.org/community

36. English in Puerto Rico http://home.earthlink.net/~apousada/id1.html

37. Bilingualism among Puerto Ricans http://www.zonalatina.com/Zldata106.htm

38. Puerto Rican Information http://www.encyclopedia.com/topic/Puerto_Rico.aspx

39. Puerto Rican Religion http://www.everyculture.com/Middle-America-Caribbean/Puerto-Ricans-Religion-and-Expressive-Culture.html

40. Puerto Rican Cultural Differences in Politics http://www.yale.edu/ynhti/curriculum/units/1980/6/80.06.08.x.html

41. Political Evolution of Puerto Ricans in America http://www.fontillas.com/dpr.htm

42. Hispanic Americans Under-represented http://www.americansc.org.uk/Online/garcia.htm

Important National Organizations

(Compiled by) Diversity Best Practices
https://www.diversitybestpractices.com/news-articles/21-latino-organizations-you-need-know

1. Association of Hispanic Advertising Agencies (AHAA) (http://ahaa.org/)

   The Association of Hispanic Advertising Agencies aims to grow, strengthen, and protect the Hispanic marketing and advertising industry by providing leadership in raising awareness of the value of the Hispanic market opportunities and enhancing the professionalism of the industry.

2. Association of Latino Professionals for America (ALPFA) (http://alpfa.org/)

   The Association of Latino Professionals for America's mission is to empower and develop Latino men and women as leaders of character for the nation, in every sector of the global economy.

3. The Committee for Hispanic Families and Children (CHFC) (http://chcfinc.org/)

   The Committee for Hispanic Families and Children aims to improve the quality of life for Hispanic children and families. CHFC has developed and implemented programs that meet the needs of low-income Hispanic families and children in such critical areas as youth development, child care, HIV/AIDS prevention and education, immigrant services, public policy, and advocacy.

4. Congressional Hispanic Caucus Institute (CHCI) (http://chci.org/)

   The mission of the Congressional Hispanic Caucus Institute is to develop the next generation of Hispanic leaders. Its vision is an educated and civically active Hispanic community that participates at the local, state, and federal policy decision-making levels. CHCI seeks to accomplish its mission by offering educational and leadership development programs, services, and activities that promote the growth of participants as effective professionals and strong leaders. In the spirit of building coalitions, CHCI seeks to establish partnerships with other Hispanic and non-Hispanic organizations.

5. Hispanic Association of Colleges and Universities (http://www.hacu.net/hacu/default.asp)

   The Hispanic Association of Colleges and Universities is a national organization representing the accredited colleges and universities in the United States where Hispanic students constitute at least 25 percent of the total student enrollment.

6. Hispanic Association on Corporate Responsibility (HACR) (http://hacr.org/)

   The Hispanic Association on Corporate Responsibility (HACR) strives to ensure that participation of the Hispanic community in corporate America is commensurate with Hispanic purchasing power. Responsible corporations endeavor to include Hispanics in employment, procurement, philanthropy, and corporate governance.

7. Hispanic National Bar Association (HNBA) (http://www.hnba.com/)

   The Hispanic National Bar Association is the incorporated, nonprofit, national association of Hispanic attorneys, judges, law professors, and law students committed to promoting the goals and objectives of the association. The HNBA has been the principal force behind the increased representation of Hispanics in all sectors of the legal profession, and has served as the legal voice for Hispanics for more than twenty years.

8. Mexican American Legal Defense and Educational Fund (http://maldef.org/)

    The Mexican American Legal Defense and Education Fund is a national nonprofit organization with the principal objective of protecting and promoting the civil rights of US Latinos through litigation, advocacy, educational outreach, and the awarding of law scholarships.

9. National Association for Hispanic Elderly (ANPPM) (http://anppm.org/)

    The National Association for Hispanic Elderly was founded to inform policy makers and the general public about the status and needs of elderly Hispanics and other low-income elderly. The organization provides direct social services and training and technical assistance to community groups and professionals in the field of aging. It also produces and distributes bilingual information on the Hispanic elderly.

10. National Association of Hispanic Journalists (NAHJ) (http://nahj.org/)

    The National Association of Hispanic Journalists is dedicated to the recognition and professional advancement of Hispanics in the news industry. The association strives to organize and provide mutual support for Hispanics involved in the gathering or dissemination of news, encourage and support the study and practice of journalism and communications by Hispanics, foster and promote the fair treatment of Hispanics by the media, further the employment and career development of Hispanics in the media, and foster a greater understanding of Hispanic media professionals' special cultural identity, interests, and concerns.

11. National Association of Latino Elected and Appointed Officials (NALEO) (http://www.naleo.org/)

    The National Association of Latino Elected and Appointed Officials empowers Hispanics to participate fully in the American political process, from citizenship to public service. NALEO carries out this mission by developing and implementing programs that promote the integration of Hispanic immigrants into American society, developing future leaders among Hispanic youth, providing assistance and training to the nation's Hispanic elected and appointed officials, and conducting research on issues important to the Hispanic population.

12. National Council of La Raza (http://www.nclr.org/)

    The National Council of La Raza, the country's largest national constituency-based Hispanic organization, was established to reduce poverty and discrimination and improve life opportunities for Hispanic Americans.

13. National Hispanic Corporate Council (NHCC) (http://www.nhcchq.org/)

    The mission of the National Hispanic Corporate Council is to provide its member corporations with the resources, market intelligence, collective expertise, education, and counsel to implement proven strategies for reaching the Hispanic community externally and leveraging Hispanic talent internally.

14. National Hispanic Council on Aging (NHCOA) (http://nhcoa.org/)

    The National Hispanic Council on Aging addresses issues of health disparities, economic security, abuse, and victimization of the elderly and their families and builds affordable housing for the elderly.

15. National Hispanic Institute (NHI) (https://www.nationalhispanicinstitute.org/)

    The National Hispanic Institute targets top Hispanics in high school and college and conducts creative leadership training to develop students' self-marketing, networking, college planning, and organizational development skills.

16. National Hispanic Medical Association (NHMA) (http://nhmamd.org/)

    The mission of the National Hispanic Medical Association is to improve the health of Hispanics and other underserved populations. As a rapidly growing national resource based in the nation's capital, NHMA provides policymakers and health care providers with expert information and support in strengthening health service delivery to Hispanic communities across the nation. This organization represents 36,000 licensed Hispanic physicians in the United States.

17. The National Institute for Latino Policy (http://latinopolicy.org/)

    The National Institute for Latino Policy (NiLP) (formerly the Institute for Puerto Rican Policy) is a nonprofit and nonpartisan policy center established in 1982. One of the leading think tanks in the Latino community utilizing an action research model, NiLP is involved in a wide range of policy issues affecting the Latino community.

18. Prospanica (https://www.prospanica.org/)

    Prospanica has hosted annual career and professional development conferences, connecting thousands of Hispanics to graduate programs, subject matter experts, corporations, and each other. Prospanica has given over $8 million in scholarships for graduate education.

19. Society of Hispanic Engineers (SHPE) (http://www.shpe.org/)

    The Society of Hispanic Professional Engineers (SHPE), founded in Los Angeles, California, in 1974 by a group of engineers employed by the city of Los Angeles, was formed as a national organization of professional engineers to serve as role models in the Hispanic community. Today, SHPE enjoys a strong but independent network of professional and student chapters throughout the nation.

20. Tomas Rivera Policy Institute (http://trpi.org/)

    The Tomas Rivera Policy Institute was founded as an independent, nonprofit research organization to foster sound public policies and programs relevant to the Hispanic community.

21. United States Hispanic Chamber of Commerce (USHCC) (http://ushcc.com/)

    The United States Hispanic Chamber of Commerce is dedicated to bringing the issues and concerns of the nation's more than 2 million Hispanic-owned businesses to the forefront of the national economic agenda. Throughout its nearly twenty-five-year history, the USHCC has enjoyed outstanding working relationships with international heads of state, members of Congress, and the current White House administration. Through its network of more than 150 local Hispanic Chambers of Commerce and Hispanic business organizations, the organization effectively communicates the needs and potential of the Hispanic enterprise to the public and private sector.

8. Learning Experience Opportunities Beyond the Classroom

CRES List of Community Organizations in the Fort Worth Area
A list of community organizations in the Fort Worth area that can serve as field trip partners or in-class-speakers for Latinx Studies-related themes.

Organizations Local to DFW

Artes de la Rosa: Cultural Center for the Arts
http://www.artesdelarosa.org/
Artes de la Rosa, formerly Latin Arts Association of Fort Worth, is the nonprofit organization that manages the historic gem of Fort Worth's Northside—the Rose Marine Theater, and Fort Worth's only Hispanic theater company—Teatro de la Rosa. Possible internship duties: Grant writing/marketing/arts.

Cesar Chavez Committee of Tarrant County
https://www.facebook.com/CesarChavezTarrantCounty/
A non-profit organization committed to promoting education, social justice, community, and civic engagement in the empowering spirit of César Chávez.

My Brother's Keeper, Fort Worth
https://www.facebook.com/mbkfortworth/
Working to improve results and opportunities for young men of color in Fort Worth, Texas.

United Fort Worth
https://www.facebook.com/UnitedFortWorth
United Fort Worth is a nonpartisan coalition that unifies people of many backgrounds, ethnicities, cultures, and neighborhoods to address local issues.

LGBTQ SAVES
Mission Statement: LGBTQ S.A.V.E.S. fosters the well-being of LGBTQ youth and allies. Provides safe spaces for social and personal development; promotes supportive learning environments; and offers resources to youth and their families.

Multicultural Alliance
Based in Fort Worth, Texas, the Multicultural Alliance® promotes inclusive communities, working toward the elimination of bias, bigotry, and oppression, and encouraging understanding and equity through shared experiences and educational programming.

Community Frontline of Fort Worth, Inc.
Community frontline's mission is to mobilize men to enter into and alleviate the suffering in their communities, beginning with east Fort Worth.

Tammy Gomez, Sound Culture
http://bikespokelove.com/
Tammy Gomez is a longtime local activist and poet. She is a great speaker to bring into class or to work with on cultural literacy projects with students of all ages.

Latino Hustle
https://www.facebook.com/LatinoHustle/
A Fort Worth-based Latinx artists collective dedicated to help bring awareness to local Latinx artists, vendors, merchants, hosts, and more in Fort Worth.

Con Mi Madre

https://www.facebook.com/ConMiMADREFortWorth/

A two-generation organization that empowers young Latinas and their mothers through education and support services that increase preparedness, participation, and success in post-secondary education. Service areas may be limited to specific schools.

Girls, Inc.

http://girlsinctarrant.org/

An organization dedicated to providing programs, opportunities, and advocacy promoting equity for girls.

Blackhouse

http://www.fwblackhouse.com/info

Blackhouse is a pioneer and purveyor of the growth and advancement of Fort Worth's creative scene. The vision of the founders was to create a creative space for artists, musicians, creators, and entrepreneurs to gain exposure, network, and collaborate. The house was built in 1915, and officially became "Blackhouse" in 2016. Since then Blackhouse has worked toward affecting cultural change throughout the city.

Thank You Darlin' Foundation

https://tydfoundation.org/

Our mission is to help disadvantaged children experience academic and personal success through the arts. We carry out this mission by partnering with schools and other organizations to provide supplemental instruction that builds confidence, literacy, and leaders.

Statewide Organizations

Mexican American Studies Texas K-12 Coalition

https://mastxeducation.com/

A website dedicated to the advancement and implementation of Mexican American Studies courses and content in K-12 Public Education throughout the state of Texas.

Tejas NACCS Foco

https://www.naccs.org/naccs/Tejas.asp

A regional network of members of the National Association of Chicana and Chicano Scholars (NACCS), which holds an annual regional conference.

RAICES Texas

https://www.raicestexas.org/

RAICES is a 501(C)(3) nonprofit agency that promotes justice by providing free and low-cost legal services to underserved immigrant children, families, and refugees in Texas.

Jolt Texas

https://www.jolttx.org/en/

Jolt is a Texas-based multi-issue organization that builds the political power and influence of Latinos in our democracy.

Intercultural Development Resource Association

https://www.idra.org/

IDRA strengthens and transforms public education by providing dynamic training; useful research, evaluation, and frameworks for action; timely policy analyses; and innovative materials and programs.

Field Trips

Local Fort Worth and Dallas

1. All Saints Catholic Church, 214 NW 20th St, Fort Worth, TX 76164

    The religious heart of Latino Fort Worth, overseen for decades by popular parish vicar Fr. Stephe Jasso.

2. The Blackhouse, 1105 Peach St, Fort Worth, TX 76102 http://www.fwblackhouse.com/info

    A Latino-owned creative event space, the Blackhouse is a pioneer and purveyor of the growth and advancement of Fort Worth's creative scene. The house itself was built in 1915, and officially became "Blackhouse" in 2016. Since then Blackhouse has worked towards affecting cultural change throughout the city.

3. *Convivio: Mural of Community and Inclusion*, at Franko's Market, 2622 Azle Ave., Fort Worth, TX 76106 https://comunidad27.wordpress.com/beautification/

    A mural created by Northside neighborhood group Comunidad 27 depicting a large mariachi band and other points of pride in the community.

4. La Gran Plaza de Fort Worth, 4200 South Fwy #2500, Fort Worth, TX 76115

    A Hispanic-themed shopping mall in Fort Worth, Texas. Opened in 1962 as Seminary South and later known as Fort Worth Town Center, it was reinvented as a center catering to largely Hispanic clientele after losing most of its major stores. The Mercado includes hair salons, real estate services, sign/print shops, clothing/apparel, embroidery/tailors, health products, candy stores, party supplies, and many other services. You will find unique weekly entertainment and special events every month. Take time to check out the original artwork from local artists posted in key spots in the mall. Tour brochures are available in the mall office, Suite 2500.

5. Manuel Jara Elementary School, 2100 Lincoln Ave, Fort Worth, TX 76164

    A FWISD campus named for a local World War II veteran and Mexican American civil rights activist.

6. Latino Cultural Center, 2600 Live Oak St, Dallas, TX 75204

    Latino arts center with a three-hundred-seat theater, an art gallery, sculpture gardens, and event spaces. Rotating exhibits at times include local Mexican American history.

7. Rufino Mendoza Elementary School, 1412 Denver, Fort Worth, TX 76164

    A FWISD school serving the North Side since 1910, it was recently renamed for World War I veteran and activist Mendoza, who also led efforts to open up educational opportunities for Latinos within the school district.

8. Pike Park / Santos Rodriguez Park, Dallas, TX 75201

    Historic city park in Dallas's Little Mexico neighborhood, featuring a Spanish-style recreation center and iron gazebo. Recently the site of demonstrations commemorating the police killing of twelve-year-old Santos Rodriguez, the city is considering renaming the park in his honor.

9. "La Pulga" (Henderson Bazar), 1000 N Henderson St., Fort Worth, TX 76107

   Weekend outdoor "flea market" featuring Latino-owned businesses and Latino-oriented products. A Fort Worth institution.

10. Rose Marine Theater, 1440 N Main St, Fort Worth, TX 76164

    Built in the 1920s, this venue hosts Hispanic performances of music, theater, and dance, plus films. Managed by Artes de la Rosa, http://www.artesdelarosa.org/.

11. St. Patrick Cathedral, 1206 Throckmorton St, Fort Worth, TX 76102

    Converted from an 1888 parish church, this beautiful cathedral downtown hosts regular Catholic church services.

12. Jesse Sandoval Park, 301 Wimberly St, Fort Worth, TX 76107

    Named for a pioneering activist in Fort Worth's Political Association of Spanish-Speaking Organizations (PASO) and other Mexican American generation groups, the park is all that is left of the historic Wiesenberger barrio near the present-day West Seventh St corridor.

13. United Fort Worth Community Justice Center, 2308 Vaughn Blvd, Fort Worth, TX 76105

    United Fort Worth is a grassroots, cross-cultural, multi-ethnic community collective that works to oppose discriminatory policy, discriminatory legislation, and oppressive systems. The mission of United Fort Worth is to ensure justice for all and improve the quality of life for marginalized communities in the 817. We believe collective action advocacy is vital in the struggle for community representation and equal justice. UFW's Community Justice Center is the city's first space where activism, community defense, political education, and grassroots social justice organizing will have a place to thrive right in the heart of Poly!

14. United Hispanic Council of Tarrant County, 2744 Hemphill St, Fort Worth, TX 76110

    A leading organization advocating for civic and political engagement on the Southside and for Latino political representation in local governments.

15. Unity Park—Parque Unidad, 4000 Townsend Dr, Fort Worth, TX 76110

    Formerly Jefferson Davis Park, the City of Fort Worth renamed this green space, playground, and pavilion in the Rosemont neighborhood after local residents protested its fictive connection to the Confederacy in 2017.

16. Vaquero de Fort Worth Statue, 1406 N. Main St, Fort Worth TX 76164

    City-commissioned bronze statue highlighting the original *Mexicano* cowboy culture and its contributions to Fort Worth.

Texas State

1. Bazán and Longoria Murders Historical Marker, Hidalgo County, Atlas Number 5507018584

   Commemorates the 1915 murders by the Texas Rangers of two prominent Tejano leaders and landowners during a period of state-sanctioned violence against Mexicans and Mexican Americans in South Texas. The marker was proposed and advocated by scholars in the nonprofit organization, Refusing to Forget, http://refusingtoforget.org.

2. Chicano Studies Program, University of Texas, El Paso, Graham Hall, Room 104, 500 West University Ave, El Paso 79968

   Founded in 1970, this is the state's first Mexican American Studies program and the only one named "Chicano Studies." It also offers the only online BA in the field.

3. Crystal City Library and City Hall, Juan Cornejo Dr, Crystal City, TX

   Hometown of renowned activist José Ángel Gutiérrez, the "first Chicano revolt" of 1963, and later el Partido de La Raza Unida (or Raza Unida Party), the library and city hall grounds stand as a testament to the nation's most successful example of Chicano movement self-determination. Local activists in this small agricultural town organized a series of political campaigns in which they took over the reins of local governments and sought to create a culturally conscious alternative to mainstream "gringo" society. Decades later, few remnants remain, but city leaders claim that their culturally relevant educational institutions and ethos of self- and community pride has resulted in the highest per capita rate of Chicano PhDs in the nation.

4. Esperanza Peace & Justice Center, San Antonio, TX

   Esperanza advocates for neighborhood preservation and community-based revitalization on the city's Westside. It hosts and sponsors intersectional events and trainings for a wide range of social justice activists. Its buildings feature large event spaces, museum exhibits, a *microtaller* (workshop) and *rinconcito* (small farm plot). Their art installations and signs—"Mi Barrio No Se Vende!"—can be seen throughout the neighborhood.

5. Dr. Hector P. Garcia Statue and Archives, Mary Bell Library, Texas A&M University, Corpus Christi, TX

   A bronze statue and the personal papers of Dr. Garcia, the founder of the American GI Forum and his generation's most recognized civil rights activist.

6. Guadalupe Cultural Arts Center, San Antonio, TX

   The city's oldest Latino cultural center in the heart of the Westside, its historic auditorium hosts music, film, theatrical performances, and more. Its complex also housed the original offices of the influential Southwest Voter Education Registration Project.

7. Felix Longoria Historical Marker, City Hall, 105 N Harborth Ave, Three Rivers, TX 78071; Atlas Number 5507016279

   Marker telling the story of Pfc. Felix Longoria, a Mexican American native of Three Rivers in Live Oak County southeast of San Antonio. Longoria was killed while stationed in the Philippines after World War II. His remains were returned to a local funeral home in late 1947, but the Anglo owners refused to receive it. News of the incident made it to Dr. Hector P. Garcia of Corpus Christi, who publicized it and ultimately succeeded in getting the junior US Senator from Texas, Lyndon B. Johnson, to intervene. Johnson arranged to have Longoria interred at Arlington National Cemetery in Washington, DC, and the case made Dr. Garcia well-known and helped give birth to the American GI Forum. The marker was previously located in front of the funeral home, but it was struck by a vehicle, and the property's current owners—who disavow its history—refused to allow its restoration on site.

8. La Unión del Pueblo Entero (LUPE), San Juan, TX

   A community union founded by César E. Chávez and Dolores Huerta, it resides in the old Texas headquarters of the United Farm Workers, which came to the Rio Grande Valley in 1966. A marker onsite commemorates the strike and a march to Austin that took place that year. LUPE continues to organize and provide services for immigrants and residents of the region's many unincorporated *colonias*. The group also hosts alternative spring breaks and other school-based service and educational trips.

9. Mexican American Cultural Center, 600 River St, Austin, TX 78701

    Center featuring exhibits, events, and programs that explore Mexican American cultural arts and heritage.

10. Felix H. Morales Funeral Home, 2901 Canal St, Houston, TX 77003

    Early Latino-owned business in the heart of the Segundo Barrio (Second Ward), an early center of Mexican American life in Houston. The home was used for meetings of the Civic Action Committee and other early civil rights organizations.

11. Museo del Barrio, El Paso, TX

    A community-based museum celebrating the Segundo Barrio of El Paso, the "Ellis Island of the West," through which millions of Mexicans passed while immigrating to the United States between the 1880s and the 1930s.

12. Our Lady of Guadalupe Church, 2405 Navigation Blvd, Houston, TX 77003

    First Latino-serving Catholic parish in Houston and home to many community gatherings in the Segundo Barrio.

13. Emma Tenayuca Historical Marker, Milam Park, San Antonio, TX

    A plaque commemorating the life of Emma Tenayuca (Brooks), a teenaged civil rights, union, and political organizer in the 1930s. A state leader in the Communist Party USA and head of the local Workers Alliance of America, Tenayuca coauthored a position paper, "The Mexican Question in the Southwest," which connected the civil rights of Mexican Americans to the class struggle. She is best known as an orator and leader of the great pecan shellers uprising of 1938, in which at least 10,000 Mexicano workers struck the seasonal industry across the Westside—and won a union contract. Milam Park was later the site of the Westside's first-ever presidential campaign rally, for Democratic candidate Adlai Stevenson, who came at the invitation of the Loyal American Democrats, a Mexican American club, in 1952.

National

1. *América – Oprimida y Destruida por el Imperialismo*, Olvera St, Los Angeles, CA

    An anti-imperialist mural by David Alfaro Siqueiros, one of los tres grandes (the three greats) muralists of the Mexican Revolution. Siqueiros completed the mural in 1934 under a commission from local elites, but the subject matter proved too controversial, and the mural was whitewashed and erased. Decades later, the white paint peeled off, revealing the original mural underneath. It has now been sealed and preserved, with both the Siqueiros mural and fading whitewash still intact. An on-site museum tells the story.

2. Boyle Heights Museum, Los Angeles, CA

3. Chicano Park, San Diego, CA

4. Escuela Tlatelolco, Denver, CO

5. Garfield High School, East Los Angeles, CA

6. *The Great Wall of L.A.*, East Los Angeles, CA

   The most extensive and impressive example of East LA's community-based Chicano/a mural movement of the 1970s and 1980s, it stretches nearly a mile.

7. Ruben Salazar Park, East Los Angeles, CA

   Formerly Whittier Park, this was the site of an all-day festival and rally led by the Chicano Moratorium Against the Vietnam War Committee in 1971. The demonstration remained peaceful until Los Angeles County Sheriff's Department deputies stormed the crowd, beating participants of all ages. After the melee, another deputy fired a tear gas canister into the nearby Silver Dollar Bar, and the missile struck and killed Ruben Salazar, the nation's leading Mexican American journalist for a mainstream newspaper. The park was renamed to honor his martyrdom.

8. San Francisco State University, San Francisco, CA

   The mythic birthplace of modern Ethnic Studies after a multiracial alliance of students went on strike in 1968 to protest their marginalization on campus. Backed by activists in the community, the students forced the administration to create the Department of Raza Studies and an entire College of Ethnic Studies.

9. Museo del Barrio, 1230 Fifth Avenue, New York, NY 10029, 212.831.7272 https://www.elmuseo.org/

   New York's leading Latino cultural institution welcomes visitors of all backgrounds to discover the artistic landscape of Latino, Caribbean, and Latin American cultures. Their richness is represented in El Museo's wide-ranging collections and exhibitions, complemented by film, literary, visual, and performing arts series, cultural celebrations, and educational programs.

10. Nuyorican Poets Café, 236 East 3rd St. New York, NY 10009 (212) 780-9386 https://www.nuyorican.org/

    Founded in 1973, the Nuyorican Poets Cafe began as a living room salon in the East Village apartment of writer and poet Miguel Algarin along with other playwrights, poets, and musicians of color whose work was not accepted by the mainstream academic, entertainment or publishing industries. By 1975, the performance poetry scene had started to become a vital element of urban Latino and African American culture, marked by the release of a "Nuyorican Poetry" anthology, and Miguel Piñero's "Short Eyes," which was a hit on Broadway. By 1981, the overflow of audience and artists led the Cafe to purchase a former tenement building at 236 East Third Street, and to expand its activities and programs from the original space on East Sixth Street.

    Over the past several decades, the café has emerged as one of the country's most highly respected arts organizations. Its programming includes poetry slams, open mics, Latin Jazz and Hip-Hop concerts, theatrical performances, educational programs, and visual art exhibits. Its weekly poetry slams draw thousands of spectators each year and have popularized competitive performance poetry. The café's educational programs (which are funded in part by the city and state of New York and the NEA) provide literacy and public speaking to thousands of students and many school groups each year. Its theater program has been awarded over thirty Audelco Awards and was honored with an OBIE Grant for Excellence in Theater.

Local and Regional Resources and Scholarships

1. Fort Worth Hispanic Chamber of Commerce (https://www.fwhcc.org/)

    The first chamber office was located downtown in the Sinclair Building, and the first meetings were held at various area restaurants. However, by 1982 interest in the organization grew enough to support a full suite of offices in the historic Stockyards section of the city. The articles of incorporation were amended November 25, 1985, and the name was changed to the Fort Worth Hispanic Chamber of Commerce. Since its founding, the Fort Worth Hispanic Chamber of Commerce has grown from the initial thirty members to hundreds of businesses and professional leaders. Today the FWHCC is a dynamic force, promoting international trade, education, opportunity, and economic mobility for all and the continuous development of its members. The chamber particularly strives to serve its members through business and professional seminars, workshops, networking opportunities, and business procurement assistance through its Economic Development Programs. The chamber also works to give back to our community through the FWHCC Scholarship fund, created in 1991. Since then, it has provided over a million dollars in scholarship awards. The FWHCC is proud to serve the business interests of the Metroplex community and will strive to seek opportunity for its membership and achieve economic benefit for all.

    Created in 1998, the FWHCC Scholarship Fund (http://www.fwhcc.org/scholarships/) has since provided hundreds of local students with financial support and encouragement, ensuring cost is not a barrier to their education. The general application for FWHCC scholarships and partner scholarships for high school students is linked on the URL above.

    ■ The Gloria J. González Memorial Scholarship
    https://www.fwhcc.org/gloriaj-gonzalezscholarship/

    The Gloria J. González Memorial Scholarship for the Advancement of Latinos in the Health Care Professions was created in memory of Gloria J. González, a former University of Texas at Austin student who was about to graduate and pursue medical school to become a pediatrician when she was tragically killed in a car accident in 1988.

    ■ The Freddie Caram, Jr. Memorial Scholarship https://www.fwhcc.org/freddie-caram-jr/

    Freddie Caram Jr. (1971-2013) was raised in the Northside of Fort Worth by a loving family. He attended All Saints Catholic School through eighth grade and ultimately graduated from Arlington Heights High School in 1989. From there, he attended Tarrant County Junior College (now Tarrant County College) and transferred to Texas Tech University, where he ultimately received his undergraduate degree in 1995. As an active member of The Fort Worth Hispanic Chamber of Commerce, Freddie not only participated in many fundraisers and networking events, he also became an ambassador and co-founder of the Latino Young Professionals group. FWHCC's goal is to honor Freddie's dedication and commitment to support his community and his encouragement of others to educate themselves, regardless of what obstacles they may face. *Applicants must meet the following two requirements: 1) have a minimum 2.75 GPA, and 2) are a graduating high school senior OR Tarrant County Community College student with plans to attend a university.*

    ■ Fort Worth Beauty School
    https://www.fwhcc.org/fort-worth-beauty-school-scholarship/

    Requirements for Enrollment at FWBS: Copy of High School Diploma (or transcript), GED, or Ability to Benefit test; Proof of Age, i.e., Driver's License, Birth Certificate, State ID card, passport, etc.; Social Security Card, if eligible non-citizen bring resident card; $100 school registration *fee waived for those who apply through the Fort Worth Hispanic Chamber of Commerce*; $25.00 prepaid debit card—to register with Texas Dept. of Licensing & Regulations; 2 small front-view pictures of yourself (Financial Aid Students: complete application for financial aid at www.fasfa.ed.gov).

■ Tarleton State University https://www.fwhcc.org/tarleton-state-university-scholarship/

With its main campus in Stephenville, an hour southwest of Fort Worth, Tarleton State University offers the value of a Texas A&M University System degree with its own brand of personal attention, individual opportunities, history, tradition, and community. Tarleton is a vibrant learning community with nearly one hundred undergraduate and graduate degrees, as well as a doctorate in education, within seven colleges: Agricultural and Environmental Sciences; Business Administration; Education; Graduate Studies; Health Sciences and Human Service; Liberal and Fine Arts; and Science and Technology. Requirements for enrollment: high school top quarter ranking, and 1080 SAT score or 23 ACT score.

2. Hispanic Scholarship Fund (https://www.hsf.net/scholarship)

The HSF Scholarship is designed to help students of Hispanic heritage obtain a university degree. Scholarships are available, on a competitive basis, to: high school seniors; undergraduate students (all years); community college students transferring to four-year universities; and graduate students. Awards are based on merit; amounts range from $500 to $5,000, based on relative need, among the scholars selected. Eligibility requirements: Must be of Hispanic heritage; minimum of 3.0 GPA on a 4.0 scale (or equivalent) for high school students; minimum of 2.5 GPA on a 4.0 scale (or equivalent) for undergraduate and graduate students; plan to enroll full-time in an accredited, not-for-profit, four-year university or graduate school, during the fall of a scholarship cycle (year); US citizen, Permanent Legal Resident, DACA or Eligible Non-Citizen (as defined by FAFSA); complete FAFSA or state based financial aid application (if applicable).

3. Hispanic Women's Network of Texas (http://www.hwntfw.org/)

The Hispanic Women's Network of Texas (HWNT) is a statewide organization made up of ten chapters across the state of Texas: Fort Worth, Dallas, San Antonio, Austin, El Paso, Denton, Houston, Corpus Christi, Rio Grande Valley, and South Texas. We are women from diverse backgrounds, each of us committed to promoting the participation of Hispanic women in public, corporate, and civic arenas. HWNT seeks to advance the educational, cultural, social, legal, and economic well-being of all women through a broader awareness of their role in society, business, and family. Members seek to celebrate the positive image and values of the Hispanic culture. HWNT is a 501(c)(3) non-profit organization.

■ Latinas In Progress (LIP) http://www.hwntfw.org/latinas-in-progress.html

HWNT Fort Worth's esteemed education series, Latinas in Progress© (LIP©), collaborates with area universities and colleges to motivate graduating high school Latinas toward achieving their dreams of a college degree. LIP not only acclimates participants and their parents to the rigors of college, but equips them with vital tools that will enrich their personal and professional lives. Latina mentors and LIP alums eagerly share their personal struggles and triumphs to create powerful visions of achievement for our ambitious young ladies. They engage in workshops such as College 101, Writing Skills, Life Skills, Assertiveness Training, and Civic Engagement. In the process, they develop networks, social skills, and confidence, and increase their community involvement by volunteering a minimum of twelve hours at community events and charities such as: Sundance Santa, toy drives, Dia de los Muertos Gala, HALOS Christmas Dance/Fundraiser, and Feed the Homeless Drives. For more detailed information, go to our program site (http://www.lipfw.org/) and scholarship site (http://www.hwntfw.org/lip-scholarship-program.html).

4. Latino Hustle (https://www.improuse.com/US/Fort-Worth/114802942344186/Latino-Hustle)

   A Fort Worth-based Latinx artists collective dedicated to help bring awareness to local Latinx artists, vendors, merchants, hosts, and more in Fort Worth. Latino Hustle was created in the winter of 2016 by local artist Jessika Guillén to bring awareness to local Latin artists in the DFW area. Latino Hustle's mission: Create supportive and welcoming spaces for local Latinx artists to showcase their work in all forms of artistic media. Events are listed at the URL above.

5. Tarrant County College – Scholarships (https://www.tccd.edu/services/paying-for-college/scholarships/)

   Student Financial Aid Services Office (SFAS) makes available various other financial aid programs/scholarships upon completion of your FAFSA/TASFA application. For more information on any of the following programs, contact your campus Student Financial Aid Services. Applications for TCC Foundation Scholarships (https://tccd.academicworks.com/) are due in November.

6. United Way of Tarrant County (http://unitedwayfortworth.org/)

   United Way of Tarrant County has worked to improve the lives of those in our communities since 1922. As a nonprofit leader, we bring together individuals, groups, donors, and service providers to help solve some of the toughest social issues affecting Tarrant County. Each year, United Way of Tarrant County helps more than 300,000 people through its resources. United Way of Tarrant County has no fees on donor designations, with 100 percent of the donation going to the selected agency or cause. United Way of Tarrant County partners with dozens of local nonprofit organizations serving a wide range of communities.

The following scholarships are specifically either for Latinx students or for first-generation, low income, and underrepresented students.

7. Terry Scholars Program (https://terryfoundation.org/affiliated-universities/)
   Full-tuition scholarship program serving thirteen different Texas colleges.

8. MALDEF Scholarships (https://www.maldef.org/wp-content/uploads/2018/11/2019-2020_MALDEF_Scholarship_Resource_Guide.pdf)

9. Collegeboard Opportunity Scholarship (https://opportunity.collegeboard.org/)

10. The Gates Scholarship (https://www.thegatesscholarship.org/scholarship)

11. Dell Scholars (https://www.dellscholars.org/scholarship/)

12. TRiO/Upward Bound (https://www2.ed.gov/programs/trioupbound/index.html)
    All program participants who go to UT-Arlington are eligible for up to $1500 per year in addition to their financial aid package. The program application is available through local high school TRiO/Upward Bound advisers. Students will also need to submit a scholarship application during the second semester of their senior year.

13. Impossible Possibilities Scholarship (http://www.ipdfw.org/scholarships/)

14. Horatio Alger Scholarship (https://scholars.horatioalger.org/scholarships/)

15. TexTesol Scholarship (http://textesolv.org/scholarship/)

16. Penrose Foundation (https://www.kellerisd.net/cms/lib/TX02215599/Centricity/Domain/2204/Penrose%20Scholarship%20for%20Hispanic%20Students.pdf)
Application shared directly with high school counselors. Award is $5,000.

17. Scholarshot Mentor Scholarship (http://scholarshot.org/)

18. Hispanic Scholar Consortium (https://www.hispanicscholar.org/apply)

19. McDonalds HACER Scholarship (https://www.mcdonalds.com/us/en-us/community/hacer.html)

FWISD Elementary History Fair

The Elementary History Fair is an opportunity for students from third to fifth grade to learn and practice essential historical thinking skills. They will learn how to analyze primary, secondary, and tertiary sources, to interrogate those sources, to recognize and explain change over time, to create and support a historical argument, and to contextualize their topics. Students can choose to research any topic that fits within the theme designated by the National History Day. Great projects will focus on unique and lesser-known topics that are meaningful to the individual student. The challenge in completing a history fair project with a topic that is not typically found in textbooks is the availability of primary and secondary sources to conduct research. This curriculum guidebook provides numerous resources that can direct students to topics directly related to Latinx Studies. Additionally, teachers can encourage students to seek out local topics. The links below can help with local research.

To engage your students in the Elementary History Fair, the district has provided a step-by-step guide to aid you in the process. https://sites.google.com/teachers.fwisd.org/fwisdhistoryfair/fwisd-history-fair-home

State and National History Day
Adapted from the National History Day Website

Texas State History Day and National History Day are opportunities for sixth-to twelfth-grade students (sixth to eighth grade is the junior level and ninth to twelfth is senior level) to learn and practice critical thinking skills, problem-solving skills, research and reading skills, and to build self-esteem and confidence. Students are able to choose a topic that is meaningful to them and display their research and argument in a variety of ways. While most students choose a traditional tryptic board, students can also create a website or documentary, write a paper, or write, direct, and star in a performance. Teachers can assign history fair in their individual classrooms and make their own judgements on which projects should advance to the regional fair of Texas History Day at the University of Arlington, typically in the beginning of March every year. Alternatively, all history teachers on campus could work together to create a school-wide fair and bring in judges (check with history majors and professors at local universities, use alumni, or partner with middle school teachers in your pyramid) to make decisions on the winning projects. From the regional fair, the top two projects in each category (every category has an individual division and group division except papers which are individual only) will move on to the Texas History Day competition held in the beginning of May each year in Austin. FWISD Social Studies department will support students who advance to the state and national competitions. The national competition takes place in June in Maryland. This curriculum guidebook provides numerous resources that can direct students to topics directly related to Latinx Studies. Additionally, teachers can also encourage students to seek out local topics. The links below can help with local research. To engage your students in history fair, National History Day has created numerous resources to guide teachers through the process.

https://texashistoryday.com/
https://www.nhd.org/

Additionally, here are some key resources for local Latinx history:

HOLA Tarrant County (https://holatarrantcounty.org/)

Latino Fort Worth YouTube Channel (https://www.youtube.com/channel/UCqHWktgiyP_szeR8K-71cCTw/featured)

Latino Fort Worth Archives (http://www.fortworthtexasarchives.org/digital/collection/p16084coll25 and https://fortworthlibrary.lyrasistechnology.org/repositories/2/digital_objects/32)

Civil Rights in Black and Brown (https://crbb.tcu.edu/)

Sam Garcia Papers, Fort Worth Library (https://fortworthlibrary.lyrasistechnology.org/repositories/2/resources/232)

9. Hispanic Heritage Month Ideas and Resources

The following online resources are intended to provide teachers and curriculum designers with ideas, material, and pedagogical tactics for strategizing ways to incorporate exercises and activities beyond the classroom relating to Hispanic Heritage Month, September 15–October 15.

Scholastic, Inc.
https://www.scholastic.com/teachers/articles/teaching-content/24-great-ideas-hispanic-heritage-month/

Community Connections: Take Your Learning Beyond the Classroom

1. Read, Review, and Recommend: Partner with a local library to create a display of Hispanic heritage-themed books. Have each student select a book and write a short review to be displayed at the library.

2. A Day in the Life of Our Class: Share your classroom culture by creating a web page filled with photos and captions.

3. Plant a Memory Forest: Plant a tree in your community for each Hispanic hero your class selects. Tag each tree with a mini biography highlighting that hero's contributions.

4. Ecuadorian *Migajon* Miniatures: Students can create tiny animals, flowers, and people just like artisans in Ecuador do. To make the dough, each student will knead one slice of white bread, crust removed, with one tablespoon of white glue. The dough will be quite sticky at first but will become manageable with kneading. Mold the dough into tiny shapes and allow to air-dry overnight. Decorate with acrylic paint and display!

5. Ponce Carnival Masks: Bring the vivid colors of Puerto Rican Carnival to your classroom with traditional papier-mâché masks of red, yellow, and black. Begin with one large paper plate for each student. Thinking of the plate as the face of a clock, cut 2-inch slits at two o'clock, six o'clock, and ten o'clock. Overlap the edges of the slits and affix with tape to make the mask 3-D. Cut two holes for eyes. Add horns to the mask by rolling small sheets of poster board into cones and attaching them with tape. Using a thin paste of water and flour and strips of newspaper, cover the mask with three or four layers of papier-mâché. Once the mask is dry, bring it to life with brightly colored paint and traditional patterns of dots. Then take your masks on parade!

6. *Papeles Picados*: Add a festive touch to the classroom with traditional Mexican punched papers called *papeles picados*. Fold thin construction paper in a variety of colors into quarters, eighths, cone style, or fan style, to achieve a variety of looks. Use scissors and hole punches to create a perforated pattern. Hang the completed papers along a string using tape.

7. Zapotec Rug Paintings: When there's not enough time to weave, recreate these beautiful geometric rugs from Mexico using paint. Begin with a sheet of poster board for each student. Using rulers and pencils, draw zigzag, stair-step, and straight lines across the poster board. Incorporate angular shapes such as diamonds and triangles. Once the pencil layout is complete, use poster paints or markers to fill in the design.

8. Grow a Heritage Garden: Plant staple crops common in many Spanish-speaking countries, such as corn, beans, squash, and peppers. Have students keep a log tracking the growth of the various plants. Extend the project by researching staple foods of other regions.

9. The Air We Share: Monitor the daily air-quality index for your city (available at AirNow, https://www.airnow.gov/). Have students study the results and look for trends. What are small actions we can take to help improve air quality for everyone on the planet?

10. Try Your Luck: Play a simple Mexican game called *Toma Todo*. Create six-sided tops and have students spin them to see if they have to take or contribute chips into the pot. Whoever scores the most chips wins! (https://www.spanishplayground.net/traditional-game-top-printable/.)

11. Adopt a City: Select a world city to "adopt," such as your city's international sister city (http://www.sister-cities.org/). Display photos of people and places, as well as a clock set to the local time. Have students report on local news events.

12. My Home Country: Celebrate diversity in your classroom by inviting ELL students to share photos of their hometowns, important cultural items, and basic phrases in their native language.

13. What's Your Heritage? Ask students to investigate their own heritage and report back to the class on the origins of their ancestors. Graph the results and discuss how the class reflects, or differs from, city, state, and national demographic statistics. For current census data, visit the United States Census Bureau (https://www.census.gov/programs-surveys/decennial-census/decade.2010.html).

14. Aztec Math: Spice up a math review activity by replacing the Arabic numerals with Aztec numbers.

15. International Outfits: Do you know how far your clothes traveled before they even reached the store where you bought them? Have students inventory the items they are wearing and the country of origin for each item. What is the total number of miles for each student? For the entire class?

16. My Spanish Dictionary: Have the class create a lively illustrated dictionary of Spanish words, complete with visual or verbal memory tricks for remembering words' meanings.

17. Label Maker: Give pairs of students a pad of sticky notes and a Spanish-English dictionary. Play festive music while students label everything in the classroom with a bilingual label. When the music stops, have students take a tour of the room and practice the new words.

18. World Alphabet Collection: Gather newspaper clippings or online printouts showcasing scripts from other languages. Create a special bulletin board celebrating the myriad of ways people write. An excellent resource is Omniglot (http://www.omniglot.com/).

19. Play Color, *Colorcito*: In this traditional Spanish street game, the child who is "It" says *"color, colorcito"* (color, little color) and then the name of a color. Everyone must run to touch something that color in order to be "safe." If the person who's "It" tags a player, he or she becomes the new "It" and play continues.

20. Move to the Beat: Reenergize students between activities with a Latin dance party. Play selections of tango, merengue, folk music, or Tex-Mex and ask students to feel the differences in the beat as they move their bodies.

21. Can You Read Mayan? Introduce students to the ancient Mayan alphabet and ask each student to write his or her name in Mayan glyphs on a sheet of paper. Collect all the sheets, then give each student a sheet to decode.

22. Write Your Own Folktale: Read one of the many traditional folktales from Spanish-speaking countries and then write new stories based on the traditions of these tales.

23. Our Heritage Album: Compile a class album of significant Hispanic Americans throughout history featuring lots of drawings, invented memorabilia, and simulated newspaper clippings. You can always help yourself and browse the Smithsonian's Hispanic Heritage Teaching

Resources (https://learninglab.si.edu/search?st=hispanic+heritage&item_type=collections& st_op=and) or take your kids to the virtual Smithsonian's Latino Center's Kid's Corner for inspiration for your album (http://latino.si.edu/KidsCorner/index.html).

24. Musical Stories: Give students the beginning paragraph of a traditional folktale, and then play a selection of Spanish music to inspire them to write the end of the story. Is the music sad or happy? On what kind of occasion would this music be played?

National Education Association
http://www.nea.org/tools/lessons/hispanic-heritage-month.html

1. National Hispanic Heritage Month, Grades K-5
   (http://www.nea.org/tools/lessons/hispanic-heritage-month-k-5.html)

2. National Hispanic Heritage Month, Grades 6-8
   (http://www.nea.org/tools/lessons/hispanic-heritage-month-6-8.html)

3. National Hispanic Heritage Month, Grades 9-12
   (http://www.nea.org/tools/lessons/hispanic-heritage-month-9-12.html)

Montgomery County (MD) Public Schools
https://montgomeryschoolsmd.org/curriculum/socialstudies/features/hispanic-heritage.aspx

Celebration

1. Hispanic Reading Room (http://www.loc.gov/rr/hispanic/)
   A wide collection of Latin American area studies resources provided by the Library of Congress.

2. Hispanic Heritage Teaching Resources (http://smithsonianeducation.org/
   educators/resource_library/hispanic_resources.html)

   Teaching resources from the Smithsonian Institution's education foundation.

3. Celebrate Hispanic Heritage Month! (http://www.educationworld.com/a_lesson/lesson/
   lesson023.shtml)

   Lesson ideas for celebrating Hispanic Heritage Month from Education World®.

4. Celebrate Hispanic Heritage (http://teacher.scholastic.com/activities/hispanic/index.htm)

   Student activities and teaching activities and guides from *Junior Scholastic*.

5. Celebrate Hispanic Heritage Month (http://www.nps.gov/history/nr/feature/hispanic/)

   National Registrar of Historic Places.

6. Hispanic Heritage Month (http://www.factmonster.com/spot/hhm1.html)

   Basic information about Hispanic Heritage Month and links to other online resources.

Cultural Interest

7. Smithsonian Latino Center (http://latino.si.edu/)

   Approaches Latinx contributions to America's history, arts, and culture from a Latinx perspective with resources for youth, educators, museum visitors, and researchers.

8. Diego Rivera Virtual Museum (http://www.diegorivera.com/)

   An online museum dedicated to the life and work of Diego Rivera.

9. Hispanic Online (http://www.hispaniconline.com/)

   A well-developed online magazine dedicated to Hispanic issues.

10. Mundo Latino (http://www.mundolatino.org/)

    A Latino news organization; in Spanish.

Research Information

11. Hispano Music and Culture of the Northern Rio Grande (https://www.loc.gov/collections/hispano-music-and-culture-from-the-northern-rio-grande/about-this-collection/)

    An online presentation in multiple format media exploring the music and culture of the Spanish-speaking residents of rural Northern New Mexico and Southern Colorado; *The Juan B. Rael Collection* provided by the Library of Congress.

12. Puerto Rico at the Dawn of the Modern Age (http://memory.loc.gov/ammem/collections/puertorico/)

    An online exhibit from the Library of Congress, American Memory, on Puerto Rico around the turn of the twentieth century.

13. Handbook of Latin American Studies (http://memory.loc.gov/hlas/)

    A database of Latin American Studies resources provided by the Library of Congress.

14. The Benson Latin America Collection (http://www.lib.utexas.edu/benson/)

    A variety of resources and online publications dedicated to Latin American Studies provided by the University of Texas at Austin Library.

15. English Only? (http://coloquio.com/english/)

    A collection of essays concerning English Only laws.

16. 1492: An Ongoing Voyage (http://www.loc.gov/exhibits/1492/)

    A Library of Congress online exhibit exploring the European discovery and colonization of the Americas.

17. Hispanic Population of the United States (http://www.census.gov/population/www/socdemo/hispanic.html)

    A collection of population and demographic statistics collected and recorded by the US Census Bureau statistics.

18. Latin America Network Information Center (http://lanic.utexas.edu/)

    A very wide variety of links to Latin American resources searchable by nation or subject; from the University of Texas at Austin.

19. Organization of the American States (http://www.oas.org/en/default.asp)

    The OAS provides a wide variety of resources, news, and information.

Hispanic Organizations

20. Congressional Hispanic Caucus Institute (http://www.chci.org/)

    Organization whose programs are designed to increase the participation of young Hispanics in the public and private sector.

21. League of United Latin American Citizens (http://www.lulac.org/)

    Organization for the advancement of Hispanic Americans.

22. United States Hispanic Chamber of Commerce (http://www.ushcc.com/)

    Organization "To advocate, promote and facilitate the success of Hispanic business."

Contributors

Michelle Bauml, PhD, is the Clotilda Winter Professor of Education at Texas Christian University. She is a former elementary school teacher whose research interests include new teacher development, teacher thinking and decision-making, and early childhood/elementary curriculum and instruction, with an emphasis in social studies education. Her publications have appeared in journals such as *The Journal of Social Studies Research, Social Studies Research and Practice, The Journal of Early Childhood Teacher Education,* and the *American Educational History Journal.*

David Colón is Professor of English and Comparative Race & Ethnic Studies at TCU. His essays have appeared in *The Cambridge History of Latina/o American Literature, The Cambridge Companion to 21st-Century American Poetry, The Routledge Companion to Latina/o Popular Culture, The Princeton Encyclopedia of Poetry and Poetics, The Journal of Latino/Latin American Studies, Critical Insights, Cultural Critique,* and many other publications. His edited anthology of Miguel González-Gerth's poems, *Between Day and Night* (2013), was named an Outstanding Title by the Association of American University Presses. He has served as a Latinx Studies consultant for the Smithsonian Institution; director of TCU's Latinx Studies Program; and vice chair of Fort Worth's Human Relations Commission.

Emily M. Farris is an associate professor of political science at Texas Christian University. Her research in American politics focuses on local politics and explores questions of representation and participation in regard to gender, racial, and ethnic identity. She received her MA and PhD from Brown University and BA from Furman University. Her published work has appeared in *Political Analysis, Political Research Quarterly, Politics, Groups,* and *Identities,* and other political and social science journals. She has worked with Cengage, developing textbook materials and contributing to their online teaching blog. She's regularly involved in public scholarship and frequently interacts with the press, having been quoted or appeared in almost forty outlets, including the *New York Times, Vox, The Guardian,* and *The Atlantic.* She is active on Twitter, with more than 18,000 followers.

Melita M. Garza is an American journalism historian who studies news as an agent of democracy, specializing in English- and Spanish-language news, the immigrant press, and coverage of underrepresented groups. Garza, an associate professor at TCU's Bob Schieffer College of Communication in Fort Worth until 2022, is the author of the award-winning *They Came to Toil: Newspaper Representations of Mexicans and Immigrants in the Great Depression* (University of Texas Press, 2018). *They Came to Toil* examines English- and Spanish-language news coverage of immigrants during the nation's longest economic downturn. Her work has been published in *Journalism History, American Journalism,* and the *Howard Journal of Communications.* She earned a PhD from the University of North Carolina at Chapel Hill in 2012, after two decades reporting for the *Chicago Tribune, Bloomberg News,* and the *Los Angeles Times.* She also holds an MBA from the University of Chicago and an BA from Harvard University. As well as teaching in the Honors College, Dr. Garza teaches journalism history, media literacy, business journalism, and diversity and the media. She was a founding faculty member of TCU's department of Comparative Race and Ethnic Studies and an affiliate of the Department of Women and Gender Studies. She is now associate professor of journalism at the University of Illinois, Urbana-Champaign.

Cecilia N. Sánchez Hill is a PhD candidate at Texas Christian University focusing on Mexican American education history in Texas and a graduate certificate student in Comparative Race and Ethnic Studies (CRES). She is the winner of the first Diversity in Research Award from the TCU's AddRan College of Liberal Arts for her master's thesis, "¿Mi Tierra, También?: Mexican American Civil Rights in Fort Worth, Texas, 1940-1990s." Prior to school at TCU, Hill taught US History and AP World History for Fort Worth ISD, served as social studies middle school specialist, helped write the curriculum for the Latina/o Studies Elective course, became a 2016 Secondary Teacher of the Year finalist, and the winner of the 2017-2018

Academic Chair for Teaching Excellence in Humanities. After she completes her PhD program, Hill hopes to continue to help secondary history teachers move beyond the traditional narrative used in history classrooms and assist these teachers in creating lessons that nurture critical thinking skills.

Gabriel Huddleston, PhD, is Associate Professor of Curriculum Studies at Texas Christian University and director of the Center for Public Education. He is also Core Faculty with both the Women and Gender Studies and Comparative Race and Ethnic Studies departments. He teaches classes in curriculum studies and qualitative inquiry. His work in curriculum studies utilizes a Cultural Studies theoretical framework within qualitative research to examine intersections between schools and society broadly and, more specifically, the relationship between neoliberal education reform and teachers. His other research interests include popular culture, spatial theory, new materialism, and postcolonial studies. He has publications in several journals, including: *Taboo: The Journal of Culture and Education; The Journal of Curriculum and Pedagogy; The Review of Education, Pedagogy, and Cultural Studies; Critical Literacy: Theories and Practices;* and *The Currere Exchange Journal.* He has also published several book chapters including: Welcome to zombie city: A full service community school and school choice in Ayres, N., Buendia, E. & Helfenbein, R. (Eds.), *Deterritorializing/reterritorializing: Critical geographies of educational reform* and The zombie in the room: Using popular culture as an apparatus in Snaza, N., Sonu, D., Truman, S., & Zaliwska, Z. (Eds.), *Pedagogical matters: New materialisms and curriculum studies.* Gabe has presented or participated in the American Education Research Association (AERA) annual conference from 2012 to 2021. He served as Managing Editor of the Journal of Curriculum Theorizing (JCT) from 2013-2018. During this time, he was also the program chair and co-organizer for JCT's annual conference, The Bergamo Conference on Curriculum Theory and Classroom Practice. Gabriel has also served as the Program Chair for the Critical Issues in Curriculum Studies and Cultural Studies SIG from 2015 to 2018 and the Section Program Co-Chair of the Section 1 of Division B from 2017-2019 (AERA).

Max Krochmal is Professor of US History and the Czech Republic Professor of Justice Studies at the University of New Orleans, where he also directs the interdisciplinary PhD program in Justice Studies. He was previously an historian and founding Chair of the Department of Comparative Race and Ethnic Studies at Texas Christian University and the Fulbright-García Robles Chair of US Studies at the Universidad Iberoamericana, Mexico City. An Organization of American Historians (OAH) Distinguished Lecturer, Krochmal is the author of *Blue Texas: The Making of a Multiracial Democratic Coalition in the Civil Rights Era* (University of North Carolina Press, 2016), winner of the Frederick Jackson Turner Award, the National Association of Chicana and Chicano Studies Tejas Foco Non-Fiction Book Award, and other prizes. He is also coeditor of *Civil Rights in Black and Brown: Histories of Resistance and Struggle in Texas* (University of Texas Press, 2021) and directed the National Endowment for the Humanities supported oral history project undergirding the volume. Off campus, Krochmal co-chaired the Fort Worth Independent School District Racial Equity Committee (2017-2021) and has served as an expert witness on voting rights in Texas. He is a native of Reno, Nevada, and majored in Community Studies at the University of California, Santa Cruz, before earning graduate degrees in History at Duke University.

Orlando Lara is a multimodal anthropologist, critical race and ethnic studies scholar, cultural worker, and writer. He is a doctoral student in Anthropology at UC Irvine working on an ethnography of citizenship, identification, and surveillance in the US borderlands. He is a member of the Sin Huellas Artist Collective, which produced "Detention Nation," a collaborative multimedia installation. He is a member of the Macondo Writer's Workshop and a founding member of the Ethnic Studies Network of Texas, a network of educators, organizers, and community leaders committed to growing Ethnic Studies in Texas public schools and colleges. He has contributed to the development of Chicanx/Latinx and American Indian/Native Studies courses in Texas high schools. Previously, he served as Associate Director of Comparative Race and Ethnic Studies at TCU and as Mexican American Studies Faculty at Lee College. He holds an MFA in Fiction from Cornell and a BA in Chicana/o Studies from Stanford.

Sylvia Mendoza Aviña, PhD, was born and raised in Yanaguana/San Antonio, Texas. She is an assistant professor in the Mexican American Studies program at the University of Texas at San Antonio in the department of Race, Ethnicity, Gender and Sexuality Studies. Her research interests center the experiences of Chicanx communities, specifically women and youth, that have historically been erased or grossly misrepresented in history through the use of Chicanx/Latinx feminist research methodologies. She has published in the journals of *Equity & Excellence in Education, Urban Education,* and *Chicana/Latina Studies: The Journal of Mujeres Activas en Letras y Cambio Social.*

Dr. Santiago Piñón, Jr. is a professional ethicist and Associate Professor of religion (PhD 2012, University of Chicago; MDiv 2001 University of Chicago; MA Abilene Christian University 1999) on the faculty of Texas Christian University since 2011. His current research is focused on the invisibility of Latinas/os in a nation that is focused on a white/black paradigm, especially in the attempt to create a place of belonging. He considers how the notion of moralism becomes the basis for exclusion, which is often based on religious and legal ideas. He also focuses on the role of trauma on men who adopt a toxic masculinity in reaction to the loss of a child. His most recent publications include "Enduring Indigenous Religious Practices in the Americas," a peer-reviewed entry in the *Encyclopedia of Religious Ethics* (2021); "Losing A Child: A Father's Methodological Plight," a chapter in *Feminist Trauma Theologies* (2020). He teaches in the Religion Department at TCU and is affiliated with both Women's and Gender Studies and Comparative Race and Ethnic Studies.

Dr. Jacinto A. Ramos Jr. was the chair of the 2019-2021 Council of Urban Boards of Education (CUBE) and the immediate past president of the Mexican American School Boards Association (MASBA). In addition to his leadership roles in CUBE and MASBA, he was one of twenty-two school board members in the country to have a seat at the National School Board Association (NSBA) table and served on the Executive Committee of the Council of Great City Schools.

Index

Adams, John Quincy, 14
African American and African Studies (AAAS) Curriculum, 49
African Americans
    in Texas, 15, 16
    Latinx Civil Rights Movement
    compared to Civil Rights Movement of, 26, 28, 30, 60
    Latinx discrimination compared to discrimination
        against, 22, 37
Africans
    enslavement of, 11
    rebellions by enslaved, 12
Agricultural Workers Organizing Committee
    (AWOC), 26, 27
agriculture
    commercial, 21
    development in Latin America of, 8
Agüeybaná II, 11
Alamo
    Siege of (1836), 112, 151
Albizu Campos, Pedro, 24, 29
Alhambra Decree (1492), 12
Alianza Federal de Mercedes, 27
All Mexico Movement, 15–16, 120
Allende, Salvador, 31–32
Alvarez, Everett, 116
American exceptionalism, 17, 36
American Federation of Labor (AFL), 22,
    25, 152
American GI Forum, 25, 60, 153, 173
American Revolution (1775–83)
    Latinx in, 3, 4, 119
Americanization, 23, 24, 25, 26
anatomically modern humans (AMH), 9
Anzaldúa, Gloria, 28
Apache, 13, 22
Arabic (language)
    influence in Spain, 10
Arbenz, Jacobo, 122
Archuleta, Diego, 4, 117
Aspira program, 154
austerity proposals
    in Puerto Rico, 34
Austin, Moses, 14, 16
Austin, Stephen F., 14, 15, 16
    historical treatment of, 16
Ayllón, Lucas Vázquez de, 12
Aztecs, 9, 49
Aztlán legend, 17

Baby Boom, 125
Badillo, Herman, 155
Balboa, Vasco Núñez de, 11
Bandit Wars, 22
Bay of Pigs Invasion (1961), 154
Beauchamp, Elías, 24
Becknell, William, 17

Belaguer, Joaquín, 30
Benavidez, Roy, 116
Betances, Ramón Emeterio, 13
Berber (language)
    influence in Spain, 10
Black Caribs. *See* Garifuna
Black Panther Party, 25, 28
Black Power, 30
blowouts, 5–6
Bolívar, Simón, 14
Bolton, Herbert Eugene
    Latinx Studies and, 5
Bonaparte, Joseph, 13
Bonaparte, Napoleon, 13
Bosch, Juan, 30
Box Bills (1928–29), 121
Bracero Program, 4, 5, 26, 125, 153, 154, 155
Brewer, Jan, 157
Brooklyn College-CUNY
    Latinx Studies program at, 6
Brown v. Board of Education of Topeka, Kansas (1954),
    27, 31, 111
Buford, Harry T. *See* Janeta Velázquez, Loreta
Burgos, Julia de
    Latinx Studies and, 5
Bush, George H. W., 156
Bush, George Prescott, 35
Bush, George W., 33
Byzantine Empire, 9

cabotage laws, 21
Caddo, 111
California State University-Los Angeles
    Mexican American Studies program at, 6
Cantú, Norma, 156
Caribs, 49
Carthaginian Empire, 9, 10
Cascajal Block, 8
Cass, Lewis, 15
casta system, 12, 52, 123
Castañeda, Carlos E.
    Latinx Studies and, 5
Castillo, Ana, 28
Castro, Fidel, 29, 122, 154, 156
Castro, Joaquín, 28
Castro, Julián, 28, 112
Castro, Rosie, 28
Castro, Sal, 29–30, 155
Catholicism
    Dominican Order, 11
    Filipinos and, 20
    Mexican government and, 14, 15, 18, 23, 151
    modern Latinx and, 35
    Romans and, 10
    syncretism and, 12–13
    in Spain, 10
    in Spanish America, 52, 119, 123, 151

League of United Latin American Citizens (LULAC), 23, 25, 27, 31, 60

Lebrón, Lolita, 24, 28

legal citizenship, 33

Legazpi, Miguel López de, 20

Lincoln, Abraham, 106

Longoria, Felix Z., 154, 173

López, Nancy, 4

López de Villalobos, Ruy, 20

Louisiana Purchase (1803), 14, 15

Lozano, Ignacio E., Sr., 23

Luzia Skeleton, 7

Machado, Gerardo, 153

machismo, 17–18

Madison, James, 36

Magellan, Ferdinand, 20

Maine, USS, 19

manifest destiny, 14, 15, 17

maquiladoras, 33, 156

Mariel Boatlift (1980), 32, 156

maroon societies, 12, 52, 123

Martí, José, 19, 152

Martinez, Susana, 35

Matanza, La, 22

matrilineal kinship
    among indigenous Americans, 9

Maya civilization (historical), 8–9, 49

Maya peoples (modern), 8, 32

McCulley, Johnston, 17

media
    Latinx, 23, 27

Medina, Eliseo, 157

Méndez v. Westminster (1947), 27

Mendez, Sylvia, 108, 110

Merchant Marine Act (1920), 21

Merchants of Labor (Galarza), 5

Mexica people, 16–17

Mexican American Legal Defense and Education Fund (MALDEF), 31, 156

Mexican American Studies, 30, 63
    origins of, 5–6

Mexican American Youth Organization (MAYO), 30, 62

Mexican Revolution (1910–1920), 22–23, 26, 125, 153

Mexican-American War (1846–1848), 15, 17, 152

Mexico
    immigration from, 23
    independence of, 13, 14
    slavery in, 13

middle schools
    adding depth to electives in, 76–77
    Latinx Studies annotated bibliography for, 142–45
    Latinx Studies core course infusions for, 105, 117–20
    Latinx Studies titles in Fort Worth ISD libraries of, 158
    scope and sequence and unit guides for Latinx Studies electives, 77–104

migrations
    Latinx communities and, 20–22, 23, 57

Minerva Delgado v. Bastrop ISD (1948), 27

Minutemen, 157

Miranda, Lin-Manuel, 4

Monroe Doctrine, 14, 17, 19

Montecristi Manifesto (1895), 19

Montesinos, Antonio de, 11

Moors
    in Spain, 10, 12, 49
    See also Islam

Moraga, Cherríe, 28

Moreno, Luisa, 25, 28

Moreno, Rita, 4, 154

Morgan, George, 3

Movimiento Estudiantil Chicanx de Aztlán (MEChA), 6, 30

multinational corporations, 33

Murrieta, Joaquín, 17

mutualististas, 125

Múzquiz, Ramón, 16

NAACP Legal Defense Fund, 31

National Chicana Conference (1971), 28

National Defense Act (1916), 21

National Farm Workers Association (NFWA), 26, 27, 154

National Hispanic Leadership Institute, 156

National Security Act (1947), 31

nationalisms
    in Latin America, 17–20
    in Puerto Rico, 24, 29

Native Americans, 109, 111, 118, 119, 124
    displacement of, 15
    forced collective labor by, 11, 13
    European diseases and, 11
    William Carlos Williams on, 5
    See also indigenous Americans; *and specific civilizations and tribes*

nativist movements, 33–34

Navarro, José Antonio, 118

Neanderthals, 9

New Laws (1542), 11, 13

New Mexico
    founding, 151

New Mexico Volunteer Infantry, 18

Nicaragua
    civil war in, 32, 122
    filibustering in, 14

Nineteenth Amendment, 110

nomadic peoples
    in Latin America, 8

non-citizen nationals, 20

Norte Chico civilization, 8, 49

North American Free Trade Agreement (NAFTA), 33, 156, 157

Novello, Antonia C., 156

Obama, Barack, 33, 111

Ocasio-Cortez, Alexandria, 4, 34

Ochoa, Ellen, 108, 110, 156

Oil Field Strikes (1917), 23

Olmec civilization, 8, 49

Operation Bootstrap, 25, 34, 153

school segregation
    of Latinx, 27, 31, 111
Second French Intervention (1861–1867), 19
second-wave feminism, 28
Seguín, Juan, 120, 151, 152
Selective Service Act (1917), 21
Servicemen's Readjustment Act (1944). *See* GI Bill (1944)
Shafer, Emmy, 156
slavery
    abolition of, 13, 151
    in Cuba, 19, 152
    of indigenous Americans, 13
    origins of, in Americas, 11
    in Puerto Rico, 19, 152
    resistance to, 12
    in Spanish America, 12, 13, 19
    in Texas, 15
Sleepy Lagoon Murder Trial (1942), 26
Smith, Adam, 36
social justice, 6, 24, 25, 27–28, 30–31
social reform, 24, 25–26
Social Studies curricula
    Anglo/European bias of, 7
    decolonization of, 7, 10, 11
Sotomayor, Sonia, 4, 34, 157
Southern Christian Leadership Conference, 28
Southwest Council of la Raza, 31
Spain
    history of, 9–10, 49
Spanish America, 10–13, 19–20, 52
    independence movement in, 13–14
    racial diversity of, 12–13
    resistance in, 11–12, 13
    slavery in, 11, 12
Spanish International Network (SIN), 27
Spanish-American War (1898), 13, 19, 54, 57, 124, 152
Spanish-Speaking People's Congress (1939), 25–26
State and National History Day, 179
sterilization, 24–25
strikes
    by Latinx workers, 23, 26–27, 27, 28
syncretism, 12–13

Taínos, 9, 11, 29, 49
Taíno-Spanish War (1511–1518), 11, 35
Tapuyas, 9
Tartessos, 9
Taylor, Paul
    Latinx Studies and, 5
Tecoac, Battle of (1876), 22
Ten Years' War (1868–1878), 13
Tenayuca, Emma, 112
Tenochtitlán, 9, 20
Teotihuacán, 9
Terán, Domingo de, 151
Texas
    Anglo settlement of, 14–15, 54
    Chicano Movement in, 30
    "great men" history of, 16

Latinx population of, 4
Latinx Studies programs in, 6
slavery in, 15
Texas Rangers (baseball team), 4
Texas Rangers (law enforcement), 15
    Mexican Americans and, 22, 172
Texas Revolution (1835–1836), 15, 118, 120
themes. *See* Latinx Studies curriculum themes
They Came Before Columbus (Van Sertima), 8
Third World Liberation Front, 6, 30
third-wave feminism, 28
Thirty-Ninth New York Volunteer Infantry Regiment, 18
Tijerina, Reies Lopez, 27
Tlatelolco Massacre (1968), 30, 122
Tonkawa, 111
Transatlantic Slave Trade
    origins of, 11
    See also slavery
transnational citizenship, 20
transnationalism, 5
Treaty of Córdoba (1821), 14
Treaty of Guadalupe Hidalgo (1848), 15, 16, 20, 27, 54, 117, 124
Treaty of Paris (1783), 3, 36
Treaty of Paris (1898), 19–20, 20, 54, 124
Trujillo, Rafael, 23, 30, 154
Truman, Harry
    assassination attempt on (1950), 24
Trump, Donald, 33, 35
Tyler, John, 15

Umayyad Caliphate, 9–10
unincorporated territory
    Puerto Rico as, 19, 34
United Farm Workers (UFW), 26–27, 27, 30, 62–63, 172, 173
United Fruit Company, 122
United States
    intervention in Latin America by, 14–17, 30, 31–32, 54, 124
University of California at Berkeley
    Ethnic Studies program at, 6
University of Texas-El Paso
    Latinx Studies program at, 6
Univision, 27
Ute, 13

Valencia de la Concepción, 9
Vallejo, Mariano Guadalupe, 152
Van Sertima, Ivan, 8
Vandals, 9, 10
vaqueros, 21, 172
Velasquez, Willie, 156
Velázquez, Janeta, 18
Veloso, Caetano, 117
Veterans Day, 106
Vial, Pedro, 17
Vietnam War
    Latinx in, 116
    Latinx protests against, 30, 175